# ERIK **Erikson**

# ERIK **Erikson**

His life, work and significance

**Kit Welchman**

**Open University Press**
Buckingham · Philadelphia

Open University Press
Celtic Court
22 Ballmoor
Buckingham
MK18 1XW

email: enquiries@openup.co.uk
world wide web: www.openup.co.uk

and
325 Chestnut Street
Philadelphia, PA 19106, USA

First Published 2000

A catalogue record of this book is available from the British Library

ISBN   0 335 20157 1 (pb)   0 335 20158 X (hb)

*Library of Congress Cataloging-in-Publication Data*
Welchman, Kit.
   Erik Erikson: his life, work, and significance / Kit Welchman.
      p.   cm.
   Includes bibliographical references and index.
   ISBN 0-335-20158-X – ISBN 0-335-20157-1 (pbk.)
      1. Erikson, Erik H. (Erik Homburger), 1902.   2. Psychoanalysts – United
   States – Biography.   3. Psychoanalysis – History.   I. Title.
   BF109.E7 W45 2000
   150.19'5'092–dc21
   [B]                                                     99–052999

Typeset by Graphicraft Limited, Hong Kong
Printed in Great Britain by St Edmundsbury Press Ltd, Bury St Edmunds, Suffolk

*To Dorothy*

# Contents

# Preface

The first impetus for writing this book came from a strong feeling that the insights and practice of counselling and psychotherapy have a valuable contribution to make to the better understanding and handling of many problems of the modern world. A crucial inspiration was hearing Scott Peck in 1993 claim that we have the 'technology' to resolve conflicts without violence if only the opposing groups can be brought together under the same roof.

Re-reading Erikson's *Childhood and Society*, I found his conception of the formation of psychosocial identity a consistent attempt to explore these problems in their individual and social dimensions and in all their complexity. I also valued the immediacy and humanity, as well as the breadth of outlook, with which he expresses his ideas and experience. At the same time his own life story, of which I had known nothing, seemed to be relevant and interesting in its connections with his concern for identity and with some fascinating and paradoxical aspects of his personality. These connections illustrate, and I hope will illuminate, Erikson's own view of the interaction of individuals and society throughout the life cycle.

Prefaces are the place where a writer can acknowledge a personal agenda as well as provide a rationale for writing the book. One fairly conscious hope I had was that studying Erikson's life and work would be an opportunity to 'fill in the gaps' in my knowledge of the history of psychotherapy in the twentieth century. This idea proved to be a vain one, since the more I began to fill in an unknown area, the wider the gaps appeared to be – and so they remain. Nevertheless, the study of Erikson and of those who shared his world and those who have written about him has been its own reward. When faced with some particularly confusing or intractable question, I could often find in returning to Erikson's writings, if not an answer, at least an insight, a thought-provoking response or a path to follow. I hope to have conveyed something of this.

The second aspect of a personal agenda is a growing sense of identification with the themes of Erikson's life which involve his concern with identity, and in particular the themes of 'a life on boundaries' (Erikson 1975a: 30) and of 'avoiding belonging anywhere quite irreversibly' (1975a: 31). It made me recognize something similar in my own life – as the son of a soldier with an inevitably peripatetic family life, and a childhood at boarding school with its alternation of term-time and holiday-time worlds. In his book on Luther, Erikson (1972) wrote that each of Luther's biographers 'concocts his own Luther'. How far and in what ways my own experience affects the view of Erikson 'concocted' here, readers may judge for themselves.

A comprehensive, authorized biography of Erik Erikson by Lawrence J. Friedman (1999) was published when the writing of this book was almost complete. Friedman has drawn on interviews with Erikson himself, his wife, family and friends, as well as Erikson's students and colleagues, and his personal papers. Friedman's book provides a wealth of detail and reflection on Erikson's personal life and on the development of his ideas. His material illuminates many of the issues considered in this book, in particular the relation of Erikson's life to his work. I have included references to Friedman's work where not to do so would have been misleading or would have perpetuated an obvious error.

Two other features of the book require a brief explanation. Erikson wrote consistently in the male gender when referring to the experience of both male and female. He has been criticized for a gender bias and these criticisms are considered in Chapter 10. Though commonly accepted usage in his time, it can give his writings a masculine tone. I have, however, left quotations in this form without comment, while trying to make sure that my own writing is as free from this bias as possible.

The second problem is that of the use of two terms (at least), 'counsellors' and 'psychotherapists', for practitioners in the psychotherapeutic field. The significance of this is considered in Chapter 11. I generally use the double term, but at times reduce it to therapist, where I feel the meaning is clear in the context. A similar problem is the corresponding use of the terms 'patient' and 'client'. For Erikson they were patients, but I also at times use the term client, where this seems appropriate.

## Acknowledgements

I particularly wish to thank Michael Jacobs, who encouraged me to write this book and gave support throughout the writing. His editing, on behalf of the Open University Press, combined careful attention to details of style and content with constructive suggestions and appreciation.

I would like to thank also all those clients, students, colleagues, supervisors and friends, whose sharing of their experience, struggles with confusion of feelings and meaning, and moments of illumination underlie and inform all that is written here. In particular I am grateful to 'Tony' for sharing his 'story'.

I wish to thank my wife, Dorothy, for her reading of the drafts of this book and for her perceptive comments and suggestions. I am grateful too for her forbearance of the less attractive aspects of a writer's absorption in a subject.

This work owes much to many others who have thought and written about the subject matter of this book, whose work may be briefly quoted in a way that does not do full justice to their work and ideas, or the degree to which their ideas have influenced my own. I thank them and apologize for any misrepresentations or oversights in acknowledging their work.

Finally, I wish to record my thanks to the Shropshire County Library Service and particularly the librarians of Oswestry Public Library who kept me supplied with a wide variety of books and sources during the writing of the book.

# CHAPTER 1

## Aims, themes and context

A young man called Jan came for counselling feeling unfairly criticized. Although he had found work which he liked and felt good at, it still seemed to him that what he did and the way he did it was not accepted or valued. 'There just doesn't seem to be a me-shaped space out there', he said, with a sense of overwhelming helplessness. In so doing he summed up a central theme both of his own life and also of our times, the theme of identity.

Caroline suffered from depression and anxiety states after her daughter left home to go to college. She said, 'I feel I don't know who I am any more.' This too can be seen as a problem of identity. But while Jan saw his problem as 'out there', Caroline felt the problem as within herself. Each person's identity can represent the most deeply felt sense of oneself and also provide a sense of belonging and a range of practical opportunities for working and living in a social context – a 'me-shaped space'. Undoubtedly this formation of identity is made easier for some than others. Jan's parents had emigrated to England and the colour of his skin and others' response to it had contributed to his feelings of alienation. Nevertheless, problems of identity are part of the experience of every individual in a world of increasing change, the disintegration of some identities and the search for new ones.

The concept of identity incorporates the age old human problem of the relation of the individual to society, the one to the many. It is a concept that bridges but can never wholly integrate the private and the public, the internal and the external, the personal and the political, the individual and society. In common use, 'identity' may be used to signify what is most particular and unique about myself; but it is also used to designate the groups to which I belong – my ethnic, racial, religious, gender, work, class, political and national identities. These group identities can be as important to me as my personal sense of self. Indeed, they are hard to distinguish from and merge into my personal identity. They are something for which people are ready to die – and to kill.

My identity is what I sense most deeply as myself, but it is also that by which I am identified and recognized. At times others seem or claim to know me better than I know myself. While we seek to hold on to and develop a secure inner sense of who we are, we also acknowledge the reality, even wisdom, in others' view of us. As Burns wrote, we would like the gift to 'see oursels as others see us' (1969: 157). There are balances to be negotiated between my own sense of identity and that which others recognize me by or impose on me.

Another source of ambiguity is the closeness of the terms 'identity' and 'identify'. Identity comes from the way others identify me, but also from the way that I identify with others. Identifications with celebrities, royalty, heroes of story, political leaders, gurus, parents or therapists are significant and powerful elements in the make-up of our identities.

While identity is experienced as being in the present, it is also recognized as part of a process of change and development through the life of an individual. The problems of identity are as old as humanity and life itself. They are the creative challenge around which all human cultures are developed, fall apart and are renewed.

Identities can be both fixed and flexible. There are elements of identity which are fixed by circumstances of birth and biological inheritance. There are those elements which are relatively fixed or beyond our choice in the context of our early years. There are also elements of identity which I can choose, discard, pass through as a phase, try out or play with. Overlapping with the wider, more or less given identities of gender, physique and nationality, there are a range of cultural, professional, work- or leisure-related, sexual and family identities. While identity implies a singularity we also derive richness and balance in our lives through the experience and deployment of such overlapping identities.

All these ambiguities between inner and outer, singularity and multiplicity, individual and group, current being and historical unfolding are essential themes in this study of the work of Erik Erikson, as they are also fundamental issues in the relation between individual and society in our time.

The concept of identity is a central thread in what Erikson (1965: 14) called his 'conceptual itinerary'. His first book, *Childhood and Society*, first published in 1950, starts with a reinterpretation of Freud's psychosexual stages in terms of *psychosocial* stages which he extends to encompass the whole life cycle. In this life cycle the transition from childhood to adulthood pivots on the formation of identity in the adolescent years. The book continues with a study of two contrasting tribes, the Sioux and the Yurok, which illustrates how adult identities are linked with patterns of child rearing. The final part, called 'Youth and the Evolution of Identity', includes reflections on American, Russian and German cultural identities in a broad psychological and historical context. The continued exploration of this theme is simply illustrated by some titles of his work: 'On the Sense of Inner Identity' (1953); 'Identity and Totality' (1954b); 'The Problem of Ego Identity' (1956a); 'Identity and Uprootedness in Our Time' (1958a); 'Identity and the Life Cycle' (1959); *Identity: Youth and Crisis* (1968a); and *Dimensions of a New Identity* (1974). Erikson pointed to the centrality of this theme when he claimed that 'the study of identity . . . becomes as strategic in our time as the study of sexuality was in Freud's time' (1965: 274).

Erikson's aim was to link the understanding of the human mind and psyche with the understanding of social, political and cultural problems. The aim of this study is to follow Erikson's exploration of identity through his personal experience, his work as a psychotherapist, his ideas and writings and his social and political context and to elucidate the significance of his ideas to crucial problems of our time.

## Contemporary issues of psychosocial identity

There are three major contemporary problems that I identify here and will return to throughout this book. They are: (a) the dependence of group identities on hostility to and exclusion of others; (b) the widespread dis-integration of established identities in the face of changing technology; (c) the problems of the transmission of viable identities from one generation to another.

### The problem of large group identities

The destructiveness of large group identities, such as nations, religions, classes and ethnic groups, is all too clearly manifested in the political conflicts and exploitations of the contemporary world. It is connected to the way in which these identities are formed by and gain their unity from their hostility and claimed superiority to others outside the group. It takes the form of various degrees of aggression, denigration, exclusion, contempt, distrust and in extreme forms the demonization and dehumanization of others, which leads to 'ethnic cleansing'. As social beings we appear to have a need for enemies as well as allies (Volkan 1988). Even those religions which value peace and brotherhood have historically revealed a capacity for conflict and violence that is made all the more intransigent by their claims to righteousness and justice.

This need for enemies may also be found in close interpersonal relation-ships and be founded on conflict within the individual. However, in large organized groups and institutions these tendencies are closely linked with elements of power, exploitation, intimidation and coercion. How such public manifestations build upon and are embedded in the inner world of the individual involves vital and as yet unresolved questions.

Large group identities thus present some of the most destructive aspects of society, as well as providing a source of pride, cohesion, security and a sense of belonging to something larger and more important than ourselves. They are the basis for oppression and victimization and the source of much intoler-ance, misunderstanding and prejudice. At the end of the twentieth century mixed elements of ethnic, national, class and religious identities are involved in recurrent violent conflict in the former Yugoslavia, in Israel/Palestine, in central Africa, in Indonesia, in parts of the former Soviet Union, in Northern Ireland, to name but a few. Such conflicts do not seem to lessen with time; neither are their causes easily understood or removed. Michael Ignatieff concludes his study of nationalism in the 1990s with the pessimistic view that between an enlightened civic nationalism, tolerant of differences, and a narrow exclusive ethnic nationalism, the latter appeared to be winning (Ignatieff 1994). We urgently need to understand better and to find ways of transcending and transforming the destructive tendencies of these basic national and social identities.

### The disintegration of identity

The second issue is the threat to a personal sense of identity from the disintegrative forces of the modern world. In a time of unprecedented change, individuals are cut off from their ancestral or cultural contexts and lose a sense of continuity and belonging that is basic to identity. Feelings of uncertainty and alienation are not new. In the early part of the twentieth century Yeats described a world in which 'the centre cannot hold' (1990: 235). In the mid-nineteenth century Matthew Arnold expressed a modern sense of alienation when he wrote of 'wandering between two worlds, one dead, the other powerless to be born' (1979). This loss of certainty has been attributed to the rational spirit of the Enlightenment or to the reckless commitment to the unknown of the romantics. These movements developed their own faiths in reason and progress, which have lost much of their certainty and confidence.

The disintegration of identity is connected throughout history to the experiences of invasion, conquest and emigration. In her novel *Accordion Crimes* (1996), E. Annie Proulx brilliantly describes how exploitable newcomers to America float in a sea of insecurity, snatching at precarious identities. This was an experience which Erikson shared, though never with such desperate poverty or helplessness. It is part of an essentially American experience. Erikson emigrated from the 'Old World' of Europe, in which long-held certainties were being fragmented and undermined, to a 'New World' where immigrants struggled to put together some form of overall American identity, sometimes with ruthless disregard for others' humanity and needs. It was an experience which gave Erikson much to reflect on.

The disruptive impact of war, poverty and persecution is combined in the modern world with the effects of the increasing pace of change and technical innovation. These disrupt the rhythms of life at work and in the home and at the same time create a proliferation of choices and an accumulation of unprocessed information and disinformation which we find it hard to absorb and digest. Individual lives seem in danger of isolation and social fragmentation. Hence the emphasis in the 1990s on the search for community in public pronouncements such as 'Back to Basics' and the need for 'stakeholding', the debates on national identities and the need for a new 'brand image' for Britain. The public response to the tragic death of Princess Diana in 1997 reflected and acknowledged a need for a communal expression of grief.

These expressions and movements may be leading to new forms of identity. The proliferation of choice through expanded means of communication presents each individual and group with opportunities to create and elaborate new identities. These may be based on traditional forms or derive from new perspectives. As I write I can watch below my window the spectacle of a village carnival. Small groups, coordinated in an impressive 'discipline of delight', to use Barry Richards's phrase (1994), incorporate the traditional and the new as Robin Hood, Celtic heroes and a Queen of Hearts follow American style cheer leaders in the parade. In these ways a sense of communal identity is created.

But there is also a sense that our creative response is all too little, too ephemeral, too unfocused to match the juggernauts of technical progress, the manipulations of the media and the pursuit of wealth and power. It is as if we are in a race where our ability to create social forms of cooperation and understanding tries desperately to catch up with our technological prowess driven by greed and insecurity. The problems of how to create and enable such new forms of mature identity are urgent and challenging.

### The generational transmission of identity

The third issue is the transmission of psychosocial identity across the generations. The problems are highlighted in three areas or stages. The first is the nature of the nurturing group for the new infant, physically and emotionally vulnerable but possessing immense inbuilt potential for individuality, creativity, adaptability and relationship. The second is the means by which a new generation is educated in the ways, skills and values of the society. The third is the more or less extended period of adolescence and young adulthood which involves the negotiation of personal and public identity, with its issues of self-worth and recognition, freedom and responsibility, independence and authority. It also involves specific social problems of crime, violence, alienation, the formation of alternative youth cultures, drugs and other addictions, deviance and unhealthy conformity.

At the same time the adolescent represents the focus of hope in society, from which can come the maturing energy to transform and create. Society renews itself through the coming together, symbolically and physically, of individuals from different families and cultures and committed partnerships and alliances. So arise new beginnings and the securing of the future as well as continuity with the past, whether in the birth of a baby or in creations less tangible but equally vital. This capacity for renewal was termed by Erikson 'generativity' (1965: 258).

Another concept of Erikson's is relevant to all the three issues I have identified. This is the concept of crisis, meaning not 'disaster' but a 'turning point' to be negotiated through the making of choices. It is not accidental that Erikson's main claim to fame may be the coining of the phrase 'identity crisis'. It is a term still frequently applied to individuals and nations and to institutions and groups of every kind, from clubs and businesses to political parties. Erikson, as will be shown, gives both the separate words and the phrase itself specific meanings. However, its wide use indicates a resonance with a way of looking at issues in the contemporary world. The three issues identified above – of intractable inter-group aggression and exclusiveness; of the disintegration of identities in the face of rapid change; and of the renewal of viable identities across the generations – may all be seen as presenting, today as much as ever, crises of identity.

## Application of depth psychology to social and political problems: the historical context

Erikson's writings are particularly concerned with the question of how psychotherapeutic ideas and practice can be applied to social and political problems such as those outlined above. His work is an important part of the history of this application. Four phases may be identified in the application of depth psychology to social and political problems in the twentieth century. The first began with a radical roar from the founders of psychoanalysis. In mid-century psychotherapy became established and the roar subsided to the respectable murmur of the consulting room. In the 1960s and 1970s there were waves of newer voices: the humanist movement, social activism, feminism and postmodernism. The last phase leads to the present, with its expansion of psychotherapy and counselling to an ever wider range of social situations, involving struggles both to establish and to resist institutionalization. In the 1990s there were renewed attempts to connect the personal with the political, to integrate psychotherapy with other disciplines and to address the place or identity of counsellors and psychotherapists in society.

Erikson's work responds to and reflects this changing historical context. Nevertheless, Erikson insisted throughout succeeding phases on the possibility and importance of applying depth psychology to social and political issues, and developed his concepts in ways which faced these issues. It is this that makes his work of continuing relevance.

*Phase 1: The radical challenge of psychoanalysis*

In the excitement of his first discoveries and the application of his insights in a new form of talking therapy, Freud felt that he had found a way of making sense of what had previously seemed irrational. He believed he had found scientifically demonstrable laws that govern the human mind and that uncovering these laws would lead to a full understanding of all aspects of human life. He enthusiastically applied his ideas to the major issues of his day – to the origins of society in *Totem and Taboo* (1912), to group behaviour in *Group Psychology and the Analysis of the Ego* (1921), to religion as a social phenomenon in *The Future of an Illusion* (1927) and to the threats to civilization in *Civilization and Its Discontents* (1930). Admired or detested, these views were read and taken seriously by many people and in a variety of intellectual disciplines.

Nevertheless, Freud's application of psychoanalysis to social problems was frustrated. His ideas were less testable than he thought and his pessimistic view of society as in constant opposition to the drives and impulses of the individual leaves his theory, as Frosh (1987) has pointed out, inadequate as a means of discriminating between societies or of formulating how society might be made better. Freud's hopes for an end to the waging of war were reduced to a wistful, poignant wish that 'mankind will become pacifists . . . though by what paths or what sidetracks this will come about we cannot guess' (1993: 362).

Towards the end of this first phase, in 1927, Erikson found himself, perhaps in both senses of the phrase, at the heart of the psychoanalytic circle in Vienna. At that time Freud was 70 and already suffering from cancer of the jaw. Erik Homburger, as he then was, was 25. He was swept along in the excitement of new ideas in an atmosphere he later described as one of 'intense mutual loyalty and a deep devotion to a truly liberating idea' (Erikson 1975a: 24). He was encouraged to train as a child analyst and had psychoanalysis with Freud's daughter Anna.

After his emigration with his American wife and two young sons to the USA in 1933, he set up as the first child analyst in Boston and he again 'found himself' in a stimulating circle with its 'flowering of interdisciplinary groups', including the anthropologist Margaret Mead (Erikson 1975a: 41). He does not particularly appear to have taken up Freud's quest to apply psychoanalysis to social problems at this time, though he was deeply concerned to understand the terrible events unfolding in the Germany he had left behind, and in particular the appeal of Hitler to German youth. His main interests were in education and childhood and he took the chance to join the anthropologist Mekeel on a field trip to the Sioux reservations with the idea of seeing how psychoanalytic theories of child development might apply in Sioux culture. In doing so he began to address two key issues presented by this phase: (a) is psychoanalysis a science or an art; (b) what is its possible contribution to social and political issues?

*Phase 2: The establishment of psychotherapeutic practice*

In this phase in the relationship between psychoanalysis and politics the main concern of psychoanalysts was that of establishing and institutionalizing the work of psychotherapy. In the USA the medically orientated psychoanalytic establishment excluded from its institutions those not medically trained. Jacoby (1983) has recorded how the socialist affiliations of emigrant analysts such as Otto Fenichel were gradually but effectively stifled. Within the psychoanalytic orthodoxy there was a move towards the ego psychology of Hartmann (1939). Hartmann's view of the ego as primarily adaptive to the outside reality of society gave it a conservative and conformist political implication. Others, such as Fromm, Horney and Reich, broke away from the orthodoxy. In the main these 'neo-Freudians' presented an ideal view of how individuals should relate to society rather than exploring how they actually do so.

In Britain there was a similar establishment of psychotherapeutic practice and concern with orthodoxy in spite of, or perhaps because of, the vigorous challenge of the ideas of Klein, Fairbairn and the object relations school, the flourishing of Jungian schools and dialogue between different groups. Work during the war led to the development of new ideas of group therapy, which became established in the Tavistock Institute, and the work of Bowlby and Winnicott affected practice in the new welfare state. These were steps towards the study of wider society and the application to it of depth psychology.

This second phase is reflected in the development of Erikson's own career. In 1938 he adopted the surname of Erikson. After the war, during which he undertook research for the war department, he went back to California where he worked for the University Institute of Child Welfare, as well as in private practice. He published his first book *Childhood and Society* in 1950 to considerable acclaim. But in the same year, in an atmosphere of communist scares, he refused to sign an extra oath of loyalty demanded by the university. Regarding it as demeaning and restricting of his work as a teacher, he resigned a secure teaching post at the university. Erikson was now an American citizen and an established figure in the field of psychotherapy, but his resignation meant that he also claimed a position as an outsider. Thus his career reflects both the key achievement and the key unresolved issues of this phase. Psychotherapy had become an established part of society but the question remained: can it at the same time stand outside society as a means of understanding and criticizing it?

*Phase 3: New waves in the 1960s and 1970s*

In the third phase new waves of ideas challenged thinking about the individual and society. These ideas may have been influenced by psychotherapy but they were inspired by other influences that in some ways confronted and opposed the established world of psychoanalysis.

Of these waves the humanist personal growth movement is the most clearly connected to psychoanalytic ideas. Many of the leaders such as Carl Rogers had trained as psychoanalysts. The basic therapeutic orientation was in terms of personal growth and individual consciousness-raising. The movement ranged from the structured self-actualization of Maslow to a variety of spiritual paths often led by gurus such as Baghwan and linked to oriental mysticism. The humanist movement dealt in certainties of faith and feeling. It was founded in a belief in the individual's basic goodness and potentiality.

The humanists believed that individual tranformation was the key to social change. Rogers and Maslow were both concerned with social applications of their ideas. In contrast to Freud's pessimistic view of the conflict between individual and society, the personal growth movement saw no such limitation to human creativity and happiness. Yet the emphasis on the individual in some ways increased the separation of individual from society.

Contemporary with the personal growth movement there was a spirit of activism manifested in the growth of CND in the 1950s, the student demonstrations of the sixties, the civil rights movement and the anti-Vietnam War demonstrations. These all challenged the existing system, including psychotherapy, believing in direct action and radical change. Feminists were developing their own challenge to the patriarchal aspects of society and saw a need for a radical political stance. At the same time postmodernist views began to challenge the basis of established systems of thought through a determination to demonstrate the relativity of all established structures, including values.

Erikson held back from the individualism and the more mystical elements of the human potential movement. Though his work seemed important to many engaged in social action in the 1960s, he held to his belief in a psychoanalytical view that did justice to both the individual and society. His ideas seem variously to align with, to resist and sometimes to be submerged by the new currents. It was as if he was experiencing a crisis of identity of his own that gave him an understanding of the experience of youth at the time – how to keep in touch with and discover one's own identity and integrity and at the same time find a coherent world view and a socially viable role. One way he explores this problem is through the study of how certain individuals in history responded creatively to their predicament in a time of great change and through the struggle created something new for themselves and society. We see this exploration in his second book, *Young Man Luther* (1972), and later in his book on Gandhi (1970a). In this phase Erikson was working to clarify and expound his ideas, reaching for an integrated view of individual and society at a time when individual and society seemed in many ways further apart than ever.

*Phase 4: The expansion of psychotherapy and counselling; renewal of political and social involvement*

The fourth phase begins with disillusion with both social activism and the hopes for an alternative society of the human potential movement. In the eighties there was a reassertion under Reagan in the USA and under Thatcher in Britain of competitive capitalism and a reaction against re-formist liberalism which had gone too far for some people and not far enough for others. With the collapse of communist regimes and economies the socialist basis for radical criticism of society had to be rethought. The alternative which the human potential movement had promised seemed to many increasingly irrelevant or even dangerous. Gaie Houston has recently written that 'the Alternative Culture grew up, unawarely fostering its own destruction in so far as it would not bridge in some way to the rest of society' (1997: 13).

Yet at the same time, and in many ways out of the seeds sown by this alternative culture in the soil of earlier traditions, psychotherapy, particularly in the form of counselling, steadily expanded in numbers, in range of prac-tices and in public profile. This has led to an increasing awareness of the need for 'bridges to society' and for psychotherapists and counsellors to take seriously the social and political context and implications of their work. For many too there is a renewed sense not only of a potential but also of a responsibility for social and political involvement.

Thus at the end of the twentieth century there is what may be termed a crisis of identity for psychotherapists and counsellors. The expansion in activity has given rise both to idealized expectations, and to resentment and fears and demands for greater public accountability. There is a struggle to match a highly personal and private activity with an increasingly public presence. It involves a dilemma between the claims for autonomy for individuals and various groups and the pressures for unity of organization and a coherent public voice. There are many unresolved questions about what it is that counsellors and psychotherapists are offering to individuals and society.

### Erikson's contribution: a psychosocial approach to the relationship between individual and society

Erikson's concept of identity will be used later to examine the current situation of counsellors and psychotherapists. However, his contribution is a wider one. Erikson is one of the few writers who provide a consistent approach to the relation of the psychology of the individual, and depth psychology in particular, to social and political issues. It is the claim of this study that his work provides a valuable foundation and a continuing contribution to the 'building of bridges' between the personal and the political. This claim will be expounded in more detail when the life and work of Erikson have been described. His approach may be summed up here in the following principles:

- The first principle is Erikson's insistence that individual and society are complementary rather than opposed. He sees the process of individual identity formation as one to which both individual and society can contribute creatively and positively as well as negatively and destructively.
- The second principle is his adherence to a psychodynamic viewpoint in two fundamental aspects – the recognition of unconscious processes and the value and power of the therapeutic relationship.
- The third is the importance of a multidisciplinary approach. This means a genuine dialogue based on respect for the validity of each discipline and a rejection of reductionism.
- The fourth is the relativity of viewpoints to their cultural context. This applies to psychoanalysis and other psychotherapies of the twentieth century as well as to individual contributions, including his own.
- Fifth, in spite of the recognition of relativities, Erikson maintained that only a committed ethical viewpoint could sustain a positive contribution by counsellors and psychotherapists to public issues.
- Sixth, Erikson insisted that human developmental psychology should be based on an understanding of healthy functioning and not simply the pathological, however important the need for healing and the insights derived from pathology may be. Healthy functioning involves a capacity for playful imagination and for mutuality in relationship.

- The seventh principle is the extension of a psychosocial viewpoint to the whole life cycle of a person, without losing sight of the important early stages of life. His pioneering psychohistorical studies extend this viewpoint to include a historical context.
- Finally, Erikson is clear that, in spite of difficulties, it is the responsibility of the psychotherapist to relate his or her ideas and life experience to matters of public concern. These included for him specific problems such as juvenile crime, racism and prejudice, uprootedness and alienation, and international conflict. Erikson wrote and spoke widely on such matters, as the following chapters will show.

Identifying such a list of principles can, however, miss the unique core of Erikson's work, which he called 'a way of looking at things' (1965: 393). Erikson's work recognizes that the connection between each element or principle is as important as the principles themselves. It is also permeated by a search for a reconciliation or balance of opposites which are nevertheless necessary and complementary to each other. This 'way of looking at things' is central to his clinical therapeutic work and his application of psychological understanding to social and political issues. It is summed up by Erikson in the word 'configurational' (1985: 21). It is an approach that sees the whole in the parts, that transcends the analytic and leaves space for what is uncertain and indeterminate in the total picture. It is a view that is similar to holistic viewpoints in physics and ecology as well as in psychology.

## Aims of the study

Bearing this total view in mind, the aims of this study may be stated as follows:

- First, *to describe Erikson's life and work and to explore the way they are connected*. His life story presents a vivid example of a struggle for identity in a confused and changing context. His personal experience provides the source of and background to the central themes of identity and integrity as they develop in his work.
- Second, *to describe and study critically and appreciatively his ideas and practice* and their place in the history of twentieth century psychotherapy and developmental psychology.
- Third, *to evaluate his contribution in bridging psychotherapy and social and political issues* and the continuing relevance of his work for psychotherapists and counsellors and for society as a whole.

I also hope that this study will stimulate the reader to reflect on and discover some new insights about her or his own sense of identity and how it has evolved. As Erikson puts it, this book invites the reader to 'consider where and how our approach touches upon his [or her] own life and work' (1975a: 10).

The next two chapters describe Erikson's life up to and following his emigration to the USA in 1933. Chapters 4 to 9 follow the development of his work and specific concepts against the background of his life and historical context. Chapter 10 is a critical assessment of Erikson's contribution to psychotherapeutic thought and practice. Chapters 11 and 12 consider the applications of his ideas to current debates: first, in Chapter 11, to issues in the development of psychotherapeutic practice and contemporary problems facing psychotherapists and counsellors; second, in Chapter 12, considering applications of his ideas to specific social and political issues and the problems this application involves. The concluding chapter reflects on the final stage of life, his own and others, in the light of all that has preceded it.

# Early life to adulthood, 1902–1933

## Life, work and context

Erikson held that individuals' ideas and work can best be understood in relation to their life and their times. There is an unfolding personal journey which runs alongside what Erikson called his 'conceptual itinerary' (1965: 14). The way in which this individual life story interacts with a historical context is an essential element in understanding the meaning and significance of his work.

Erikson's life story presents a vivid example of the struggle for identity in a confused and changing social context (Lutheran, German, Danish, Jewish, American) and this indeed forms the central concern of his work. Erikson himself points to such connections: 'Maybe the fact that I am an immigrant to this country made me feel that the problem of identity holds a central position in the disturbances we encounter today' (Evans 1964: 29). There is, however, a guarded feeling about his discussion of his own identity which illustrates what Erikson himself acknowledges, in line with the concepts of his psychoanalytic teachers: that there are aspects of ourselves which we do not easily perceive or which consciously or unconsciously we keep hidden. Whatever we write or say reveals both more and less than we had intended. How far and in what ways it is possible to explore beyond the overt into the hidden content of a person's own account of their life is a problem with which Erikson grapples in his psychohistorical studies, such as that of Gandhi (1970a).

There is no doubt that Erikson was seen by many of his contemporaries as a leading figure. When he died in 1994 his obituary in the *New York Times* declared that he 'profoundly reshaped views of human development'. In the *Guardian*, Haste (1994) wrote that his work had been 'a major influence on developmental psychology, cultural studies and psychohistory'. It was held that he 'pioneered new relationships between psychoanalysis and social science' (*Current Biography Yearbook* 1994: 645). In his critical study of Erikson, Paul Roazen concluded that he was 'unquestionably one of the most creative thinkers to have emerged out of the psychoanalytic movement' (1976: ix). Erikson's work has been praised for its originality, comprehensiveness, style, balance and humanity.

However, any critical assessment of the influence and relevance of Erikson's work has to consider certain questions. Are his ideas too vague to be verifiable? Is his a literary rather than a scientific vision? (And does this matter?) Does he stick too loyally to the concepts of Freud and Anna Freud? Or does he dilute the power of their insights? How far can his vision and concepts sustain new enquiry and practice? Do his ideas challenge established society and thinking or do they tend to support the status quo? Is he a pioneer and leader of opinion or is he a maverick, a marginalized figure? Is he a popularizer or an originator? Does he simply reflect his times or can he transcend them?

These critical questions are also questions about the man himself. There is something enigmatic about a man who can be seen in such ambiguous ways, as maverick or moderate, radical or conservative, original or popularist. I have noted how he acknowledged his own experience as important to his concept of identity. But how do we comprehend the cost which the struggle for identity involved for him? Using his own terms, what balance of trust and fearfulness, confident autonomy and doubt, competence and inadequacy, identity and confusion, intimacy and isolation, generativity and stagnation, integrity and despair, sustained or eroded his life's work and experience? The search for identity is a search for the meaning and power of concepts but also a search for understanding of an individual.

## Life history, 1902–1933

Erik Erikson was born on 15 June 1902, near Frankfurt-am-Main. His mother Karla (née Abrahamsen) came from a prominent Jewish family in Copenhagen (Friedman 1999: 39). Little seems to be known of his father, not even his name. In his autobiographical account written in his sixties, Erikson says that his father was 'a Dane who had abandoned her [his mother] before my birth' (1975a: 27). His biographer, Coles, says that his parents were both reared in Copenhagen, that they 'separated' before Erik was born and that his pregnant mother 'left Denmark for Germany to be near friends' (1970: 13). It is not clear how Erikson felt about his father's abandonment of his mother, let alone about the unacknowledged but equally real abandonment of his baby son. Friedman has shown that in spite of lifelong concern, Erikson never discovered his father's identity and that his mother kept the secret until her death (Friedman 1999: 39). For Erikson his natural father remained the unknown, 'mythical father' (1975a: 29).

When he was 3 his mother stopped to 'rest' at Karlsruhe in southern Germany, where Coles says 'she knew a number of people' (1970: 13). There she met a local pediatrician, Dr Theodor Homburger. According to Coles Erik had become ill and was taken by his mother to Dr Homburger. They fell in love and married. So at 3 Erik became Erik Homburger. The secret of his natural father was kept from him. Erikson later comments that 'as children will do, I played in with this and more or less forgot the period before the age of three, when mother and I had lived alone' (1975a: 27). This is a strange comment in view of the fact that few children do remember before the age of 3. He seems to be implying that there was a sense of not quite belonging or of being different and of separating off the time before and after the new life with his stepfather.

Considering how significant the first three years of life are for psychodynamic psychology and, indeed, in Erikson's own developmental stages, and how these years cover the first two and a good part of the third out of his eight stages, it is curious to have so little information about this period of his life. The relationship between the single parent whom Coles describes as 'the wandering Danish woman' (1970: 13) and her only child, as well as his fantasies and feelings about the unknown father, cannot but be of immense significance for the life of the future Erikson. It is worth spending a little time to consider and speculate on what there is of historical data and Erikson's own impressions and reflections.

The first thing to note is the courage and determination needed to be a single parent at that time, whether by choice or not. The alternatives may have been to give the child up at birth or to have some arrangement within the family. Karla was in her mid-twenties. As a single parent she would have to cope with the physical and emotional strains of exile, of travelling in conditions far rougher than today, of making temporary homes in new places. Erikson says that 'my mother first raised me among strangers' (Coles 1970: 180). Friedman writes that she was sent by the Copenhagen Abrahamsens to stay with 'three aging spinster aunts' (1999: 30). The support of her friends and relatives must have been vital to her and her child's survival, but so must her independent toughness.

Karla Abrahamsen was an educated and cultured woman of her time. She read philosophy and poetry. Was Erik's father similarly serious, was it a casual affair or had the relationship been arranged with family involvement and a view to marriage? Was the decision to leave Denmark Karla's or was it forced on her by unsupportive and critical parents? Was Karla Abrahamsen a rebel against a strict upbringing or was she a liberated young woman like one of the Bohemians in *La Bohème*, an opera first performed in 1896.

She certainly seems to have been no ailing Mimi. The picture we glimpse from Erikson's notes is of someone strong, serious but reserved. He visualizes the mother of his early years as 'deeply involved in reading what I later found to be such authors as Brandes, Kierkegaard and Emerson' (1975a: 31). This indicates wide-ranging interests. Brandes was a writer on and advocate of European culture, who left Copenhagen after accusations of atheism. He later returned and became Professor of Aesthetics in 1902, the year of Erikson's birth. Erikson also remembers his mother as 'pervasively sad' (1975a: 31). He says that 'her ambitions for me transcended the conventions which she, nevertheless, faithfully served' (1975a: 31). She seems to have been neither a radical nor a rebel but a woman with thoughts of her own, which she kept mainly to herself.

The impression of this solitary, pensive person, strong in a passive kind of way, is balanced by the recorded facts of the friends in Frankfurt and the 'people she knew' in Karlsruhe. What sort of friends were these – family connections, perhaps, or a network sharing literary and artistic interests? We have a glimpse of one of these groups as described by Erikson; 'Then [when my mother and I lived alone] her friends had been artists working in the folk style of Hans Thoma of the Black Forest' who 'provided my first male imprinting' (1975a: 27).

In a memoir written on the death of the anthropologist Ruth Benedict in 1949, Erikson includes a portrait sketch of a woman called Karla Homburger (1987: 719). Neither Erikson nor his editor refers to this woman as Erikson's mother. The portrait faces that of Ruth herself and Erikson says that as he sketched Ruth he thought of four others who 'had evoked in me – a dealer in words – this irresistible urge to document a face by drawing it.' The first of these faces, that of Karla Homburger, had been 'of an old Jewish woman from Mt Carmel in the State of Israel'. 'Visiting California, she had impressed us all with the new sense of dignity and identity which her work had given her: the work of tending her grandchildren, freeborn Jews in their own State' (1987: 717). It is just possibly a sketch of another woman with the same name as his mother. However, the likelihood of a personal relationship is affirmed by the fact that he signs this drawing Erik while all the others are signed EHE.

It shows a strong, almost masculine face with marked eyebrows, determined chin, firm mouth and large, intent but not particularly sad eyes. The masculine effect is balanced by a feminine softness in the scarf tied loosely at her throat and in the flowing unruly hair. If it is the face of his mother, a survivor of Nazi Germany with a new-found identity as an Israeli grandmother, Erikson seems to express a detached admiration. His deeper feelings for the mother he had left in Germany in 1933, now visiting him in *his* New World, remain obscure.

Such is the picture that may be gleaned of this first carer and 'provider of identity'. What then might be supposed of the vital relationship between the infant and this mother and what may be discerned of its effects on his life history?

Erikson identified the first basic task of the infant and mother as to establish trust and contain its counterpart of mistrust. From our impression of his mother it would seem that she would provide an enduring presence and adequate strength and consistency in a changing background. Erikson demonstrated in later life a fundamental optimism and trust in the capacity of the world around him to provide and respond. At the same time there is in his mother a feeling that the strength is passive rather than active and that while never withdrawn altogether it might be a reserved or muted presence. Erikson's abiding memory of her as 'deeply involved in reading' might be taken to imply a passivity that would push a child to find his own sources of stimulation rather than expecting it from his mother. If we look back from the experience of the adult man we may tentatively see a correspondence between this relatively distant relationship and a lifelong restlessness; as though to stay too long in one place or to rely on one source of interest might lead to disappointment, or too strong a closeness to the 'pervading sadness' inherent in living.

The second task identified by Erikson in these years of vital dependence on a single carer is the establishment of autonomy; that is, the foundations of a sense of self as a separate entity. Erikson does seem to have had in later life a reasonably secure sense of who he was, of inner identity. The negative counterpart of autonomy is doubt, and this may be manifested in Erikson in a sense that the self is safer when not too close to others or happenings, in the search for wide perspectives and a doubt about the solidity of what is apparently so. This may be connected to the experience of reserve in the relationship with his mother. These issues around autonomy may also form a continuing element in his search for identity as it re-emerged in adolescence and which formed the focus of Erikson's adult creative work.

Shame is the 'brother' of doubt at this stage, according to Erikson (1965: 245). Throughout Erikson's life his abiding sense of self may have been threatened by a vulnerability to shameful feelings, kept mostly hidden, but capable of being stirred by situations of attack or rejection – situations which he would mostly try to avoid.

The marriage of his mother to the doctor who made his house their home was a major event in Erik's life at the age of three. It is at the beginning of that period which Freud called the Oedipal stage and Erikson characterized as one of initiative versus guilt. It is also developmentally significant as the threshold of self-consciousness and the establishment of lasting memory. The fact that it coincided with the arrival of a stepfather into the family relationships would ensure that this person and this stepfather relationship had a major impact on Erik's development and provided continuing themes throughout his life.

The ambivalence of the relationship from the beginning is vividly expressed by Erikson nearly seventy years later. 'I had to come to terms with that intruder, the bearded doctor, with his healing love and his mysterious instruments' (1975a: 27). This conveys some of the resentment at the intrusion and its inevitability. It is particularly significant that this age has been characterized by Erikson as one of intrusiveness. The rising 3-year-old, now able to 'move independently and vigorously' (Erikson 1965: 80), is dominated by this intrusive mode which includes 'the intrusion into other people's bodies by physical attack; the intrusion into other people's ears and minds by aggressive talking; the intrusion into space by vigorous locomotion; the intrusion into the unknown by consuming curiosity' (p. 81). But the child also has to cope with the aggressive responses of others when he or she overreaches and with the more powerful and seemingly irresistible capacity of others to intrude themselves into the child's life and developing sense of self. Feelings of guilt, fear and rage accompany such relationships. According to Erikson a ratio of confident initiative to guilt, fear and diffidence is set up which resonates through life. The relationship with his stepfather involves a feared and resented intrusion into his relationship with his mother, but also the consequences in guilt and fear of punishment over his abundant and energetic intrusiveness and growing initiative.

What sort of man then was this bearded doctor and how did he relate to the young 3-year-old who had intruded upon *his* life? Erikson speaks of him warmly as 'anything but the proverbial stepfather' (1975a: 27). He emphasizes the efforts he and his mother made to make him feel 'thoroughly at home in their home' (1975a: 27).

As a pediatrician Dr Homburger must have considered his place in the spectrum of contrasting ideas and practice in relation to children at that time. At one end of the spectrum was the strict authoritarianism which believed children must be trained or even broken in before they could become acceptable members of society and redeemable sinners. Alice Miller has devastatingly described this as the 'poisonous pedagogy' (Miller 1983). 'Two attitudes run in counterpoint throughout the nineteenth century – those who like children against those who do not; those who trust nature versus those who fear God; those who discipline lightly opposed to those who believe that pain is good for the young; the Age of Reason confronting the Puritan Ethic' (Robertson 1974: 422). Towards the end of the century a number of elements emphasized the value and significance of childhood. There was a nationalist flavour, as politicians but also doctors began to worry over high infant mortality and see children as future citizens of competing empires in a world influenced by social Darwinism (Abt and Garrison 1965). At the same time a new element 'manifested itself with scientific throroughness in the starting up of laboratories for experimental work in child psychology and journals to disseminate the results' (Robertson 1974: 422). Another element was a softer more romantic view of childhood as a time of innocence in need of protection. These elements had contributed to social legislation to protect children and to the founding of a separate profession of pediatrics and of children's hospitals (Abt and Garrison 1965). An even newer element was the recognition of the child's intellectual and imaginative potential which was to flower in the work of Maria Montessori in Europe, in John Dewey in the USA and in the illumination of the realities of childhood sexuality in the work of Freud and his colleagues.

The indications are that Dr Homburger was somewhere in the middle of this spectrum. He seems to have been a kindly man but by no means radical; conventional, respectable and not particularly interested in new ideas. F. H. Garrison summed up his experience of pediatricians in the early years of this century as 'for the most part genial, helpful, unassuming men, inclined to minimize their own talents, a trait rare in physicians' (Abt and Garrison 1965: 170). This may be somewhere near the mark for Dr Homburger.

Erik sensed the kindness but felt himself somehow not quite to belong to this 'intensely Jewish small bourgeois family' (1975a: 27). As he observed the first floor of the house 'filled with tense and trusting mothers and children' and the 'healing love' devoted to them, he says that he had fantasies that he himself 'had been altogether a foundling' (1975a: 27). This was perhaps an echo of that past life with his mother and the secret of the unknown father. There may also have been a yearning that he too could receive some of that seemingly unconditional paternal love that his stepfather devoted to these strangers.

Nevertheless, the environment seems to have been good enough for Erik to develop a reasonably positive ratio of initiative to guilt; Erikson later described such a ratio as crucial for the development of an individual's capacity for purposive activity. His room, says Coles, overlooked the castle and the grounds around it. He had 'ample space to walk, run, or play and a solid, comfortable home waiting upon his return' (Coles 1970: 13). He lived 'in a country and a region which presented to its middle-class citizens a rich tradition of culture, solidly transmitted by its educational system' (p. 14). His family belonged to a closely knit Jewish community but one which at that time was mainly respected and did not feel itself unduly rejected or separated from the German middle-class culture. Another world available to him was that of the painters who had been his mother's friends from the early years. 'I enjoyed going back and forth between the painters' studios and our house' (Erikson 1975a: 27). Coles says that his mother 'entertained many artists of the region' (1970: 14). Erik may have valued most the contrast between the two worlds, the one comfortable and secure, the other more relaxed, informal and exciting. In one of his last works he also recalls sunny summer visits to Danish uncles that included boat trips in the Ore Sund (Erikson 1978a: 4).

Roazen maintains that in the family picture Erikson presents he has 'constructed what Freud would have called a "family romance"'' (1976: 96). He implies that there may be suppressed unhappiness and dark secrets behind the respectability of the bourgeois home. In Erikson's own theory the establishment of a good enough initiative is developed against an inevitable counterpoint of guilt and 'infantile fear' which 'accompanies him through life' (Erikson 1965: 395). I do not think it likely that Erik was maltreated or neglected, though there will undoubtedly have been times of loneliness and distress. The possibility of cruelty or mistreatment has to be recognized, however, in view of the way in which an authoritarian childhood can condition a child, as Miller (1983) has convincingly shown, and because Erikson's own reticence on his childhood leaves room for doubt.

Nevertheless, it seems to me that an overall positive sense of initiative and purpose was established; and that he was able to surmount this third stage or crisis by facing or expressing his fears through his imaginative fantasies and perhaps often solitary play and the normal daily reality of a good enough home. On the other hand, from these early struggles issues remain, throughout life, of his relationship to authority combined with a yearning and anxious uneasiness about where he might truly belong. Erikson himself summed this up as a stepson theme, in which he became the 'habitual stepson' who would use his talents to 'avoid belonging anywhere quite irreversibly' (1975a). He claims that he counteracted this by 'a conceptual turn to social and historical implications, and . . . to religious actualists such as Luther and Gandhi' (1975a: 31). These were people who could teach him to say 'Here I stand'. They were also guides to two other lifelong themes arising from this period: that of the need to feel approval from others and ultimately from himself, and a search for some secure ethical basis for his identity. In the unfolding of his life and work these themes will be revisited and recalled.

Before we pass on to the next stage of Erikson's life, there is another element to be considered. In the *New York Times* obituary (1994) two surviving sisters are named, one living in Manhattan and one in Israel. In Erikson's account of his childhood there is no mention of them. Assuming that they are the children of his mother and stepfather, their arrival, whatever age Erik then was, must have had considerable intrusive impact on his life. His silence emphasizes, perhaps, his sense of not fully belonging to his step-family and a clinging to the time when he had his mother to himself. It suggests to a powerful degree the ambivalent feelings already noted in response to the intrusion of his stepfather into his life.

Erik attended *Vorschule* (primary school) from 6 to 10 and from 10 to 18 went to the local *Gymnasium*. In this socially extended environment he found it difficult to be at ease with who he was and who he was expected to be. There were many and contradictory identifications – as a German, a Jew, a Dane, with his respectable bourgeois home, with the sick children on the first floor, with the group of artists who befriended him. There were his father's wish for him to be a doctor and his own leanings to art and history. How acute these feelings of confusion were in the primary period he does not say, but he records that 'identity problems sharpen with that turn in puberty when images of future roles become inescapable' (Erikson 1975a: 27).

He perceives this particularly as a dissonance between himself and his stepfather's world. 'My stepfather was the only professional man (and a highly repected one) in an intensely Jewish small bourgeois family, while I (coming from a racially mixed Scandinavian background) was blond and blue eyed, and grew flagrantly tall. Before long I was referred to as the "goy" [gentile] in my stepfather's temple; while to my schoolmates I was a "Jew" ' (Erikson 1975a: 27). He does not say whether this name calling involved particular cruelty or betrayal. It must at least have been confusing and is part of what he called a 'whole roster of problems related to my personal identity' (p. 26). He comments that this may be related to the focus on identity in his work. 'My best friends will insist that I needed to name this crisis and see it in everybody else in order to really come to terms with it in myself' (p. 26).

At this vulnerable period of puberty between 12 and 16, Erik was growing up in a nation at war, a 'Great World War'. Nationalism was both a cause of that war and heightened by its outbreak. He says that he 'tried desperately to be a good German chauvinist'. It was with relief from an impossible tension that he 'became a Dane when Denmark remained neutral' (Erikson 1975a: 28). A curious trace of nationalism surfaces years later when he recalls that 'the Danes wanted to steal Schleswig-Holstein' (Coles 1970: 180), a dubious piece of history but a very Bismarckian viewpoint. Or is he being ironic?

The nationalism of war may or may not have heightened feelings of anti-Semitism. It may be that during the war enmity was directed more towards other nationalisms, French, English and Russian. Nevertheless, to be a nationalist at that time in Germany, as has recently been said (e.g. by Daniel Barenboim in relation to Wagner), was almost inevitably to be anti-Semitic. But though the tensions were great, many retained the liberal belief that somehow progress and enlightenment would be able to resolve them. It was a confidence that was shattered by Nazism.

In spite of his natural talents and intellectual curiosity Erik was not a particularly good student. This may have been because of the tensions of identity confusion, because of his reaction to the 'strict and formal atmosphere' of the classically based Gymnasium or because of rebellion against his father's wish for him to become a doctor. His favourite subjects were art and ancient history. He later said he was grateful to the *Gymnasium* for its thorough classical *Bildung* (general education). At this time he says that he 'became intensely alienated from everything my bourgeois family stood for' (Erikson 1975a: 28).

So he left school without any commitment to a future career as his family would have wished. After a year of wandering with a knapsack full of 'distilled passages' of 'Laotse, Nietzsche and Schopenhauer' (Erikson 1975a: 26), he took up a place at art school in Karlsruhe, feeling he had enough talent to consider being an artist. It was 'at least a passing identity' (p. 26). But he was not settled. He often had a kind of 'work disturbance' and set off again on what he called later 'interminable hiking' (p. 26). He enrolled for a time in the art School in Munich, where he exhibited huge woodcuts alongside works of Max Beckmann. Then he dropped out again to go to Italy. Looking back, Erikson is grateful to his parents for their attitude at this time. They 'had the fortitude to let me find my way unhurriedly in a world which, for all the years of war and revolution, still seemed oriented towards traditional alternatives' (p. 31). It was a way of life sanctioned not only by his parents but also by society in what he defined later as a 'moratorium', a 'well-institutionalized social niche' in which 'adolescent and neurotic shiftlessness could be contained in the custom of Wanderschaft' (p. 25). It was a time of 'isolation shared only by a few like-minded friends' (p. 26).

One of his closest friends, perhaps his only close friend at this time, was Peter Blos, who later emigrated to the USA and became a distinguished psychoanalyst with special interest in the development of children. They both came from Karlsruhe and both had bearded physicians for fathers. Erikson says of Peter's father that his wide interests were never constricted by professional custom and tradition, implying perhaps a contrast with his own stepfather. Erikson in his reminiscences of Peter Blos (1987: 709) evokes their world of lofty romantic aspirations and immersion in what he calls *Geistigkeit* – 'an intrinsically German preoccupation with matters on the borderline between the spirit and the mind' (p. 710). It had its English counterpart in what were once called, with half-mocking seriousness, the 'eternal verities'. An essential element in *Geistigkeit* is the romantic feeling for nature: 'Geistigkeit could mean a very special relationship to philosophy, to art and above all to nature . . . We walked *in* nature, and somehow nature seemed to know about it' (p. 710). *Wanderschaft* involved the pleasure of exploration and physical well-being combined with a feeling of liberation, sensory delight in the natural beauty and misty philosophical intimations so well expressed in Herman Hesse's *Wandering* (1920), which Erikson and Blos might well have read. In Florence they 'could absorb principles of artistic form and of the human measure' (Erikson 1987: 711), and 'endless time was spent soaking up the southern sun and the ubiquitous sights with their grand blend of artifact and nature'. As he says with perhaps a touch of wistfulness, 'I was a "Bohemian" then' (Erikson 1975a: 28).

Much of this may have been enjoyed with the carefree spirit of youth. But he was also vaguely but disquietingly aware that commitment to adulthood could not be put off forever and that the lofty world they immersed themselves in was neither totally real nor totally secure. 'Such cultural and personal narcissism', he wrote later, could be 'a young person's downfall unless he found a compelling idea' (Erikson 1975a: 28). Something was missing from the endless wandering unless there was a goal at the end of it. In part this narcissism took the form of a 'total neglect of the military, political, and economic disasters then racking mankind' (p. 28). In Italy they encountered the growing hold of fascism which we took 'in our stride; it could only be a passing aberration from the classical spirit' (Erikson 1987: 711). He was also perhaps too well trained in the virtues of work not to be happy without a challenging and recognized focus for his industriousness.

If Erikson recalls his neglect of the political and social issues surrounding him, he is totally silent on that other typical preoccupation of youth, sex and sexuality. The accounts we have mention neither sex nor any intimate relationships. What he does say is this: 'I will not describe the pathological side of my identity confusion, which included disturbances for which psychoanalysis seemed, indeed, the treatment of choice' (Erikson 1975a: 26). These disturbances, he says, assumed 'a "borderline" character – that is, the borderline between neurosis and adolescent psychosis' (p. 26). The reference to the treatment of choice seems to me to imply that the disturbances related not only to his relationships with his family figures but also to his sexuality and capacity for intimacy. Roazen points out that in an earlier draft of this autobiographical account (Erikson 1970b: 742) Erikson did say that the problem was 'psychosexual' (Roazen 1976: 94). Whatever he experienced of sexual feelings and encounters and of the intensity of youthful intimate relationships, as well as the personal insights he may have gained in his therapy, Erikson keeps to himself.

Erikson indicates that his pathological disturbances were a part of his identity confusion. If what is suggested above is correct it is at least as deeply involved in issues of intimacy. His experience at this time of late adolescence must influence his later delineation of two separate stages and crises: identity and intimacy.

In 1927, at the age of 25, Erik was back in Karlsruhe, resigned to the need to settle down to the job of teaching art in his home town. It was a letter from Peter Blos which 'came to my rescue'. He invited Erik to join him in the running of a small school in Vienna. 'With his help, I learned to work regular hours, and I met the circle round Anna Freud – and Freud' (Erikson 1975a: 29). In this way he was to find work as a teacher which absorbed him, a 'compelling idea' in psychoanalysis to which he could be committed, and the 'treatment of choice' for his late adolescent disturbances. He was also to find a partnership in a marriage that lasted the rest of his life.

The small school he came to was founded by Dorothy Burlingham, an American in Freud's circle who employed Peter Blos as tutor for her four children. She founded the school for some twenty children in a school room built in the back garden of the house of Eva Rosenfeld, another of the Freuds' circle. This was a time and place of remarkable flowering of experimental ideas in education encouraged by the Austrian Minister for Education Otto Glöckel. He advocated 'a new educational system based on democratic principles and respect for the needs of individual children. Audacious new methods were applied . . . so that for a number of years Vienna was a kind of Mecca for modern pedagogues' (Ellenberger 1970: 588).

While Peter Blos developed the 'project method' following the ideas of John Dewey that children learn best when their interest is fully engaged, Erik undertook to study the methods of Maria Montessori with her skilful harnessing of children's ability to learn by doing and the 'absorbent mind' (Montessori 1912). Erikson's Montessori diploma was the only further educational qualification he ever acquired. In a Christmas journal of 1929 designed by the children, one writer records that 'to illustrate the lessons Herr Erik drew so many posters that by the end of the year they covered all of the walls' (Erikson 1987: 5).

Fundamental to his future was the school's connection with Freud's circle. He was chosen according to the informal procedure of the time as suitable for analysis with Anna Freud. She was particularly keen to find someone interested in working, as she was, with young children. He undertook the lengthy process of analysis and of training as a child psychoanalyst and attended the intensive seminars and informal discussions.

Thus he became one of Freud's Vienna circle in the autumn of its founder's life. Freud was in his early seventies though still productive of new ideas, particularly on the social and cultural implications of psychoanalysis. Erikson remembers mushroom picking expeditions on the Semmering mountain near Vienna and sometimes acted as chauffeur for drives in the country. Freud had recently had an operation for cancer in the upper jaw and his attempts at speaking caused him pain, which must have increased both his remoteness and the awe which a young man would have for the father-founder.

Erikson's main response seems to have been of great relief at finding somewhere he felt accepted, although there was a characteristic tinge of feeling in some way on the edges and never quite wholly belonging. He had found what he was looking for in his 'truly astounding adoption' by the Freudian circle (Erikson 1975a: 29). He accepted this in a spirit of 'a kind of positive stepson identity that made me take for granted that I should be accepted where I did not quite belong' (p. 29). It was a sense of not belonging that he himself even welcomed and nurtured. 'I had to cultivate not-belonging and keep contact with the artist in me' (p. 29). He keeps his detachment in recalling his analysis with Anna Freud. 'I often wonder whether this prone and wordy procedure is good for people who have not been ambulatory and generally curious first.' It did, however, give him a 'certain inner sturdiness' (Coles 1970: 180). He also recalls how Anna Freud affirmed his visual and configurative talent. 'When I declared once more that I could not see a place for my artistic inclinations in such high intellectual endeavours, she said quietly: "You might help to make them see" ' (Erikson 1975a: 30).

In this new circle the patriarchal Freud was immensely important to him. He was the 'great doctor who had rebelled against the medical profession', as Erik had rebelled against his father's wishes for him to become a doctor. Yet now he had undertaken the 'kind of training which came as close to the role of children's doctor as one could possibly come without going to medical school'. So there was, in his attachment to Freud, a strong (and ambivalent) 'identification with my stepfather, the pediatrician, mixed with a search for my own mythical father' (Erikson 1975a: 29). Erikson says that his psychoanalytic identity was not settled until much later, when 'with the help of my wife I became a writing psychoanalyst' (p. 29).

There is no doubt that the young man became deeply involved and entranced with the psychoanalytic movement in spite of his sense of not quite belonging. He describes enthusiastically the 'small intense seminars' with their 'devotional atmosphere in which no clinical detail was too small and no theoretical insight too big to merit intensive presentation and debate' (p. 33). It was an atmosphere of 'intense mutual loyalty and a deep devotion to a truly liberating idea, if often also of deeply ambivalent mental upset' (p. 24). There was also 'a high degree of common sense and humane humour' which clinical writings rarely reflect (p. 33).

Erikson remained committed to the basic ideas of Freud for the rest of his life. He listed them in 1975 as the concepts of resistance, regression, the unconscious, the significance of sexuality, the importance of infantile experience and the therapeutic use of transference. Nevertheless, in reviewing his years in the Freudian circle in *The Life Cycle Completed* (1985), Erikson notes three particular ways in which his views diverged from the orthodox and which were to be the foundation of his later developments in the USA. The first is his view of the autonomy of the ego. Erikson attributed this to his work with children. He could not help observing them 'outdoing all adult expectations in their directness of playful and communicative expression' (Erikson 1985: 20). The children he taught 'revealed, along with the child's intense conflicts, a resourceful and inventive striving for experience and synthesis' (p. 21). He points to the influence of Heinz Hartmann, one of his teachers in Vienna as well as a leading analyst, in the understanding of ego autonomy in the development of ego psychology (Hartmann 1939). However, he can claim that Freud, too, had remarked on the ' "Strahlende Intelligenz" (the "radiant intelligence") displayed by children who for some moments are permitted (by themselves and by circumstances) to function freely' (Erikson 1987: 13).

Second, he saw a divergence between the clinical and the theoretical basis of psychoanalysis. 'The mechanistic and physicalistic wording of psychoanalytic theory . . . came to puzzle me in my early training' (Erikson 1985: 19). It was a contrast particularly underlined in the climate of the clinical seminars which were 'alive with a new closeness to social as well as inner problems' (p. 20) and through the work with children. 'The clinical and the theoretical language seemed to celebrate two different attitudes toward human motivation' (p. 20). It is clear which attitude Erikson favoured.

The third element of divergence is what he calls the *'configurational attention to the rich interplay of form and meaning'* (Erikson 1985: 21). It is linked for him to being trained, as an artist, 'more in visual than in verbal communication' (p. 22). One of his first psychoanalytical papers written while in Vienna was on children's picture books (1931). He links a configurational way of thinking to Freud's therapeutic approach of equal attention and suspension of judgement. He claims that *The Interpretation of Dreams* (Freud 1900) is the model for this approach (Erikson 1985: 21). It was the intuitive and artistic aspects of Freud as shown in his writing style, his 'indomitable visual curiosity' (Erikson 1975a: 30) and his 'freedom and enjoyment of enquiry' (p. 40) that appealed most to Erikson. The configurational approach was, he says, easily transferred to the observation of children. If dreams were Freud's royal road to the unconscious, children's play, Erikson claims, was his own royal road to the understanding of young persons' 'creative self-renewal in truly playful moments' (p. 39).

Another teacher at the Dorothy Burlingham School was Joan Serson, 'Canadian-born, American-trained – then a dancer and a teacher' (p. 40). She was researching the new dance movements in Europe for a doctorate thesis. It is said that they met at a Mardi Gras masked ball in 1929 (Coles 1970: 24). They fell in love and were soon married. Their relationship and partnership as professionals and parents became a lasting and influential part of the rest of his life and his work. If it was indeed difficulties over sexuality and forming intimate relationships which was the core of his psychoanalytic therapy, then it can be claimed that the treatment worked. Erikson recalled forty years later in his memoir of Peter Blos that in Vienna 'we found our wives, a Swede and a Canadian respectively. We solemnly approved of each other's choices and, what is more, we still do, knowing full well that our wives have saved us from our wandering selves and from *too much Geistigkeit*' (1987: 711).

In a short memoir written together they give a glimpse of the school and their early married life (Erikson and Erikson 1987). 'We lived on the Kueniglberg, above the school. When our son Kai was born . . . we daily carried him between us in a laundry basket to the tiny schoolyard or the Rosenfelds' back porch. It became routine that the children would tell us during class when he was crying, and in the intermission some watched him being nursed' (p. 5). They also recall 'a memorable old English Christmas – Yule log, carols, acrobats, dancers, and a boar's head and mistletoe – at the Burlingham's house, and "the Professor" [Freud] appearing to watch it' (p. 5).

In 1933 Erik Homburger had completed his analysis and graduated as a trained child psychoanalyst from the Vienna Institute of Psychoanalysis. 'The idea of moving on and working independently seemed an invigorating as well as politically advisable idea' (Erikson 1975a: 38). What this meant to him and the circumstances and consequences of his decision to leave Vienna and emigrate are considered in more detail in the next chapter.

# CHAPTER 3

# Immigrant to author, 1933–1950

Erikson's early life had prepared him for a concern with the formation of a psychosocial identity in a number of ways: the wandering life with his single mother to the age of 3, with its mixture of closeness and remoteness; the unresolved ambivalence towards the intrusion of his stepfather; the confusion of ethnic, cultural and religious backgrounds linked to uncertainty as to where he really belonged; his search for himself as a wandering artist, as a teacher and as a child therapist in the Freudian circle in Vienna.

These themes from childhood and young manhood re-emerge as his life unfolds in the new context of the United States. For the next twenty years Erikson's life will never be without the circumstance of being an *immigrant*, one who assimilates and is assimilated and who seeks to find a place in a new world. At the same time he is also an *emigrant*, one who has left behind the world of his birth, his childhood upbringing, language, culture; and who left those who had been nearest to him to the persecution and brutality of the Nazi regime. The connection between this context and his work is the main focus of this chapter.

In a review of his life, Erikson acknowledged the impact of this experience on the formation of his ideas, 'It would seem almost self-evident how the concept of "identity" and "identity crisis" emerged from my personal, clinical and anthropological observations in the thirties and forties.' These terms 'seemed naturally grounded in the experience of emigration, immigration and Americanization' (Erikson 1975a: 43).

When we stop to wonder what this experience meant to Erikson himself, we find we are kept at a distance. When he writes of the experience of American immigrants, he leaves us to guess in what ways this experience was also his. 'Emigration can be a hard and heartless matter, in terms of what is abandoned in the old country and what is usurped in the new one. Migration means cruel survival in identity terms, too, for the very cataclysms in which millions perish open up new forms of identity to the survivors' (p. 43). In this moving passage his personal experience has been subsumed in the problems of millions. Nevertheless, it leaves us wondering what in *him* was 'abandoned' and in what ways the new 'usurped' the old in order that he might become one of the successful survivors. What sort of identity did he gain a hold on, wish for or feel a loss of during this period and how did it contribute to his survival?

In any attempt to enter personal experience, the individual's own accounts are an essential starting point. Erikson did not leave, as did Freud and Jung, detailed self-observations. There are no records of his dreams and only rarely any direct self-observation. There are also few accounts or observations of him by others. We have, then, to rely on indirect sources and clues; on what can be sensed in what he says of others; on characteristic themes or uncharacteristic expressions or a single word, such as 'usurp' or 'abandon', which seems to carry an extra emotional charge; on what he does not say; on inconsistencies, idealizations, denigrations, projections or denials which may indicate some anxiety or hidden inner conflict. We may take note of subjective responses to his writing, our own or others' – whether uplifted or mesmerized by his long unfolding sentences, charmed or irritated by his self-deprecation, alienated or inspired by what may be felt as preachiness. From such a variety of sources we can converge tentatively on a likely but never wholly certain conclusion. In Erikson's own words we may find something 'retrospectively intelligible, retrospectively probable' (1965: 33).

One rare example of self-analysis may provide a useful starting point for an exploration of Erikson's experience during these years. In 1959 he gave an address to the World Federation of Mental Health. It was called 'Identity and Uprootedness in our Time' (1964: 83), and 'followed intensive discussions of the plight of emigrants and refugees all over the world'. It was given at the University of Vienna. Erikson was returning as an American citizen to the home he had left 25 years before. He began the talk by recounting in the manner of Freud (1901) a 'symptomatic bit of everyday pathology'. He had noticed himself in the previous weeks obsessively humming and being 'haunted by' a melody from Dvořák's *New World* symphony.

> When I stopped and listened it was hard not to perceive that I was arming myself for the moment when I would speak about identity and uprootedness. The *New World* Symphony, that blend of American horizons and European valleys served as a bright reassurance against the symptoms and scruples attending my own emigration. But most of all, I think it was to reassert my status as an American immigrant. This term soon after my migration gave way to the term *refugee* – even as such terms as *settler* or *pioneer* had already become mythological, giving way to *migrant* and *itinerant*.
>
> (Erikson 1964: 83)

The passage expresses still recurring anxieties connected to emigration and immigration: *after* immigration, the anxiety of an immigrant who has just escaped being a refugee, but who still needs some reassurance of his status; *before* immigration, anxiety manifested in scruples and symptoms attending emigration. He does not describe what these symptoms and scruples are, but recognizes their connection to an anxiety sufficiently powerful to require the lulling reassurance of the 'repetitious melodies'. 'It is clear', he says, 'that this symphony, in view of the grim and complex facts of all emigration, is also an historical lullaby' (Erikson 1964: 84).

Later in the address he refers to one possible source of hauntingly recalled scruples. 'I cannot offer my contribution to these problems . . . without one word of remembrance for those who could not join us in the migration: the dead . . . To them even flight was denied; and our image of man must forever include the hell which was their last experience on earth' (1964: 85). It is still painful to remember that he is talking of men and women and children some of whom he had known personally. It is not too fanciful to suggest that this return to Vienna provided an opportunity to relive and retrieve some of the hidden feelings that accompanied the process of emigration, immigration and Americanization – in particular that part of it which involved a sense of irretrievable loss and a sense of guilt for what had been left behind.

## The stages of migration

The Spanish psychotherapists, Leon and Rebeca Grinberg, have developed a psychodynamic view of emigration and immigration (1989) which provides a useful framework for the consideration of Erikson's experience. The Grinbergs divide the experience of emigration/immigration into the stages of: premigration; journey; arrival and assimilation. Erikson's experience will be considered at each of these stages.

*Premigration*

The impact of the experience of emigration usually starts well before the journey itself. If it is in any way chosen, as Erikson's was, there is a period overshadowed by weighing up of options, discussion and decision making. Various reasons are given for leaving, whether the appeal of the future or fear of, or dissatisfaction with, the present. There are conflicting feelings of hope and excitement, anxiety and doubt, and accompanying symptoms of the stress involved.

A common symptom which also seems to have affected Erikson is the difficulty in making the decision. Coles (1970: 31) tells how a crucial element in the decision to go to Boston was a chance meeting on a railway platform. Hans Sachs, who had already emigrated to Boston as a psychotherapist, reassured Erikson of a welcome and opportunity to work there. America was not Erikson's first choice, although Coles says that his American wife Joan's 'ancestral roots prompted consideration of America' (p. 30). Erikson wrote, 'I had first attempted to regain my Danish citizenship and to help establish a psychoanalytic training center in Copenhagen. When this proved then impractical, we had emigrated to the US and settled in Boston' (1975a: 40). The decision to move to the USA was strongly influenced, according to Friedman (1999: 108–9), by Joan's mother offering to help the family relocate in Boston, where she now lived. Erikson later recalled that it was Joan who 'decided to take us to America' (Friedman 1999: 109). We can only guess what his feelings were about the failure to regain the citizenship of his unknown father and to settle in his mother's birthplace; and what conflicts there may have been between his professional ambitions and the needs and interests of his wife and two young sons, Kai and Jon.

Of his motivation for leaving Europe Erikson wrote, as already noted, that the 'idea of moving on and working independently seemed an invigorating as well as politically advisable idea' (1975a: 38). Politically there was the threat of fascism in Italy, Germany and Austria itself. One of the first actions of Hitler's government on coming to power in Germany in 1933 was to burn Freud's books. Erikson later expressed irritation, combined with concern, at the way 'Vienna at that time chose not to foresee the power of National-Socialist advances' (1975a: 38), although some had already left. At the same time he was feeling restless in the Viennese circle. 'The student could not help sensing in the didactic milieu a growing conservatism and a subtle yet pervasive interdiction of certain trends of thought' (p. 38). We may assume he shared these feelings and was therefore ready to look for something more 'invigorating'.

He describes his mood as one of 'rather vague uncertainty and curiosity' (p. 38). This conveys something common to those who make the decision to emigrate, with its momentous but unpredictable consequences. The Grinbergs write that 'even people who feel able to tolerate the changes that are part and parcel of migration . . . must go through a difficult developmental process, including the inevitable wavering, until they make the final decision to leave' (Grinberg and Grinberg 1989: 59). If Erikson shows such 'symptoms' of indecision and vagueness, what might be the 'scruples' concerning those he would be leaving behind? He tells us nothing of this directly. The urge to move on, however, could not be complied with without some sense of loss and guilt. In his silence may be seen perhaps the strongest symptom of the powerful feelings involved.

At such times of heart-searching and decision there may be a convergence of feeling and thinking about essential issues in a person's life. Erikson later summed up the issues which he says that he was only 'dimly' aware of at the time (1975a: 39). Psychoanalysis, he says, had broken through to much that had been neglected in all previous models of human personality. It had turned inward (to the inner world), backward (to the past and childhood) and downward (to instinctual tendencies). What he felt then, if only dimly, was the urge to move in the opposite direction. To move outward (to mutuality and commonalty), forward (to the anticipation of new possibilities) and upward (from the unconscious to the enigma of consciousness) (p. 39). It is perhaps this inner urge for a new direction that took him, for whatever outer reasons, from the home in Vienna and his earlier home in Karlsruhe towards the 'wide horizons' of the New World.

*Journey and arrival*

The journey itself may be a time of elation but also of disorientation. 'Far from the shore they live in an unreal state shared only with shipboard companions' (Grinberg and Grinberg 1989: 74). It must have been a time of excitement for the young family. The only glimpse we have of Erikson is his meeting with a young diplomat, George Kennan. Together they 'gloomily speculated . . . about beleaguered Europe' (Coles 1970: 32). Erikson himself recalled how he discussed with Kennan some notes he was writing on the appeal of Hitler to German youth. 'My original purpose was to explain this phenomenon to myself . . . These German youths had turned Nazi and were, in fact, killing off my Jewish friends. They might have disposed of me if I had been there' (Evans 1964: 65). So his thoughts were still with the traumatic events he had escaped. At the same time, in enlisting Kennan's help in translating his notes, he was turning towards the future.

From the moment of arrival the New World begins to turn from fantasy into reality. From now on the experience is one of interaction with this New World. For Erikson it was, by all accounts, a good time. He was welcomed to a degree that surprised him, not only by psychoanalytic colleagues but also by those in medicine and other disciplines at Harvard. 'To the immigrant with a desirable specialty . . . this country proved, indeed, a land of unlimited possibilities' (Erikson 1975a: 41). He was given a position at Harvard Medical School and also at the Massachusetts General Hospital, and thus a 'vastly expanded clinical experience' (p. 41). There was the stimulating circle of professional connections in the 'flowering of interdisciplinary groups' (p. 41). He set up in private practice in a prestigious part of old Boston. He was also invited to work at the Judge Baker Guidance Center with 'the poor and delinquent boy or girl who at ten or twelve is already in trouble with school officials and the police' (Coles 1970: 33). In 1934 he began a research project with Harvard students. He was thus in touch with the main movements in child therapy, child care and youth research which had been developing in the USA since the beginning of the century.

There is no reason to doubt that his experience was substantially positive in these years. However, the gratitude which he undoubtedly continued to feel may also have contributed to the need to idealize the experience, and to dismiss the less comfortable aspects of it. According to the Grinbergs, 'at first a person's most obvious tendency is to idealize the new country . . . and to undervalue the old' (1989: 78). We may trace some of this idealization in Erikson's view of the 'unlimited possibilities' of the American horizons.

It is likely, however, that there were rejections as well as welcomes in the early years. There is some evidence that he met with discouragement from the leading analyst in New York, A. A. Brill. He also attempted to gain an academic qualification in psychology, but gave this up and decided to 'weather the future without belated degrees' when the Yale Medical School gave him a full-time research appointment (Erikson 1975a: 42). While he dismisses this failure, it may have its part in the sense of inadequacy that persists in relation to his intellectual ability and academic status. 'I proved inept in theoretical discussion . . . and was apt to neglect ruefully the work of my colleagues' (p. 40). In *Childhood and Society* he deliberately rejects the academic apparatus of references, although he shows both interest and ability in theoretical discussion.

There is a hint of anxiety as well as relief in Erikson's reiterated referral to having just made it in time. It was his 'luck' to get accepted as a psycho-analyst just before 'the medical professionalization of psychoanalysis in the United States would soon thereafter lead to the expulsion of non-medical candidates from training' (1975a: 41). In his Vienna address he noted the significance of the status of immigrant, which 'soon after . . . gave way to that of refugee' (1964: 84). How easily, he seems to be saying, he might have been a refugee, how easily excluded from psychoanalytic practice. These are thoughts which provide a sense of relief in retrospect but at the time must have been real anxieties.

Erikson's work as a child therapist and adult analyst seems to have been successful and his reputation grew rapidly (Friedman 1999: 117–18). However, he was uneasy about the empirical direction of the psychological research projects in which he became involved, while his subjective and configurational approach disappointed and frustrated some of his colleagues (Friedman 1999: 122). It seems likely that Erikson, like any other freelance with a young family to support, had his anxieties about whether he would actually make it and doubts about whether they had made the right choice in coming to America.

The Grinbergs also point to the part the 'receptor group' may play in encouraging the idealizations of the immigrant. 'Sometimes the receptor group reacts very positively to a newcomer who has unconsciously been cast as an omnipotent and idealized image and "should be able to" resolve or help resolve intricate problems afflicting the community' (Grinberg and Grinberg 1989: 84). A reaction of this kind may be seen in Erikson's reception in Boston with his 'desirable specialty'. Someone who works with children, who carry so many of the deeply unresolved problems in human civilization, and one who comes from the fountainhead of psychoanalysis, is likely to be the recipient of some attributions of omnipotence or even Messianic hopes. 'In these cases the newcomer is seen as a kind of Messianic leader and is treated with the utmost cordiality and kindness' (Grinberg and Grinberg 1989: 84). The problem is that 'since the newcomer can never satisfy the expectations, the receptor group may react with disappointment and hostility' (p. 85). The insecurity of wondering whether the welcome would come to an end and be replaced by hostility may have been among Erikson's anxieties.

*Language and the immigrant*

While the immigrant is working through the shock of adjustment, he or she may deny the negative aspects of experience and the value of what has been lost. One of the most significant aspects is that of language. What is interesting in Erikson is the extraordinary facility which he acquired in the new Anglo/American language. He records how in the 'small and intense meetings' of the interdisciplinary groups in Boston he 'slowly learned to speak and write in English' (1975a: 41). Yet by the time of writing *Childhood and Society* he shows astonishing mastery of the language and literary skill.

The Grinbergs point out that 'language change is one of the most difficult problems facing the immigrant'. It takes 'a great effort' for the immigrant to

change his or her language because it is 'the fruit of the culture that nour-
ished him' (1989: 99). It is embedded in their relationships with parents,
with earliest consciousness and the sense of self. For the immigrant Erikson
the successful struggle with a new language parallels and to some extent
reiterates his childhood struggles for communication, relationship and agency.
Erikson put it this way: 'Maybe as an immigrant . . . I faced one of those very
important redefinitions that a man has to make who has lost his landscape
and his language and with it all the "references" on which his first sensory
and sensual impressions . . . were based' (Evans 1964: 41). The significance of
the struggle is intensified by its incorporating also an adolescent rejection of
the parental world which the native language represents.

Roazen says that Erikson's native language was German, though it may be
that he learnt Danish from his mother and some Jewish language. This points
to an already existing ambivalence involved in his 'mother' tongue. The
intense creative effort in learning the new language may have been a way of
resolving these resultant anxieties. The Grinbergs say that some immigrants
'show a marked facility for assimilating a new language which, besides being
a specific talent, may have to do with defensive motivations' (1989: 110). They
note also that eventually as the language becomes part of a new integrated
identity the assimilated newcomer 'makes space within himself for more
diversity, which enriches him and may enrich others' (1989: 112). Erikson's
self-curative creative response to the challenge of immigration was the formation of his identity as a psychotherapist, as an American and also as a writer
who could reflect in the English language the real conflicts, gains and losses
of his immigrant experience.

### The continuing process of assimilation

The process of assimilation as described by the Grinbergs has much in
common with bereavement. There is denial, disorientation, mixed feelings
of anger, fear and sadness, guilt and despair. There is a time of depression
and a gradual reinvestment in the new relationships and interests. It is a
process that takes time. There is, however, a significant difference between a
bereavement and an emigration, particularly if the emigration is a deliberate
choice. From the moment of arrival the immigrant is caught up in a new
world in which he or she has invested hope, whereas the bereaved has no
such investment. For the emigrant it is the choice of something new that has
brought about change. From the beginning interaction with the environment plays a dominating role. In a bereavement, by contrast, there has been
no choice and the focus remains primarily on the past until gradually loss is
accepted and a new life can become a reality. This does not mean, however,
that working through losses is not an important part of the adjustment of
the immigrant.

This process of assimilation also has similarities with the formation of
identity in childhood and adolescence. Erikson describes this as the 'gradual
integration of all identifications' (1965: 233) into a settled assumption of
identity. The immigrant, like the child, develops identifications with individuals,

with groups, with images from the new context and its history. Erikson could identify with the intellectual elite of Harvard, the anthropologists and educators, and with the political aspirations of the New Deal. He also identified with the pioneers, with other immigrants and with the discarded elements in society, such as the Sioux.

Erikson's visit to the Sioux appears to mark a significant phase in his assimilation process which is underlined by Erikson himself in his accounts of the development of his ideas. It is first of all a pioneering activity. Coles says it is possible that in Erikson's trip 'psychoanalysis made its deepest penetration into rural America' (1970: 37). For Erikson it was an affirmation of his competence to observe a part of American life on behalf of an American public service. The Bureau of Indian Affairs, recently under new liberal direction, was looking to him for enlightenment in a baffling problem. It was a confirmation of his status as a psychoanalyst. Yet this American identification was only partial. From another viewpoint he was still Erik Homburger who could so easily have been a Nazi victim or a refugee. He identified with the Indian's tragic sense of being corralled in a present with no escape except into the past, and having to confront passively the powerful, arrogant and acquisitive forces of American society. As Erikson himself put it, 'they were both denied the right to remain themselves and the right to join America' (1975a: 45).

His visit to the Pine Ridge reservation was followed by a number of events which seem interrelated: a move to California, the decision to take American nationality, the decision to change his name and the involvement in working for the official 'Committee for National Morale', set up in response to the threat of war in Europe. A fifth event just before leaving New Haven was the birth of their first American-born child, a daughter, Susan.

Erikson says of the move to California, 'I spent the forties in California, having been invited to abstract life histories of a cross section of Berkeley children then being studied by the Institute of Child Development' (1975a: 42). It was another migration, if an internal one, but there are few clues as to why he moved or what his feelings about it were.

The decision to become an American citizen and the decision to change his name are significant steps in his assumption of American identity. Roazen (1976: 93) states that 'when he became an American citizen in 1939, he changed his name to Erik Homburger Erikson', and says that 'his choice of a last name is obviously significant'.

He suggests that it may have represented an identification with the early Norwegian explorer of America, Leif Erikson – a link with his Scandinavian origins and with the pioneering side of his nature (Roazen 1976: 93). He also suggests a link between the choice of name and the theme of the absent father in Erikson's life – being Erik's son implies being a father to himself – in line with the theme of the American self-made man. Roazen also tells the story that the Homburger children were being called 'Hamburger' and that his son suggested the name Erikson because he was Erik's son (Roazen 1976: 98). The name Homburger could certainly have attracted hostility at this time.

Roazen explores some of this inconsistency, looking at Erikson's response to the publicity and controversy that followed the publication of his auto-biographical essay in 1970. In a review of this in the *New York Times*, Marshall Berman accused Erikson of disguising his Jewishness (1975: 22). Roazen comments that 'when Erikson says that he has "kept my stepfather's name as my middle name out of gratitude . . . but also to avoid a semblance of evasion" . . . he does not realize how hollow this rings . . . The mere initial "H" on the title page of all his books seems less than an expression of straightforward fidelity or love' (Roazen 1976: 99). Roazen claims therefore that the choice of name was 'an act of repudiation of his German-Jewish stepfather, as well as the mother who had secured a legitimate name for her son' (p. 99).

What is at work here, however, seems to me not so much repudiation as the unresolved ambivalence which has already been suggested towards 'the intruder, the bearded doctor, with his healing love and mysterious instruments' (Erikson 1975a: 27). Erikson's feelings about his past may also have been influenced by the conflict between these two aspects, the German and the Jewish, with their entanglement as persecutor and victim. To claim affinity with one would seem to involve rejecting the other. Moreover, whatever his mother and stepfather may have represented of Jewish tradition and German culture, they also represented the hope or assumption that they could live together. It was this liberal confidence, the foundation of his parents' security, which was shattered by Nazi power. In this way Erikson's parents could not provide a secure source of identification or world image. It was partly to replace this failed integration that Erikson sought out an alternative, first in psycho-analysis and then in the New World. With such feelings involved it may have been safer for Erik Homburger to opt for a neutral Danish past, or for no past at all as a 'self-made man', than to face at this time of incomplete assimilation the apparently irreconcilable conflicts of his German and Jewish identities.

It was not only events reaching back into his childhood or the trauma of Nazism, however, but also contemporary America that made it difficult for him to claim a German-Jewish identity. It was not long since there had been rabid anti-German feelings during the First World War. It was even less time since the revived Ku-Klux Klan reached a peak of four million members in 1925, on the basis of hostility to Jews, Catholics and foreigners as much as to blacks (Brinkley *et al.* 1991: 716). Both past experience and present context contributed to edging Erikson towards his American identity and a turning away from the past.

In this historical context his official work for the Committee for National Morale may have both assuaged and disturbed the still ambivalent feelings about his German-Jewish past. Between 1939 and 1944 Erikson wrote papers for this committee on internment camps (1940a), Nazi mentality (1940b), Hitler's speeches (1942), the interrogation of German prisoners of war (1943) and submarine group psychology in the American Navy (1940c). This work provided an affiliation with the USA at war. As Erikson put it, 'we immigrants could tell ourselves that America was once more helping to save the Atlantic world from tyranny' (1975a: 44). It also acknowledged the value of his German background and affirmed the value to society of his psychoanalytic viewpoint.

## Themes of identity

For Erikson becoming an American meant identifying with those images and themes of American life which reflected earlier issues from his personal experience. Two themes central to American historical experience are those of expansion and of emancipation. Expansion is a part of the experience of the pioneer seeking new territory but also a new home. It involves a tension between the desire to settle and the urge to move on. When the opportunities of the geographical frontier are exhausted, its place is taken by the urge for technological and commercial expansion. This has its own tension between the ideology of unlimited expansion and its ultimate frustration through recognition of its consequences.

The theme of emancipation or liberation is also deeply embedded in American history. It is expressed in the imagery of the Statue of Liberty, the words of the Declaration of Independence and the experience of the formative War of Independence and the Civil War. The belief in scientific progress may be seen as an attempted emancipation from nature. Emancipation has its own conflicts when the emancipation of one individual or group is grasped at the expense of another. The shadow counterparts of expansion and emancipation are rootlessness, alienation and exploitation.

Erikson's identification with these themes looks both backward to issues in his personal experience and forward to his work as a writer and his life as an American citizen and the continuing search for a wider, more inclusive identity. The themes of expansion and emancipation are related by Erikson, as is expounded more fully in the next chapter, to the psychosocial stage of childhood which focuses on the task of developing initiative and also on the experience and urges of vigorous locomotion and explorative intrusiveness. This stage is linked to Freud's psychosexual stage of Oedipal conflict with the father. Following Freud, Erikson also identifies this stage as one in which the unlimited urge to explore and intrude is contained through confrontation with external limits and the internalized experience of shame and guilt. These experiences are part of Erikson's continuing life issues and are formative issues in American childhood as life experience is transmitted across the generations.

Erikson's process of assimilation as an immigrant was both completed and balanced by his finding an identity as a writer and psychoanlayst as well as an American. He comments that the ambivalence attached to his psycho-analytic identity 'was not settled till . . . with the help of my American wife, I became a writing psychoanalyst' (Erikson 1975a: 29). The identity of a writer provides a basis for a claim not only to be a part of society but also to stand aside from it, to observe it and to criticize it. In this way becoming a 'writing psychoanalyst' is a reworking, and to some degree a resolution, of the child-hood theme of the stepson who avoids 'belonging anywhere quite irreversibly'. Just as the psychoanalyst is both involved in and detached from the experi-ence of a patient, so the writer has a viewpoint from which to observe unresolved issues in himself and to connect them with those of society. It was the writing, he seems to be saying, which was significant in reconciling some of the lasting ambivalencies of the stepson who became an analyst. Even then there is a touch of uncertainty when he adds, 'if in a language which, again, had not been my own' (1975a: 29).

Erikson called his first book, *Childhood and Society*, a 'conceptual itinerary' (1965: 14). The word itinerary seems to me a strangely dry one, associated with a route preplanned by others rather than an exploration. Hidden in it may be an association with the 'itinerant', the wandering beggar – what the pioneer becomes when he no longer has a social sanction. Yet another association is that of the itinerant preacher. He is still a wanderer but one who is sanctioned in his 'job of enlightenment' (p. 414).

Through his struggles with the experience of immigration and emigration, Erikson's work has continuing contemporary significance. This is partly because the experience of migration, whether brutally forced, voluntary or under economic pressure, is still part of the experience of millions of people. But the challenges of immigration have a wider significance. Almost every human individual and group is faced with a degree of transition between cultures owing to the pace of technological change and the developments in communication. We are all to some degree confronted with a kind of cultural migration experienced in individual lives and between the generations. It involves an increasing multiplicity of choices confronting the human capacity for creativity and destructiveness, for exploitation and for cooperation and affirmation. How Erikson began to grapple with these issues in *Childhood and Society* is examined in greater detail in the next two chapters.

## Neil Erikson

Erikson's struggle to find an identity in the New World reflected themes that were central to that world and also to his personal past. In the years preceding the publication of his first major work, *Childhood and Society* (1965), he was also affected by events which have only recently been made public (Friedman 1999: 22–3 and 208–15), and which threatened to shatter his personal life.

In 1944 Joan became pregnant and gave birth to a third son. After a difficult birth, the hospital staff told Erik that the newborn was a Down Syndrome baby, in those days termed a 'Mongolian Idiot'. The doctors said he was only likely to live one or two years and recommended that he be placed in an institution. Erik accepted their judgement and the baby was transferred before Joan recovered consciousness (Friedman 1999: 209). Joan went to see the baby and was shocked by his lack of response to her. She had him transferred to a smaller home that looked after Down Syndrome children. When he was nearly 1, the parents complied with the doctors' and other professionals' recommendations that he should be transferred to 'a special public hospital north of Berkeley' (Friedman 1999: 210). Neil, their third son, never lived with the family and died in an institution in 1965 (Friedman 1999: 334).

The Eriksons told their other children that the baby had died. Friedman says that the Eriksons 'followed the pervasive response of parents of Down Syndrome children during those years – silence, shame, and profound sorrow'

(1999: 211). The decision to hide the truth about their son from their other children also seems a tragic repetition of Erik's mother's and stepfather's hiding of the truth about Erik's real father.

The strain of this situation affected the Eriksons' marital relationship. During the mid-1940s there were times when they 'contemplated divorce' (Friedman 1999: 211). It affected the parents' relationship with their other children, shattering the family image of which they were so proud and sapping their confidence as parents. It led to an inevitable loss of trust when the children did find out the truth (Friedman 1999: 213–14).

Erikson's response seems to have been a passive retreat into himself, perhaps similar to the way his mother had responded to her predicament. The feelings of shame surrounding Neil are likely to have awakened earlier feelings of shame and doubt and weakened his sense of autonomy and confidence. The uncovering of secrets, with its potential for healing and growth, were central to Erikson's work and success as a therapist. It cannot but have disturbed him that he was unable to apply his skills and insight in his own intimate relationships.

Friedman also suggests that the experience of the birth of this fourth child and all it involved, influenced the work on which Erikson was engaged during the first six years of Neil's life, in both positive and negative ways (Friedman 1999: 215–20). On the positive side, as Erik and Joan worked through the crisis in their relationship, they seemed to emerge with a new sense of equality and closeness. Erik turned to Joan for the first time as a real collaborator in his work, rather than as the supportive editor and sustainer of the family which she had been until now.

Joan's influence enriched *Childhood and Society* in two ways. First, she urged and assisted in the extension of the life cycle model to include the later stages and crises of human development – adolescence, adulthood and old age. Secondly, her perceptions and experience of the growth of their 'healthy' children added immediacy and reality to the descriptions of the successive life stages. It may be that Erikson's reexperiencing of his childhood struggle with shame and guilt also helped to shape his descriptions of childhood experience.

On the negative side, the shutting away of the apparently irreparably damaged child may be reflected in the urge to create a comprehensive scheme of 'normal' development. In Friedman's view, 'Erik and Joan had an emotional stake in placing Neil at the fringe of the map just as he remained distant from the family' (1999: 219). The insistence on a universally applicable normality in the stages of development can all too easily lead to the exclusion of what is perceived to be abnormal, shameful and irredeemable.

*Childhood and Society*: **triple bookkeeping,
the concept of identity, clinical and
cultural contexts**

After the end of the war Erikson continued working in California as a private child analyst and undertaking research. His professional standing was confirmed by becoming a training analyst and he began the four-year task of putting together his ideas and experience into a book. Coles says that for four years from 1946, at the age of 44, Erikson 'disappeared from psychiatric and psychoanalytic journals' (1970: 113). 'In the midst of a busy analytic career he kept one day a week to himself, and used it to write and work . . . in the empty beach house of a friend' (p. 113). In 1950 *Childhood and Society* was published and in the same year Erikson accepted a professorship at the University of California. He was one who had 'made it' in the 'land of unlimited possibilities' (Erikson 1975: 41).

*Childhood and Society* is in four parts, each with an introduction and a linking passage of summary and reflection. These parts approach the main theme of the search for psychosocial understanding from very different angles. In spite of the linking material there is a feeling of discontinuity between the separate blocks. Yet there are two consistent themes which run through the whole. The first is the gradual shift of focus from the concept of the ego as part of the psychoanalytic trio of id, ego and superego to the concept of identity, a psychosocial concept which, however difficult to define, is seen as indispensable to the individual as he or she develops as a member of society. In this movement from ego to identity, however, Erikson is concerned not to replace one term by another but to extend Freud's concept of the ego without losing hold of the essence of it. Thus he arrives at the concept of ego-identity, a hybrid concept which includes the ego as organizing principle and identity as the product being formed by the ego process as well as influencing it. Erikson explores the theoretical aspects of these terms in Part III of the book and they are discussed more fully in the next chapter.

The second main theme is the constantly expanding viewpoint, a succession of moves into new territory. Erikson referred to this when he summed up his work as a 'conceptual itinerary' (1965: 14). In the first part Erikson expands clinical psychoanalysis to include an essential social element. In the second he expands the psychoanalytic view of child development to include the study of whole societies. In the third part he expands the stages of human development to include the whole life cycle. In the fourth part he extends his study to consider the life and development of three individuals in separate social and historical contexts.

In this expanding vision there is a tension between what, in his study of two Indian tribes, he describes as centrifugal and centripetal tendencies. The centrifugal tendency is to expand in ever widening circles. The centripetal tendency is to be drawn back to the centre or confined to a limited space. In Erikson's book the centrifugal is dominant but there is always a counter-movement to return to the centre, a holding on to the inner individual experience as theorized and explored in psychoanalysis. The strain of holding these two forces in balance is sometimes evident. It was suggested in Chapter 3 that this tension between expansion into new territory and the holding on or return to the centre has its parallel in Erikson's personal experience and in the American experience of the migrant and the pioneer.

### *Childhood and Society* **Part I**

*The psychoanalytic practitioner*

Erikson begins the book with an example of his clinical practice, which appears at first sight to be the orthodox psychoanalytic approach typical of his time. In this and the six or seven detailed case studies in the book we can get a good idea of his practice. He likes to involve the family in the therapy before, during and after treatment, although the sessions themselves are usually held in a play/consulting room with himself and the child. Before sessions he joins a family meal. He notices how the 4-year-old quickly sees through his cover as a family 'acquaintance', when the child opens a conversation with him by saying, 'in a decidedly artificial tone', 'Aren't dreams wonderful?' (1965: 48). He encourages parents to recognize how their own tensions (over a father's loss of work or a grandmother's death) may be unconsciously and dangerously interpreted and reflected in the child's world. He values parents' initiatives during treatment and after the sessions. He also works with medical specialists in the use of drugs.

In the interactions of the playroom he uses the child's ability to express feelings and problems through play and is aware of the inadequacy of words and the child's readiness to convert what is going on within into actions or play as a means of containment, restoration or communication. He also uses the child's transference of feeling and behaviour on to the therapist as an alternative parent with whom to act out unspoken feelings of rage and fear. He values the child's precious but precarious trust in him as someone who might just understand and be able to help.

He seeks in psychoanalytic fashion to make the links between body and mind, past and present. He seeks out the hidden, the misunderstood, and, like a detective, the overlooked. He believes in the power of bringing unconscious

or repressed material into the light of consciousness and of making interpretations in order to do this. Such methods were standard in the often quite
flexible practice of his time. He does not claim infallibility for them but he
appears confident and perceptive in their use with his young patients and
their families.

Even in this first case, however, Erikson is challenging an orthodox approach
which he sees as too limiting. Sam a 4-year-old, suffers from epileptic attacks
and has outburts of aggressive cruelty (Erikson 1965: 21). Erikson is concerned
with the 'relevance and relativities' of what is happening, and this is the title
of his first chapter (p. 19). What makes material relevant is the way it can be
seen to link up to form some kind of pattern or configuration. By relativity
he means the connectedness of things (not to be confused with the relativity
of behaviour or ideas to their cultural or social context). Thus the relevant
material here includes: the physical and behavioural symptoms of epilepsy
and violence; the maturational stage of 'rapid increase in locomotive vigour'
and 'increased intolerance of restraint' (p. 27); the pressure the parents themselves are under; a grandmother's visit and sudden disappearance and the
clumsily attempted denial of her death. But beyond these Erikson sees also
the relevance of the family's recent move from the security and familiarity
of a Jewish neighbourhood in the East to being the only Jewish family in a
new suburb in the West. 'The family had dared the Jewish fate by isolating
itself in a gentile town.' He notes how this 'fate' has included 'the chosen
but dispersed Jewish people's unarmed helplessness against the surrounding
world of always potentially violent Gentiles' (p. 26). He notes how the culture
encourages a certain mental and physical toughness, which was now appearing in Sam in very inappropriate, and apparently inexplicable, 'bad' ways at
a time when fantasies of omnipotence, fears of retaliation and impatience of
restraint were all issues for him.

*Triple bookkeeping and the concept of identity*

In this 'specimen' of a human crisis, Erikson identifies the relevance of three
distinct but closely linked processes: 'the somatic process, the ego process,
and the societal process' (1965: 32). The therapist has to undertake a kind of
'triple bookkeeping' (p. 41). The meaning of each relevant item 'which may
be "located" in one of the three processes is co-determined by its meaning in
the other two' (p. 33). The processes are not causes but there is a 'convergence
in all three processes of specific intolerances which make the catastrophe
retrospectively intelligible, retrospectively probable' (p. 33).

Erikson illustrates this further by another case, this time from his experience
with a war veteran, diagnosed as suffering from war neurosis. He sees 'three
contemporaneous processes which instead of supporting one another seem
to have mutually aggravated their respective dangers' (p. 38). The somatic
process was generated by the overwhelming stress of bombardment and subsequent fever. The group process involved being one of a group which, from
having a clearly defined identity in the armed forces, suddenly found itself

leaderless. The ego process included the belief that he could 'take anything'. When the other two processes broke down, as the group disintegrated under the pressure of defeat on the battlefield, and he reached his physical limits, 'this occurrence opened the floodgate of infantile urges which he had so rigidly held in abeyance' (p. 39). Erikson concludes that:

> being unable to arrive at any simple sequence and causal chain and a clear and circumscribed beginning, only triple bookkeeping (or if you will a systematic going round in circles) can gradually clarify the relevances and relativities of all the known data. The fact that this may not lead to a . . . well founded prognostic formulation is unfortunate for the appearance of our files, but it may be just as well for our therapeutic endeavour; for we must be prepared not only to understand but to influence all three processes at the same time.
>
> (Erikson 1965: 41)

Erikson is challenging the adequacy of existing psychoanalytic approaches. He is pointing to the over-simplistic view, popular perhaps rather than professional, of psychoanalysis as 'originology', the search for one traumatic event which started it all. He is pointing out the limitations of the focus on psychosexual developments in childhood as the main cause of present problems. He is insisting that the matter is more complex and that, in spite of difficulties, only a wide ranging triple bookkeeping can begin to form an adequate understanding of what is going on.

He is aware that this leaves him vulnerable to charges of vagueness both in conceptual structure and in procedure. It is an uncertainty that the phrase 'systematic going round in circles' may disarm but cannot quite dispel. In venturing into a new complexity he has lost some of the clarity which orthodox analysis provided. Id and superego are little mentioned and ego has become increasingly important but detached from its position between id and superego.

It is at this point, in connection with the case of the war veteran, that Erikson introduces the concept of identity.

> What impressed me most was the loss in these men of a sense of identity. They knew who they were; they had a personal identity. But it was as if, subjectively, their lives no longer hung together – and never would again. There was a central disturbance of what I then started to call ego identity.
>
> (Erikson 1965: 37)

## The theory of infantile sexuality

As if to reassure himself, or perhaps his psychoanalytic colleagues, of his hold on his psychoanalytic foundations, Erikson now returns to the Freudian framework of psychosexual stages and seeks to extend them in a way that will accommodate his 'triple bookkeeping'. He describes in detail two cases from his clinical practice in which the presenting problems are soiling and bedwetting for a 4-year-old girl and boy respectively. These presenting problems show a clear connection to a body zone and to the stage in Freudian theory known as the 'anal' stage, in which the elimination and retention of body wastes, the pleasure taken in them and the use made of them by child and parent in their relationship represent an important development.

Erikson is concerned to illustrate how the focus on the particular body zone, whose importance he does not deny, is part of a simultaneous development of muscular control and a general ability 'to hoard things and to discard them, to cling to possessions and to throw them out of the window' (1965: 76). 'All of these seemingly contradictory tendencies, then, we include under the formula of retentive-eliminative modes.' He goes on to indicate a further social aspect which he calls the social modality. It is seen in the way a child will 'snuggle up and how ruthlessly he will suddenly try to push the adult away'. This social modality he describes as a 'simple antithesis of *letting go* and *holding on*' (p. 76). Thus the psychosexual stage focused on the anal–urethral zone and on elimination and retention is to be seen as one aspect of, as contributing to but not determining, a wider range of developments at the same time, which include the physical, the sexual, the mental and the social.

On this basis Erikson builds a complex chart, which becomes the prototype for his later life cycle in eight stages. Here, however, he confines the chart to those stages covered by Freud's early life psychosexual stages. The first, 'oral', stage is linked to a generalized 'incorporative' mode which may include taking in and grasping not just with the mouth but with the eyes and all the senses. (Erikson divides this stage into two substages.) For this stage there is a social modality of getting and receiving – of *'getting what is given'* (Erikson 1965: 70).

The second stage, as we have seen, is linked to a generalized ability to hold on and let go. The third stage, Freud's phallic or oedipal stage, Erikson calls the locomotor–genital stage. This has the generalized quality of intrusiveness: 'intrusion into other people's bodies by physical attack; the intrusion into other people's ears and minds by aggressive talking; the intrusion into space by vigorous locomotion; the intrusion into the unknown by consuming curiosity' (p. 81).

But perhaps the most outstanding and original feature of the thinking in this chapter is the way he delineates the successive stages as a sequence of 'nuclear conflicts' in the developing personality. This nuclear conflict implies a balance that is never fully resolved between positive and negative aspects of development. In the concept of these nuclear conflicts Erikson transfers the focus of development from a physical to a social or relational basis.

In the first, 'oral', stage, the mutuality of giving and receiving between parent and child, which forms the basis of the infant's trust, is inevitably undermined by situations in which this mutuality breaks down. 'There are stages marked by such unavoidable developments of rage and anger that mutual regulation by complementary behaviour cannot be the pattern for meeting them. The rages of teething, the tantrums of muscular and anal impotence, the failures of falling, etc. – all are situations in which the intensity of impulse leads to its own defeat' (p. 73). Thus, 'even under the most favourable circumstances, this stage leaves a residue of a primary sense of evil and doom and of a universal nostalgia for a lost paradise' (p. 74). The basic sense of trust is balanced by, and never fully free from, an opposing basic sense of mistrust. This is the first nuclear conflict or crisis.

Erikson describes in similar terms the nuclear conflicts of the second and third stages. For the retentive/eliminative stage, he sees a conflict between autonomy – a pride in one's sense of inner goodness and ability to stand on one's own feet – and a sense of shame and doubt: 'that sense of having exposed himself prematurely and foolishly which we call shame' and 'that secondary mistrust, that looking back, which we call doubt' (p. 79).

The third, phallic or locomotor–genital, stage is characterized by the nuclear conflict between initiative and guilt. Initiative is formed by the new found ability to explore vigorously, to have goals and achieve them, which is matched by the inevitable overreaching this involves and the impossiblity of attaining what is desired, including the fantasies, secrets and fears of retaliation of the primal parental scene.

Erikson has thus extended and built on the basic psychosexual stages of Freudian analysis to form a complex configuration of more generalized modes, of social modalities and of nuclear conflicts between counterbalancing attitudes and responses to life.

In creating a new viewpoint of the interrelation of the biological, the psychological and the social processes Erikson has called into question some of the Freudian presuppositions. One question is whether the development of the individual is really as linked to the body zones as Freud held it to be in his psychosexual stages. Erikson still seems convinced of the influence of the body zones, but he has changed the balance and weakened the link. He treats the body zones as metaphorical as well as literal.

A second problem arises over the dependence of Freud's theory on the concept of libido and the theory of drives. Erikson is seeking to get away from the 'scientific' imagery of hydraulic energy which he believes that Freud used under influence from the scientific milieu of his time, but which is now outdated.

A third problem that arises from Erikson's adherence to a Freudian ground plan of the body is the implications for the differentiated social development of the sexes, particularly in the third or phallic phase. Erikson says that girls have a similar or equal development to boys in terms of initiative and intrusiveness which are characteristic of this stage. He allows for a specifically feminine initiative of '*inception* and *maternal inclusion*' (Erikson 1965: 82). But he also says that although girls' 'locomotor, mental, and social intrusiveness is equally increased and adequate as that of boys, they lack one item: the penis' (p. 82), and he links this to a 'general exploitability which has been women's fate' (p. 84).

Erikson's concern with the gender differences and their dependence on the body plan is underlined by his ending this chapter with an account of his work with children's imagery, which was part of a large-scale study undertaken at the University of California. Working with a play table and a random selection of toys he invited boys and girls of 10 and 11 to 'construct on the table an exciting scene out of an imaginary moving picture' (Erikson 1965: 92). One of the main conclusions that emerged to his surprise was a significant difference in the way boys and girls used the blocks. 'In the boys, the outstanding variables were height and downfall and strong motion', while the girls demonstrated 'static interiors, which are open, simply enclosed, and peaceful or intruded upon' (p. 99). He concludes that 'the spatial tendencies governing these constructions are reminiscent of the *genital modes* and ... closely parallel the morphology of the sex organs' (1965: p. 100).

He is aware of the dangers of jumping to false conclusions. Such emphases or parallels may be only those of a temporary stage. They may be the result of social influences and expectations. Nevertheless, he concludes that the results of the study 'incline me to think that the dominance of ... genital modes over the modalities of spatial organization reflects a profound difference in the sense of space of the two sexes' (p. 100).

It is a conclusion about which he seems to feel uneasy and which indeed has led to continued criticism. The feminist criticism of his work is considered more fully in Chapters 9 and 10. However, he sees the evidence as conclusive that 'experience is anchored in the ground plan of the body', that there is a 'male and female experience of space' and that this illustrates the 'interpenetration of the biological, cultural and psychological' (Erikson 1965: 102). He is saying that sexual differences are something which social institutions do not and cannot ignore. He sums up his views in a way that perhaps raises more questions than it answers, but which sets out the main issues facing society and the individual in relation to sexual difference: 'Cultures ... elaborate upon the biologically given and strive for a division of function between the sexes, which is, simultaneously, workable within the body's scheme, meaningful to a particular society, and manageable for the individual ego' (p. 102).

The significance of sexual difference lies both in itself and as part of a wider problem of difference which underlies many of the issues inherent in the attempt to integrate individual and society. Differences provide the basis for individuality and identity as well as for cooperative action; for interdependence as well as for isolation, exclusion and exploitation in both personal relationships and in institutions. In the final chapter of *Childhood and Society*, Erikson writes of 'the existential oppositions such as Male and Female; Ruler and Ruled; Owner and Owned; Light Skin and Dark, over all of which emancipatory struggles are now raging both politically and psychologically' (1965: 407). The first of these existential oppositions, however, is that between 'the polarity Big–Small', the child and the adult. It is to the working out of this opposition and its effects in a whole society through its child rearing practices that he turns in the next part of his book.

## *Childhood and Society* Part II

Part II of *Childhood and Society* consists of studies of two so-called primitive societies, from the standpoint of psychoanalytic child psychology. Erikson visited the Sioux in 1936 and the Yurok in 1942. His aim was to see how the life of the people and the functioning of their society might be linked to their child caring and child rearing practices and how his psychoanalytic understanding of children's development might throw light on this connection. These studies represent a further expansion and a testing out of his viewpoint in two contrasting cultures, which are themselves in contrast to the dominant American white culture.

For Erikson himself the first visit to the Sioux must have been an exciting time, a confirmation of his growing reputation and an opportunity to break out of the mould of the professional psychoanalytic world. It might also have been an opportunity to see the reality behind the fantasy image of America, which the Indian, particularly the plains Indian such as the Sioux, represented for European children of his time. The Sioux had once roamed on the prairie and hunted vast herds of buffalo. Now they lived on reservations supported mainly by handouts from the state, for the buffalo had long been extinguished and the right to roam had been removed. These Indians on their reservations were the subject of considerable concern to the American Bureau of Indian Affairs for their apathy and indifference to the education, welfare and training in child care which the authorities provided. They were not openly hostile, but passively accepted what was offered, which they sloughed off like a skin as soon as they left the institutional context of school or clinic. So they bewildered and infuriated their well-meaning social workers and teachers. Erikson was therefore invited not simply as an interested observer but as someone who might be able to provide some explanations or new ideas for how to cope with these people.

By listening to the women talking about their child rearing now, and what they had been told by their mothers and grandmothers, Erikson is able to show fairly convincingly how the child rearing practices are oriented towards a social context of the past. They are designed for a hunting and warrior people, who need courage, endurance and cunning and an ability to pursue without limits when the opportunity comes on the open plains. It is a culture which Erikson calls centrifugal. White man's education in individual competition, delayed gratification and accumulation is irrelevant. The present is seen as only an intermission before the old days will return and the old ways will be re-established.

Erikson identifies three aspects of child rearing as oriented to such a past. First, the very late weaning gives a sense of limitlessness in the oral phase, a basic trust and feeling of being cared for and provided for. This also provides a basis for the nostalgia for a lost paradise that, against the appearances of the present, still maintains its hold in the hope that some day these conditions will be restored.

Second, in the mother's aggressive reaction when the child begins to hurt her with his teeth while still nursing at the breast, Erikson sees a way of channelling the child's frustrated rage towards an external prey, whether animal, tribal enemy or unprotected woman. It is also a basis for the warrior who will need a reservoir of fierce courage and cruelty, an ability to hurt or sustain hurt whether in hunting or battle. The Sioux warrior directs a similar cruelty towards himself in his development as an adult. This development involves an acceptance of pain as part of life and a valuing of self-discipline, endurance, self-punishment and self-reparation.

Third, the use of the cradle board is seen by Erikson as similarly channelling rage and frustration by restricting movement. These early characteristics are further strengthened towards the needs and context of the world image of the tribe through the anal and genital stages. Thus, through each stage of psychological development, 'cultures . . . elaborate on the biological given' in a way that is 'meaningful to the particular society, and manageable for the individual ego' (1965: 102).

Erikson listens and responds to these people with sympathy and respect, though he also sympathizes with their frustrated teachers. He comments on the personal sensitivity and courtesy his Indian companion maintains in spite of his sense of helplessness. He warms to the mothers' feeling for their children which the white officials so misunderstand or deny, and he empathizes with the passive despair of the men, deprived of all identity except that which they retain as a vague memory of what once was and through their tribal dances, in which only the older men can now participate with any conviction.

The Yurok salmon fishers of the Klamath river in California are different in temperament, in their economy, their history and their relation to the dominant American culture; their childhood training is correspondingly different. Where Erikson describes the Sioux as characteristically centrifugal, the Yurok are centripetal. They live in a river valley circumscribed by mountains. The river provides the main source of food and wealth as each season the salmon make their way from the sea to the spawning grounds high up in the mountains. The Yurok are suspicious of strangers but well used to bargaining. They have had their own form of money since before the white men came. Making a good bargain and avoiding being outdone by others is central to their life and culture. Nevertheless, they are capable of large-scale communal enterprise when each year they build a dam across the river to catch salmon.

Erikson notes that a feature of their child rearing is abrupt weaning and a general discouragement 'from feeling too comfortable in, with and around his mother' (1965: 170). He links this to the preparation for life as a fisherman 'who has his nets ready for a prey which (if only he behaves nicely and says "please" appropriately) will come to him' (p. 170).

He notes that in his 'official behaviour' the Yurok shows 'compulsive ritualization; pedantic bickering; suspicious miserliness; retentive hoarding' (p. 172) – all the traits which Freud and Abraham found associated with 'anal fixations'. Yet Erikson now comes up against the fact that in Yurok society 'there seems to be no special emphasis on faeces or on the anal zone' (p. 172). He is forced to question the connection between childhood training in terms of body zones and the explanation of social characteristics.

However, he does not give up the connection entirely. He points to a pervasive avoidance of contamination caused by supposed antagonistic fluids, a kind of holding apart rather than holding back. This is a kind of retentivity which 'may be already well developed in connection with orality' (Erikson 1987: 437). Erikson concludes that 'the configuration of Yurok retentiveness seems to be as much alimentary as it is anal' (1965: 177). This 'configuration' is powerfully expressed in the geographical imagery of the river valley as a 'tubular food-carrying passage' (1987: 438) with its mouth opening to the sea.

Erikson is keen to point to the relativity of personal and social characteristics to the culture in which they are found. What may be inappropriate in one culture may be a source of strong personal functioning in another. The characteristic ability of the Yurok to shed tears, either in order to persuade the gods that control the supply of salmon or in personal bargaining, may be seen by outsiders as a sign of childish weakness. But Erikson says that such 'institutionalized helplessness' is 'neither a trait nor a neurotic symptom' (1965: 177). 'It is probable that the really successful Yurok was the one who could cry most heartbreakingly . . . in some situations and be full of fortitude in others' (p. 177). Similarly, 'anal' characteristics which may be 'neurotic' symptoms in our society must be seen quite differently in the context of another culture.

One individual with whom Erikson identified among the Yurok was the 'doctor' or tribal healer he called Fanny. He says she laughed heartily when told about psychoanalysis, the main principles of which can 'easily be expressed in her terms' (1965: 165). On the second day of interviews with her, Erikson noticed that Kroeber, the anthropologist who had introduced him to the Yurok, was absent. Erikson asked where Kroeber had gone. 'The old woman laughed merrily, and said, "He give you chance to ask alone. You big man now"' (p. 166).

Fanny's therapeutic method involved sucking the 'pain' from the body of the presenting patient in the presence of his or her extended family. When all the pains have been taken out and 'vomited' into a nearby basket, there comes the Yurok version of an interpretation. Fanny 'sees' how one of the present members of the family has been behaving in some inappropriate way. That is why the child is sick. It is usual for the individual named to admit to whatever is named. The 'doctor' has identified, as Erikson sees it, 'the main source of ambivalence in the family and has provoked a confession in public' (1965: 169). Thus, in psychoanalytic terms, the therapist has been the container and catalyst for the healing of the individual and has taken the further step of returning the problem to its social context.

Erikson has extended his concepts of triple bookkeeping into an analysis of child development as related to society in two 'primitive' cultures with some conviction. However, as a way of conceptualizing childhood and society this presents a dilemma. These two tribes are, or in the case of the Sioux were, self-contained or 'homogeneous' societies which can be said to 'synthesize their concepts and their ideals in a coherent design for living' (p. 179). But modern societies, whether in America or elsewhere, are not 'homogeneous'. They are fragmented, complex, constantly changing and interdependent. Erikson says that 'we may do well to try to understand these "instinctive" blueprints, as mankind works towards a different kind of adaptation, at once more rational, more conscious and more universal' (p. 180). There is, however, a very large gap between the 'instinctive blueprints' of the past and the kind of conscious social integration he envisages, which might belong to the future. Finding a way to bridge this gap is nevertheless the task with which Erikson perseveres in the second half (Parts III and IV) of *Children and Society*, the subject of the next chapter.

## *Childhood and Society*: ego and identity, the stages of the life cycle, the historical evolution of identity

### Past III, ego and identity

The third part of *Childhood and Society* is called 'The growth of the ego', but might equally well be called the growth or formation of identity. The relation between ego and identity, which Erikson sometimes calls ego identity or psychosocial identity, is a central concern of his book.

Erikson's conception of the ego was influenced by the work of Anna Freud and Heinz Hartmann. The ego, as Erikson sees it, is an inner guide to individual development, an 'inner institution' (1965: 188) which guides the individual in relation to society. Identity is the result of the work of the ego. Thus Erikson says that a strong ego is an 'individual core firm and flexible enough to reconcile the necessary contradictions in any human organization, to integrate individual differences, and above all to emerge from a long and unavoidably fearful infancy with a sense of identity and an idea of integrity' (p. 179).

Erikson is aware, however, that the reality is more complex than this. Ego cannot be seen simply as something that produces identity because the two are interactive; the ego not only produces a sense of identity but is itself dependent on the formation of an emergent identity. The formation of identity starts at the very beginning of life. There is a 'budding identity' (Erikson 1965: 232), there are 'infantile steps towards identity' (p. 227) and a 'rudimentary sense of ego identity' (p. 239), as well as a 'lasting ego-identity' (p. 238) and a 'psychosocial identity' which 'develops out of a gradual integration of all identifications' (p. 233).

Erikson illustrates the complex unfolding interaction of ego and identity thus: 'A lasting ego-identity cannot begin without the trust of the first oral stage; it cannot be completed without a promise of fulfilment which from the dominant image of adulthood reaches down into the baby's beginnings and which . . . creates at every step of childhood an accruing sense of ego strength' (p. 238). If this is not altogether clear it makes two important points: that ego and identity are linked at every stage; and that both an inner ego process and an appropriate social context are indispensable to the growth of individual identity.

In attempting to define identity Erikson emphasizes three vital elements – 'continuity, consistency and sameness of experience provide a rudimentary sense of ego-identity' (p. 239) in the infant – and these three continue to be basic to an established sense of identity. However, he finds it easier to describe what he means by identity by what is missing and by its indispensability than by a positive definition. In the case of the war veteran in connection with whom Erikson first started to use the term ego-identity, what had impressed him had been the 'loss in these men of a sense of identity' (p. 37).

In describing the case of a 5-year-old he says that 'there is no feeling of being alive without a sense of ego-identity' (p. 232). 'Should the child feel that the environment tries to deprive him too radically . . . he will defend it [his identity] with the astonishing strength encountered in animals who are suddenly forced to defend their lives . . . Deprivation of identity', he says starkly, 'can lead to murder' (p. 232).

The loss or deprivation of identity can, then, be a desperate state; but what it is is still hard to clarify. Looking back on his ideas on identity nearly twenty years later, Erikson wrote that 'the more one writes about this subject [identity], the more the word becomes a term for something as unfathomable as it is all-pervasive. One can only explore it by establishing its indispensability in various contexts' (1968a: 9). More recent explorations of identity have developed this view (Woodward 1997: 1). In *Childhood and Society*, nevertheless, Erikson is still struggling for a 'better description and definition of what we mean by identity' (1965: 227).

In the first chapter of Part III Erikson describes the case of Jean, a 'schizophrenic' who was almost 6 years old when Erikson first saw her. He characterizes the case as one of early ego-failure. It is the bleakest of the cases described in the book and the only one which Erikson sees ultimately in terms of failure. He conveys some of the intense pain that is endured by the child, her parents and all who care for her. He describes the chilling but poignant impression of 'her beautiful dark eyes which seemed like peaceful islands within the anxious grimace of her face' (1965: 189). He conveys the feeling of helplessness of the parents in their untiring struggle to find a way of remedying what seems an incurable defect. He conveys too his own sense of helplessness when she 'quickly lost what she had gained in the years of her mother's heroic effort' (p. 200).

He describes how one can 'live with schizophrenic thought only if one can make a profession out of understanding it' (p. 196). Each member of the household 'in being forced to take a glance into Jean's mind, characterized as it was by the alternation of naked impulsiveness and desperate self-negation, was endangered in his own equilibrium and self-esteem' (p. 196). In spite of the occasional breakthrough in communication and emotional expression and the discovery of an unusual musical talent, those around her are ultimately defeated by what Erikson calls her 'cruel self-punitiveness and paralysing perfectionism' (p. 200).

Whatever the parents may have done in triggering off the first attack when they denied her access to the bedroom where her mother was ill, or in employing an obsessively tidy nurse, Erikson sees no cause to blame the parents; rather, he admires their courage and care. Nor does he blame the failure on himself or the other therapists involved, though I guess he must have felt like doing so at times. He concludes that this girl was one of those who are damaged in the core of their ability to integrate as individuals. 'It is not that they fail to be able to learn, to remember and to excel ... It is that they cannot integrate it all; their ego is impotent' (Erikson 1965: 200).

Erikson is pointing to the crucial importance of the integrative functioning of the ego, as an 'inner institution', for the formation of identity and relationships. How this actually works or fails to work is elusive. However, he is also saying that the functioning of the ego, or its failure, cannot be understood on its own but has to be related to the other elements of the triple bookkeeping, the biological givens and the social context of relationships. Drastic failure in any one of the three areas may cause, but is also influenced by, strengths or weaknesses in the other two areas.

By contrast to Jean, Erikson turns to a situation which illustrates the 'capacity of the ego to find recreation and self-cure in the activity of play', and to a therapeutic situation 'in which we were fortunate enough to be able to help the child's ego to help itself' (1965: 202). After a discussion of various aspects of play Erikson describes in detail how 3-year-old Mary was able to dramatize her relationships, which involved overwhelming fears and frustrations, rage and envy. At first she used the toys available in the consulting room. Then she contrived a situation in which she shut Erikson into his own consulting room, shouting 'Thtay in there!' (1965: 224). These were the first words she had spoken to him. In this way her feelings in relation to her father, who had shut *her* out, became explicit and more manageable and her assurance in her world was restored.

In Jean's case Erikson showed how if the ego is not functioning properly a functioning identity cannot develop. In Mary's case the natural creative and self-curative functioning of the ego is restored if supported by the world around. But what if this is not the case and the potentially functioning ego is faced with a totally inadequate or destructive environment? Erikson's conclusion on this is clear: 'Therapy and guidance by professionals are doomed to failure where the culture refuses to provide an early basis for an identity and where opportunities for appropriate later adjustments are missing' (1965: 233). The ego by itself is not enough.

For an example Erikson turns to a whole group in society which is forced to suffer a 'permanent loss of identity' (1965: 233). Such, as he sees it, is the case of black American children whose heroes or heroines were always, in his time, presented as white. Their own denied elements become associated with their blackness and the stereotypes forced on them by the dominant society. Their 'identity fragments' become 'dominant in the form of racial caricatures which are underscored and stereotyped by the entertainment industry' (p. 234). This predicament of black American children 'is only the most flagrant case of an American minority which by the pressure of tradition and the limitation of opportunity is forced to identify with its own evil identity fragments' (p. 236).

## 'The eight ages of man'

From the struggle to clarify the 'unfathomable' complexities of ego and identity and the apparently intractable identity problems forced on minorities, Erikson emerges in the final chapter of Part III with what is probably the best known and most influential part of the whole book, his concept of a life cycle in eight stages, which he calls the 'eight ages of man'. This framework is one that he continued to work on for the rest of his life. In fewer than thirty pages it embraces human life in an outline that combines complexity with clarity, subtlety with authority, a coordinating overview with a sense of immediacy and reality. The later stages of the life cycle were apparently added at a late stage of writing the book. They were formulated for a paper which he prepared with his wife Joan for a conference on the development of the healthy personality in 1950 (Evans 1964: 63). This leaves open, but difficult to answer, the question of his wife's contribution to this most influential aspect of all Erikson's work.

I shall outline the scheme and comment on the features which make it effective. I then note some of the unresolved problems involved in it. This summary, however, is no substitute for reading this part of Erikson's book in its entirety.

The first three stages to some extent recapitulate their description in an earlier chapter. The crucial change of perspective is that the nuclear conflict between positive and negative attitudes at each stage or 'crisis' becomes the central feature on which all other elements converge.

### Basic trust versus basic mistrust

In this first stage 'the firm establishment of enduring patterns for the solution of the nuclear conflict of basic trust versus basic mistrust . . . is the first task of the ego' (Erikson 1965: 241). Trust is a state of being and responding. It is a trust in the 'sameness and continuity of the outer providers', but also trust of 'oneself and the capacity of one's own organs to cope with urges' (p. 239). 'Näiveté' and 'mutuality' are characteristics of this trust (1965: p. 239). The relationship with the provider creates the sense of trust. The quality of the relationship and not the extent of frustration or deprivation is crucial even at this first stage. 'Ultimately, children become neurotic not from frustrations, but from the lack or loss of societal meaning in these frustrations' (1965: p. 241).

The 'alternative' attitude to trust is mistrust. Erikson points out how strong is the basis for mistrust which arises out of the inevitable natural frustrations, parental inadequacy and absences. It is also a result of the defensive splitting which characterizes the process of differentiating inner from outer, self from not self, with all its accompanying distortions of reality, projections and introjections. It is thus against a 'powerful combination of a sense of having been deprived, of having been divided, and of having been abandoned that basic trust must maintain itself throughout life' (Erikson 1965: 242).

### Autonomy versus shame and doubt

This stage, as we have seen, is linked to a physical development of muscular maturation and to the generalized modes of holding on and letting go. Autonomy is the growing ability to control oneself, to hold on and let go with discretion, to 'stand on his own feet' (Erikson 1965: 244).

The alternative is shame and doubt. Shame is particularly associated with the experience of 'being completely exposed and conscious of being looked at', as in dreams of nakedness or of being seen 'with one's pants down' (p. 244). Doubt is the 'brother of shame', associated with consciousness of having a front and a back, an area behind that one cannot see, but which may be the source of evil and decay, the 'small being's dark continent' (p. 245). It is a source of paranoid fears of being attacked from behind and of secret persecution. Shame and doubt are experienced individually but are also channelled or exploited by the adult world. The decisive ratio between these two will determine, subject to later experience and revisitations, whether there is a 'lasting sense of goodwill and pride' or 'from a sense of loss of self-control . . . a lasting propensity to doubt and shame' (1965: 246).

### Initiative versus guilt

This stage is linked to the physical 'ambulatory stage and that of infantile genitality' and a general social modality of 'being on the make' (p. 247). Initiative is the typical example of 'that pervading quality' which at every stage attends a 'new miracle of vigorous unfolding, which constitutes a new hope and a new responsibility for all' (p. 246). Erikson distinguishes initiative from autonomy in that initiative adds to autonomy 'the quality of understanding, planning and "attacking" a task for the sake of being active and on the move' (p. 247).

The alternative is a 'sense of guilt over the goals contemplated and the acts initiated in one's exuberant enjoyment of new locomotor and mental power', including 'acts of aggressive manipulation and coercion' (p. 247). Such overreaching provokes a reaction from parents and siblings and comes up against the inherent dangers and intractability of the environment. This leads to the internalization of a sense of guilt. A new found imagination in story, myth and play and the search for explanations of the growing absorbent mind provide a means of containing and expressing new experiences but also of secret terror, guilt and misunderstanding. It is not just hurt, frustration and deprivation but a sense of badness and fear of punishment that accompany the growing powers at this stage.

Also involved is the identification with the parent of the same sex and jealous attachment to the parent of the opposite sex which Freud typified in the oedipal relationship. The 'oedipal' stage results in the 'oppressive establishment of a moral sense'. Nevertheless, in Erikson's view it also 'sets the direction towards the possible and the tangible which permits the dreams of early childhood to be attached to the goals of an active adult life' (p. 250).

## Industry versus inferiority

This stage corresponds to and draws on Freud's stage of latency. For Erikson the child has now experienced 'a sense of finality regarding the fact that there is no workable future within the womb of his family' (p. 250). He is ready for the mastery of the skills of production, communication and cooperation. He 'develops a sense of industry' and learns to 'win recognition by producing things' (p. 250).

The child's danger at this time lies in a sense of inadequacy or inferiority. If he 'despairs of his tools and skills' or is 'discouraged from identification' with his 'tool partners', he may consider himself 'doomed to mediocrity or inadequacy' (p. 251). Erikson points to another danger that the child may identify too completely with the world of skills and work and so become 'the thoughtless slave of his technology and of those who are in a position to exploit it' (p. 252).

## Identity versus role confusion

In this stage Erikson's exploration of identity finds a new formulation within his stages of nuclear conflict. Until now the sense of identity has been only partial, emerging or budding, held within a framework of economic and emotional dependence in the family, a series of identifications rather than an identity. Now is the time for the formation of a lasting identity which is 'more than the sum of childhood identifications' (p. 253). It is 'the accrued experience of the ego's ability to integrate all identifications with the vicissitudes of the libido, with the aptitudes developed out of endowment, and with the opportunities offered in social roles' (p. 253).

The 'danger' of this stage is one that Erikson describes as role confusion. He particularly emphasizes the importance of occupation at this stage. 'In most instances . . . it is the inability to settle on an occupational identity which disturbs individual young people' (p. 253). Falling in love is seen as an 'attempt to arrive at a definition of one's identity' (p. 253).

Erikson introduces two other ideas around the adolescent identity crisis here which he explores in later work. The first is the idea of the psychosocial 'moratorium' (p. 254), a socially sanctioned period in which the adolescent can be allowed to flounder and explore before settling on a more permanent identity, a time of extended play and experiment between childhood and adulthood. The second is the concept of ideology as a 'defined world image' (p. 254) by which the young adult finds some sense of order and orientation. It is this need for ideology, Erikson suggests, that makes adolescents so susceptible to the exploitation of totalitarian creeds, which offer a world view rather than simple commandments, but in a polarized way that excludes those who do not think as we do.

*Intimacy versus isolation*

For Erikson intimacy depends on and therefore follows a sense of identity. Intimacy is the 'capacity to commit . . . to concrete affiliations and partnerships and to develop ethical strength to abide by such commitments, even though they may call for significant sacrifices or compromises' (Erikson 1965: 255). He sees this stage as contrasting with as well as building on the establishment of identity. 'The young adult, emerging from the search for and insistence on identity, is eager and willing to fuse his identity with that of others' (p. 255). In this stage 'true genitality' is expressed in mutuality of relationship (p. 256).

The danger is that the individual may avoid commitment to intimacy and this may lead to 'a deep sense of isolation and consequent self-absorption' (p. 255). This isolation extends into wider social relationships through what Erikson calls distantiation: 'the readiness to isolate and, if necessary, to destroy those forces and people whose essence seems dangerous to one's own' (p. 255). On the other hand, the experience and differentiation of 'adult duty', 'competitive encounter' and 'sexual embrace' may lead to that '*ethical sense* which is the mark of the adult' (p. 256).

*Generativity versus stagnation*

Erikson says that this stage is, or should be, a central one because it is the crucial link between the generations. He believes that the 'fashionable insistence on dramatizing the dependence of children on adults blinds us to the dependence of the older generation on the younger one' (1965: 258). Generativity is 'primarily the concern in establishing and guiding the next generation'. Erikson makes it clear that by generativity he does not mean exclusively having and raising children, but includes creative contribution to society of all kinds. However, he also sees it as 'an essential stage on the psychosexual as well as the psychosocial schedule', in which 'the ability to lose oneself in the meeting of bodies and minds leads to a gradual expansion of ego-interests' (p. 258).

Failure to develop such an 'enrichment' of interests may lead to a 'pervading sense of stagnation and personal impoverishment' (p. 258). This sense of stagnation is the alternative to the positive sense of generativity. Such stagnation is the more significant because at this stage it affects not only the individual but successive generations; for adults may convey their own lack of trust, or may impose excessive demands that the child can somehow redeem or restore what the adult and parent has failed to find for himself or herself.

*Ego integrity versus despair*

Integrity is the 'fruit of these seven stages'. It can be found 'only in him who in some way has taken care of things and people and has adapted himself to the triumphs and disappointments adherent to being, the originator of others or the generator of products and ideas' (p. 259). Integrity involves 'a proclivity for order and meaning', 'post-narcissistic love' and 'acceptance of one's one and only life cycle'. It allows for 'participation by followership as well as the acceptance of the responsibility of leadership' (p. 261). The possessor of integrity is aware of the 'relativity of all the various life styles' but 'is ready to defend the dignity of his own style against all physical and economic threats' (p. 260). This style is deeply personal and individual and at the same time something shared with others – 'a style of integrity of which he partakes'. It is the style of integrity 'developed by his culture or civilization', and Erikson sees this as typified by certain specific ideal types: 'a wise Indian, a true gentleman, and a mature peasant' (p. 260).

Lack or loss of integrity brings an alternative sense of despair which 'expresses the feeling that the time is now short, too short for the attempt to start another life and try out alternate roads to integrity' (p. 260). For Erikson this despair is 'signified by fear of death'. For the person of integrity 'death loses its sting', because a particular style of integrity 'becomes the "patrimony of his soul"' (p. 260; quoted from Calderon, original in text). So Erikson brings the final stage into relation to the first. Integrity is both the completion and the foundation of infant trust. 'Healthy children will not fear life if their elders have integrity enough not to fear death' (p. 261).

### Features of the life cycle

We have followed Erikson's scheme stage by stage, but the impact of the scheme depends not only on the detail of its stages but on what characterizes it as a whole. It is, Erikson claimed, 'a global form of thinking and rethinking which leaves details of methodology and terminology to further study' (1965: 265). He attempted to summarize this as shown in Figure 1. The principal features of the whole scheme are as follows:

1 It embraces a complete life cycle viewed within a sequence of generations.
2 It consistently applies a threefold process linking biological, psychological and social processes in its formulation of human development.
3 The 'epigenetic' sequence provides an original contribution to the nature versus nurture dilemma in human development. I discuss this in more detail below.
4 Each stage is described in terms of a nuclear conflict between opposing or alternative attitudes. Each crisis, by which Erikson means a turning point, must be resolved in a balance between positive and negative. Nevertheless, the negative is important in its own right.
5 The stages are interrelated. The ratio or resolution of each stage sets a pattern that is never complete. Each stage is prefigured in and affected by earlier stages and will continue to affect and be modified in later stages. This interrelationship is particularly illustrated by the empty boxes in the chart, each of which has its significance.
6 The scheme is focused on normal rather than pathological development.

|   | 1 | 2 | 3 | 4 | 5 | 6 | 7 | 8 |
|---|---|---|---|---|---|---|---|---|
| H maturity | | | | | | | | ego integrity v. despair |
| G adulthood | | | | | | | generativity v. stagnation | |
| F young adulthood | | | | | | intimacy v. isolation | | |
| E puberty and adolescence | | | | | identity v. role confusion | | | |
| D latency | | | | industry v. inferiority | | | | |
| C locomotor– genital | | | initiative v. guilt | | | | | |
| B muscular– anal | | autonomy v. shame, doubt | | | | | | |
| A oral sensory | basic trust v. mistrust | | | | | | | |

*Figure 1* The life cycle 1. (From Erikson 1965: 264.)

7 The scheme is intended to show a pattern of healthy development. This appears at times to be considered synonymous with normal.
8 Erikson outlines a link between the stages and institutions of society, e.g. between stage 1 (trust versus mistrust) and religion.
9 A feature which appears in the second edition is the linking of a particular ego quality deriving from the nuclear conflict at each stage, e.g. hope from trust versus mistrust, fidelity from identity versus role confusion (1965: 266n). Erikson says that these strengths or 'virtues' are the 'lasting outcome of the "favourable ratios"' between positive and negative aspects which emerges from the successful negotiation of a crisis at each stage.

## Issues arising from the eight stages

The 'eight ages of man' scheme raises important issues of human development in three main areas. The first concerns the view of life as a sequence of stages. The second concerns the nature of the nuclear conflict or crisis at each stage. The third concerns the relationship of individual to society as suggested by the scheme. These three areas may be seen as reflecting the problems in the biological, the ego and the social processes respectively, and in their relation to each other.

### Issues involved in the sequence of stages

The main issues here are: how far is the sequence of stages predetermined and how far is it modifiable by the environment and the activity of the individual ego? Is a negative or unfavourable ratio at one stage retrievable in another? Are the stages fixed in their order, and if so has Erikson defined the stages and their order correctly? How much flexibility is there in the timing, order and overlapping of the stages?

Erikson described the sequence of stages as 'epigenetic'. What does he mean by this? Epigenesis is a term which apparently derives from nineteenth-century embryology, with its disputes as to whether development in the womb is dependent on preformed parts which emerge in sequence according to a predetermined timetable, or whether development depends more on the interaction between the organism and its environment (Bateman and Holmes 1995: 50). It is a version of the nature versus nurture debate. Erikson's version is characteristically an attempt to combine the two viewpoints. He states the principle of epigenesis as that 'anything that grows has a ground plan, and that out of this ground plan parts arise, each part having its time of special ascendancy, until all the parts have arisen to form a functioning whole' (Erikson 1968a: 92). This sounds very much like a predetermined viewpoint, and indeed Erikson uses the word predetermined. He says that personality 'can be said to develop according to steps predetermined in the human organism's readiness to be driven forward, to be aware of, and to interact with a widening radius of significant individuals and institutions' (p. 93). Nevertheless, Erikson modifies this 'predetermined' view in a number of ways.

The first way is by saying that what is predetermined is a 'readiness' as in the quotation above, a potentiality. Thus the 'inner laws of development' create 'a succession of possibilities for significant interaction' (p. 93). His scheme allows for both predetermined 'parts' in a 'ground plan' and the possibility of modification as these develop in interaction with the environment. Bateman and Holmes (1995: 51) suggest that Erikson's theory implies that there are 'many different possible developmental pathways' owing to the potentialities involved in each stage.

The second modification is that the ground plan 'makes room for variations in tempo and intensity' (Erikson 1965: 263). Such acceleration or retardation 'is assumed to have a modifying influence on all later stages' (p. 265). This leads to the third major modification of the predetermined nature of the sequences, the interrelationship and interaction between them. Erikson is particularly concerned that his stages should not be misunderstood as 'an achievement, secured once for all at a given state' (p. 265n). 'Each item of the vital personality . . . is systematically related to all the others.' The relation includes the way 'each item exists in some form before "its" decisive and critical time normally arrives' (Erikson 1968a: 93). They also continue their influence on later stages. As Bateman and Holmes put it, 'the "stages" are not superseded . . . but remain active as phases or "developmental lines" throughout life which may be activated at times of stress' (1995: 51).

The interrelationship between the stages is signified by the empty boxes in the epigenetic chart. The article which Erikson wrote with Joan Erikson in 1950, on which the 'eight ages' chapter is based, includes a version of the chart in which the boxes relating to the stage of identity versus identity confusion ('role confusion' in *Childhood and Society*) are filled in (see Figure 2). Box V/1, for example, illustrates how the earliest phase may surface during the adolescent crisis of identity in the form of 'time confusion' as a persisting element of mistrust in the environment. Erikson points out how there may be a regression to a time 'when time did not exist' (1968a: 181) in the adolescent, who finds it 'hard for him to go to bed and face the transition into a state of sleep . . . hard for him to get up' and 'hard to come to the therapeutic appointment, and hard to leave it' (p. 169).

Box I/5 indicates how in stage I, if there is massive breakdown of trust, the infant may attempt to resolve this by 'autistic isolation'. This represents a premature resolution of identity without any of the resources needed for this resolution. 'Mutual recognition', on the other hand, provides in embryo form the basis for a later emergence of identity, in which the recognition of his or her identity by the world around will play a vital part.

At the other end of the scale, V/8 indicates how the concern for ultimate values essential to stage 8 is already in some way, and in some individuals most intensely, anticipated and prefigured at the stage of adolescence. Erikson was later to become absorbed in this aspect in his studies of Luther and Gandhi.

Nevertheless, in spite of this awareness of the interrelationship of stages, Erikson maintains that 'while such interaction varies from culture to culture, it must remain within "the proper rate and the proper sequence" which

| | 1 | 2 | 3 | 4 | 5 | 6 | 7 | 8 |
|---|---|---|---|---|---|---|---|---|
| VIII | | | | | | | | **Integrity v. Despair** |
| VII | | | | | | | **Generativity v. Stagnation** | |
| VI | | | | | | **Intimacy v. Isolation** | | |
| V | Temporal perspective v. Time confusion | Self-certainty v. Self-consciousness | Role experimentation v. Role fixation | Apprenticeship v. Work paralysis | **Identity v. Identity confusion** | Sexual polarization v. Bisexual confusion | Leader- and followership v. Authority confusion | Ideological commitment v. Confusion of values |
| IV | | | | **Industry v. Inferiority** | Task identification v. Sense of futility | | | |
| III | | | **Initiative v. Guilt** | | Anticipation of roles v. Role inhibition | | | |
| II | | **Autonomy v. Shame, doubt** | | | Will to be oneself v. Self-doubt | | | |
| I | **Trust v. Mistrust** | | | | Mutual recognition v. Autistic isolation | | | |

*Figure 2*  The life cycle 2. (From Erikson 1968a: 94.)

governs all epigenesis' (1968a: 93). Each stage has a time when its special theme 'comes to its ascendance, meets its crisis, and finds its lasting solution' (p. 95). Some confusion and misunderstanding concerning the 'achievement' of each stage seems unavoidable here. While wishing to acknowledge and allow for the interaction between stages, Erikson also has a powerful sense based on his own experience of children, and perhaps of himself, that there are decisive encounters linked to a particular developmental stage. It is based on his observation of how 'a crisis more or less beset with fumbling and fear' is resolved 'in that the child is suddenly seen to "grow together" both in his person and in his body . . . He appears "more himself"' (Erikson 1965: 246). Whatever reworkings and resonances there may be at later stages, for Erikson the ground plan ensures a series of specific crises which are 'not a threat of catastrophe, but a turning point, a crucial period of increased vulnerability and heightened potential' (1968a: 96).

The ambiguity around the rigidity or flexibility of the sequence of stages is reflected in the implications for therapy. On the one hand, Erikson seems to be an optimist who sees the aim of therapy as the restoration of a naturally healthy ground plan and ability for self-cure. On the other hand, the epigenetic scheme implies that a stage once missed cannot be remedied. Erikson is pessimistic in the sense that he sees the development of a strong ego as dependent both on natural endowment and on favourable social context. This seems to rule out the heroic view of the human spirit as able to triumph over adversity in any circumstance.

Apart from these general considerations about the sequence of stages, there are questions to be considered about the validity and accuracy of his descriptions of each stage. Is the formation of trust primarily located in the first stage of development? Is his model male-centred? Is industry an adequate term for the developments in the 'latency period'? Is the formation of intimacy correctly placed after rather than contemporary with or before that of identity, as feminist therapists among others have questioned? Erikson has provided a general outline and its value lies in its subtlety and complexity and in the stimulus for testing and comparison, both with personal experience and with empirical observation. Criticisms of Erikson's scheme, and of stage theory in general, and more recent developments and modifications based on his life cycle are discussed more fully in Chapter 10.

### Issues arising from the concept of nuclear conflict

In Erikson's concept of the nuclear conflict or crisis there is ambiguity as to whether the polarities in the conflict are to be seen as positive and negative in absolute terms or whether they are in some way complementary. Mistrust, for example, is seen as a danger that destroys or impairs trust, or alternatively as something that the healthy individual also needs because it provides a 'readiness for danger and an anticipation of discomfort' (Evans 1964: 15). Erikson's view on this seems to vary. In the eighth stage, for example, he seems to see despair as a destructive negative without any redeeming value. Role confusion, however, is sometimes seen as providing a valuable quality of openness to different possibilities in the formation of identity. In general his view is that while the task of the ego is to work through the conflict to a 'favourable ratio' of positive over negative, experience of the negative is an essential element in human experience and development.

### Issues arising between individual and society

The third area to consider in Erikson's outline of human development is in the relation of individuals to society. The main issue here is the dependence of the individual on society's ability to provide an adequate context for the development of his or her sense of identity. Erikson allows for the possibility of exploitation of the individual, but in some ways the eight ages of man model assumes that society generally does provide a context for the development of a healthy identity. It leaves unanswered the question of what an individual can do when faced with an environment that is hostile to her or his developmental needs. Erikson later explored this problem in the responses of individuals such as Luther and Gandhi to their historical context. In the fourth part of *Childhood and Society*, to which I now turn, Erikson explores the predicament of adolescents facing the challenge to form an identity in three different historical contexts.

### Part IV, Youth and the evolution of identity

In Part IV of *Childhood and Society* Erikson further expands his exploration of the identity problems of youth, now placed in a historical context. While he is seeking to 'reconcile historical and psychological methodologies' (Erikson 1965: 393), he protests that he does not have the necessary knowledge 'to approach in any systematic fashion the relationship between ego qualities, social institutions, and historical eras' (p. 270). The exploration of this relationship, however, if impressionistic rather than systematic, is just what he proceeds to undertake.

He focuses on 'the problem of ego identity and on its anchoring in cultural identity' (p. 271). This anchoring takes place primarily at the stage of adolescence. The formation of identity is for the *individual* 'the only inner arrangement which prevents the superego's permanent alliance with the unreconstructed remnants of latent infantile rage' (p. 271). At the same time this arrangement provides for the *society* a means of transmission to a new generation and also of renewal. For each generation 'can and must revitalize each institution even as it grows into it' (p. 271). Erikson examines the problems of identity connected with the entry into industrial production of three countries: the USA, Germany and Russia.

A paradox in this part is that while Erikson's viewpoint encompasses a wider perspective of different times and cultures, it also becomes more subjective and more personal. For each country he chooses an individual to represent the predicaments and processes of a whole society in change. For Germany, he examines the early life story of Adolf Hitler. For Russia, he chooses the childhood of Maxim Gorky as seen through the medium of Donskoi's film trilogy, which is based on Gorky's autobiography. For the USA, rather than choosing a specific individual, he creates an impression of a typical representative: 'our boy', 'our adolescent'.

Erikson describes American identity as formed between two historically polarized needs: for expansion, pioneering and moving on and for settlement, staying put and finding one's place. He sees a particular problem for the American adolescent in the tendency to keep open both options as far as possible and not to foreclose either. He relates the position of the dominating American 'Mom' to her response to this problem and her attempt to resolve the tension between moving on and staying put and so creating some stability for her children. Fathers are seen by Erikson in this generation as failing to provide an adequate basis for identity for their sons.

As he expounds this theme, insightful and convincing as it often appears, one cannot help wondering how far he is describing his own struggle to reconcile the urge to pioneer and push beyond old boundaries with the need for a settled place and identity.

Erikson then examines the story of Hitler's early years from his account in *Mein Kampf*. He points to its 'fairy tale' qualities (1965: 318). The details are distorted and contradictory. For example, his father is 'a faithful civil servant' (1965: 318), but also a brutal husband and a contemptible failure. Erikson is concerned to explain the problem of why Germans followed Hitler, as much as how Hitler became what he did. He sees Hitler as the leader of a gang to whom he gives licence not to grow up but to remain within the repeating rebellious circle of adolescent fantasy. Any authority other than his own is denounced as either pathetically weak or threatening the rights of the gang member. Hitler is the Führer, the leader, who excludes and replaces paternal authority.

The film trilogy which is based on Gorky's autobiography depicts the story of a Russian family with brilliant intensity and detail. It is a vivid portrayal of chaotic impulsiveness and self-destructive brutality. Through all this the 'hero', Alyosha, learns to survive and to draw his own conclusions about the identity to which he will commit himself. In the chaos of the family the redeeming feature is the mother. She represents the primal passive strength and capacity for compassion of the mothers, the bedrock of the Russian peasants' capacity to endure and survive. It is a redemption which, Erikson says, Alyosha must reject because to accept it is to be drawn back into the primitive helplessness and victimhood of the Russian people. The identity Alyosha chooses, presented to him by a travelling revolutionary, is one of hardness, rejection of roots in the past and a commitment to revolutionary action. Erikson also sees this as a protestant form of identity in its claim to make one's peace with life and death, without the intermediate patronage of priests or tsars.

Erikson intends to show how in each of these situations an individual is facing a personal crisis which is a part of and a response to a wider social crisis. There are unique elements to each individual and each historical context. However, Erikson also identifies similarities between all three situations which may form a basis for mutual understanding. For instance, he appeals to Americans to understand the protestant nature of the Russian commitment to revolution. From a very long-range point of view 'their protestantism is ours, and ours theirs' (1965: 392).

In Erikson's analysis an underlying problem in all three situations is what might be termed the problem of the father. In each case there is a failure of the father to provide a firm source of identification as a basis for the identity of the sons. In Germany, Hitler's power is seen to depend on the usurpation of the personal authority of the despised father by the leader of the gang. In Russia, Alyosha's father has disappeared and the grandfather declines from a threatening bully to a pitiful outcast in the street. In America, Erikson points to the powerful image of the grandfather, the pioneer who knew who he was, by contrast with the father who seems to have abdicated authority. It is left to the mother to provide an ideology which the sons can respect or fear but with which they cannot identify. The dislocation which this creates in the formation of identity for a new generation of sons is a theme which is reflected, as we have seen in Chapter 3, in Erikson's own experience of fathers.

### Conclusion: beyond anxiety

In the concluding chapter of *Childhood and Society*, Erikson returns to psychoanalysis to consider what light it can shed on the problems of society. Psychoanalysis, he says, is the study of the origins and manifestations of anxiety. He distinguishes anxiety from fear. While fears are 'states of apprehension which focus on isolated and recognizable dangers', anxieties are 'diffuse states of tension . . . which magnify and even cause the illusion of an outer danger, without pointing to appropriate avenues of defence or mastery' (Erikson 1965: 396). Thus the individual 'remains ready to expect from some enemy, force or event in the outer world that which, in fact, endangers him from within' (p. 396). The study of anxiety provides a link between the problems of the individual and the problems of society, because it is the 'arsenal of infantile anxiety' (p. 396) which provides the means for exploitation by unscrupulous leaders or indeed by political and religious institutions (p. 397). Erikson's concern with the political exploitation of anxiety draws particular significance from the fact that while he was writing the book between 1945 and 1950 America was swept by its fears of communist subversion, which had a direct impact on Erikson's life.

What, then, can psychoanalysis do to illuminate or help these social and political problems, given that its primary basis of work is with the individual? Erikson's answer is that it can best contribute through assisting in the formation for both individuals and society of a different, more fully realized, more inclusive and more rational identity. The main element of this identity he sums up as 'judiciousness'. This is 'a frame of mind which is tolerant of differences, cautious and methodical in evaluation, just in judgement, circumspect in action and – in spite of all this relativism – capable of faith and indignation' (Erikson 1965: 406). Its opposite is prejudice, an outlook 'characterized by prejudged values and dogmatic divisions' which makes exploitation possible and is destructive of mutuality (p. 406).

While he believes that psychoanalyis can contribute in theory and practice, he remains cautious about the possible abuse of its power. Psychoanalysis too can 'make man more exploitable by reducing him to a simpler model of himself' (p. 409). Psychoanalysis cannot work alone but has its place in concerted efforts which 'should focus on a relaxation of unconscious superstition in the handling of infants and on the reduction of political and economic prejudice which denies a sense of identity to youth' (p. 407).

Nearing the end of the chapter, he describes the 'dimensions of a psychoanalyst's job' (p. 412) in terms of matching pairs: cure–research, objectivity–participation, knowledge–imagination, tolerance–indignation. It is a characteristic search for balance between opposites. At the end of his 'conceptual itinerary' he returns to that aspect of his identity, as a psychoanalyst, with which perhaps he feels most at home. He concludes with a plea that the analyst be ready to analyse his or her own choice of identities, 'to discard archaic rituals of control and learn to identify with the lasting value of his job of enlightenment' (p. 414).

*Childhood and Society* begins with a challenge to psychoanalytic theory which describes individual development in terms of id, ego and superego. In its place, or as an extension of it, Erikson suggests an interaction of three processes: somatic, ego and societal. The book ends with a commitment to the work of enlightenment based on psychoanalytic insight in cooperation with other disciplines.

Through the concept of identity Erikson has brought into focus fundamental issues of individual autonomy and dependence in relation to society. This new focus implies that the conflicts of adolescence and of adulthood are as significant for the individual and society as the earlier struggles of childhood, even as they are a continuation of them.

Shortly after *Childhood and Society* was published, Erikson was confronted by the historical reality of an America in conflict over the supposed threat of communist subversion. Erikson's personal response to this confrontation led to another migration and further explorations of identity. It led to a focus on youth's struggle for identity and a search for an ethical basis for adult life that is relatively free from the compulsions of childhood. It involved a return to and reconsideration of his own roots in Europe and in the work of Freud. It also led to a search for a wider identity that can encompass difference and competing cultures. These themes are followed through his life and work in the following chapters.

# CHAPTER 6

---

# The 1950s: youth and the identity crisis

## Prelude: the oath of loyalty

In June 1950 the Governors of the University of California decreed that their staff should undertake an additional oath of loyalty. There had always been a loyalty oath to the constitution of the United States and to the State of California for those taking up a post. The additional oath was part of a growing reaction throughout the USA to the supposed threat of communist subversion.

The glow of victory at the end of the Second World War had been followed by disillusion as the Cold War developed. Hopes of a new world order of peace under the United Nations faded as East confronted West in Europe. The pride of Americans in their economic system and democratic government as the progressive force in world affairs was undermined. As after the First World War, the wish to use American power to uphold the new world order based on the American model struggled with a wish to be left alone to enjoy the benefits of victory and affluence. There also persisted the underlying trauma and grief for the scattered dead, in bomber missions in Europe, battleships in the Pacific, the jungles of the Solomon Islands or the lanes of Normandy.

Communists, suspected or real, became the focus of resentment and fear of all who might disturb American society with radical thinking or demands for change. There was in Erikson's words a ' "bunching together" of all that seems undefinably dangerous: spies, bums, Communists, liberals, and "professors" ' (1987: 619).

In 1947 the House Un-American Activities Committee began a series of 'widely publicized and inflammatory investigations' to prove that the nation 'had allowed communist subversion to reach alarming levels' (Brinkley *et al.* 1991: 847). It caught the popular feeling. The spotlight was turned on Hollywood and many suspects were barred from work or even jailed for refusing to answer questions. In February 1950 Senator Joseph McCarthy made a speech claiming to have the names of dissidents in the State Department.

The Fuchs spy revelations gave credibility to his charges. In June 1950 the outbreak of the Korean War added a further dimension to world confrontation. The rattled Democratic administration responded by setting up 'Loyalty Boards', authorizing the dismissal of employees judged as bad security risks. As the fever intensified, states and public bodies launched loyalty programmes of their own. Such was the loyalty oath demanded of university employees in California in April 1950.

The oath required an annual declaration that 'I am not a member of the Communist party or any other organization which advocates the overthrow of the Government by force or violence and I have no commitments in conflict with my responsibilities with respect to . . . free pursuit of truth' (Coles 1970: 156). About ninety members of the university senate refused to sign. Under pressure, two-thirds reluctantly gave way. Erikson seems to have wavered. He declared himself a non-communist. The remaining few who still refused to sign were dismissed. Erikson then resigned his newly won professorship. His resignation statement was read to the American Psychoanalytical Association that winter and published in May 1951 (Erikson 1987: 618).

Erikson gave a number of reasons for his decision. First, the constitutional oath was sufficient to affirm loyalty. 'I still resent being asked to affirm that I meant what I said when I signed the constitutional oath' (p. 619). Public hysteria is more likely to increase than be allayed if 'professors themselves tacitly admit that they need to deny perjury, year after year' (p. 620). He pointed out the oath's ineffectiveness, as a real subversive would sign the oath without scruple.

His main reason, however, was that to sign would harm the very people he was committed to serving, the students. What would young people, 'rightfully suspicious and embarrassingly discerning', make of the fact that the professors 'who are to teach them to think and to act judiciously and spontaneously must undergo a political test'? (p. 619). His particular work with students included the study of just such hysteria as was being manifested, including the 'tremendous waste in human energy which proceeds from irrational fear'. He could not therefore with a good conscience participate without protest in a 'vague, fearful and somewhat vindictive gesture devised to ban an evil in some magic way' (p. 620).

For Erikson and his family the resignation and protest were followed by another uprooting and a return to the eastern states. It is true that he was not long in finding a new post. Coles says that 'other institutions began to bid for him' (1970: 159). He was offered and accepted, 'after much deliberation' (Coles 1970: 159), a post at the Austen Riggs Center in Massachusetts as director of research, psychotherapist and training analyst.

The decision had not been easy, however. Recalling the event 25 years later, Erikson said that 'when the papers told us foreign-born among the non-signers to "go back where we came from," we suddenly felt quite certain that our apparent disloyalty to the soldiers in Korea was, in fact, quite in line with what they were said to be fighting for' (1975a: 42). Nevertheless, there is also a sense of hurt and of vulnerability. In a memoir written on the death of the friend Robert Knight, who had offered him the new base in New

England, Erikson recalled how 'we non-signers found ourselves unsupported by the students and abandoned by most of our colleagues' (1987: 734). This, more than the attacks of extremists or the media, may have been the hardest to take.

There was an element of uncertainty surrounding Erikson's protest. Friedman had concluded that while Erikson certainly resigned his professorship, he continued working for the university for a while and signed 'a new form of contract containing the very loyalty oath language that he publicly opposed' (1999: 250). 'This contradiction', writes Friedman, 'had to produce unease' (p. 250).

Erikson had chosen an American identity and citizenship and had begun to feel comfortable in it. Now this identity was threatened in its continuity and in its integrity. He was confronted with an expression of American feeling that branded any difference of background or thought that was 'un-American'. It could not but revive the immigrant's, and perhaps an even deeper Jewish, sense of insecurity; that the belonging is conditional and that a new homeland can at any time turn and reject you.

It also brought into focus the fact that being an American was not simply homogeneous. Erikson says that the incident was a test of his American identity, a test from which he emerged clearer. But it also made him aware that American identity was conflictual and fragmented, as well as rich and diverse – at times struggling for harmony, at others solidifying into exclusiveness and hostility. It was no longer a question of being an American, but what sort of American he could claim to be and what sort of American might be acceptable. The immigrant's conditional belonging continued to heighten his sensitivity to the conflictual nature of a discordant identity struggling to see itself as whole; and of the fragility of the myths, ideals and imagery on which this identity rested.

Erikson's work through the 1950s follows two main themes. The first is a focus on adolescence and young adulthood in terms of the psychosocial stage and crisis of identity versus identity confusion. The second is the revisiting of his German past and his reconsideration of the work of Freud, the subject of the next chapter.

Erikson approached the problems of youth and the crisis of identity in two ways. The first was based on his work as a psychotherapist and sought to delineate from individual cases a pattern of symptoms that could be recognized as a 'syndrome called *identity-confusion*' (1964: 64). His second approach describes the identity crisis as a normal and healthy, if often conflictual and distressing, stage of development. Although the two approaches are in many ways complementary, they do not always lie easily together, and this can be a source of confusion.

## Psychotherapy and the identity crisis

Throughout the 1950s Erikson worked at the Austen Riggs Center as psychotherapist and researcher. This work provided the basis for his psychotherapeutic view of identity. The Austen Riggs Center was a private clinic providing residential care and treatment. Many of Erikson's patients were college students who were failing in the transition to emotional and economic independence and occupational identity. The clinical setting and the multidisciplinary team work provided an almost ideal testing ground for Erikson's psychosocial therapeutic approach, as well as for research into the problems of young adulthood. On the other hand, it was, as Erikson himself commented, almost too perfect, causing amazement and some envy among colleagues at professional conferences. He simultaneously worked in a very different clinical setting in Pittsburgh and in various ways extended his experience beyond the circumscribed environment of Austen Riggs.

In a lecture to a conference at the Massachusetts Institute of Technology on the theme 'evidence and inference', Erikson gives a detailed account of therapy with one young adult in terms of an identity crisis. His talk was entitled 'The nature of clinical evidence' (1958b), and was an exposition to a mainly scientific audience of the ways in which psychotherapists use evidence and the qualities and limitations of that use as compared to that of scientific method. This account provides a detailed illustration of Erikson's psychotherapeutic approach, and a powerful metaphor for his concept of identity crisis.

The patient was a student at a theological college preparing for a ministry as a missionary. He had encountered a crisis of faith and confidence in himself and his vocation, not uncommon in such a setting. But he had become almost literally paralysed in his inability either to continue his chosen vocation or to reject it and start a search elsewhere. The initial assessment (by another therapist) concluded that he had 'border-line psychotic features in an inhibited, obsessive-compulsive character'. He seemed 'to be struggling to strengthen a rather precarious control over aggressive impulses, and probably feels a good deal of anxiety' (Erikson 1964: 60).

Erikson's account of the psychotherapy centres on a dream which is described as follows: 'There was a big face sitting in a buggy of horse-and-buggy days. The face was completely empty, and there was horrible, slimy, snaky hair all around it. I am not sure it wasn't my mother' (1964: 57). Erikson uses the two main images of the dream – the faceless face and the horse and buggy – as the basis for an exploration that becomes an 'interpretation', which was in turn 'strategic for the whole treatment' (1964: 59). For Erikson interpretation was part of a process of exercising 'free-floating attention', a wide ranging listening to associations and feelings concerning past, present and future and a gradual confluence of all these into 'recurring themes' which, 'first faintly but ever more insistently, signal the nature of the patient's message and its meaning' (p. 59). From these themes emerges the formulation of a '*unitary theme*' (p. 72).

This is an intuitive process but it is also one which the therapist is prepared for by training, experience and his or her thought structures. These give the therapist an 'implicit inventory' (p. 62), a schedule of 'expectable mental states' (p. 60), of links and interpretations against which to test not only what is being said but what is being left out, the significant omissions (p. 62).

Thus ' "free-floating" clinical attention and judgement lead him to all the *possible* faces which may be condensed in this one dream face', and then to decide its *'probable meaning'* (p. 63). This process is one of mutual effort which 'joins the patient's and the therapist's modes of problem-solving' (p. 72). It is a process described by Erikson to his scientific colleagues as *'disciplined subjectivity'* (p. 53).

The process involves holding back premature thoughts and ideas and opening out possibilities; it also involves a sense of urgency and the need for decision by the therapist. The dream presented was no ordinary one, but one which continued to haunt the young man through the daytime. The therapist had to decide whether it was indeed a 'sign of an impending collapse' or on the contrary 'a potentially beneficial clinical crisis' (p. 61). The decision to continue the dream's exploration involved a risk for the therapist matching that of the patient in reporting the dream.

Erikson says that at the heart of the young student's confusion are feelings of dread at a seemingly inevitable abandonment by those very people who meant most to him and on whose recognition and affirmation his sense of himself depended. Erikson puts it as 'Whenever I begin to have faith in somebody's strength and love some sickly and angry emotions pervade the relationship and I end up mistrusting, empty, and a victim of anger and despair' (p. 71).

This emerging unitary theme is linked through the dream to four distinguishable phases in the young man's life. The theme is recognized in early childhood as 'the desperate wish to keep alive in himself the charitable face of his mother in order to overcome the fear, guilt, and anger over her emotions' (p. 71), which are his response to similar unbounded emotions in her. They are glimpsed through the half-denied 'veiled presence' of his mother in the dream (p. 69). The second phase is his later childhood, in which the image of horse and buggy represents the world and presence of his grandfather, in place of an absent father, nostalgically idealized by his mother and himself. It represents a past strength, but one that cannot be assimilated into the very different technological and ideological reality in which the young man now has to live. The third phase is his immediately preceding religious crisis – his 'abortive attempt at finding through prayer that "presence" which could cure his inner void' (p. 71). His dread is now manifested in the feeling that God's face is turned away from him (1964: 65).

The fourth and perhaps most crucial link lies in the relationship with the therapist. It is crucial because it has an immediacy that can be faced here and now with another person who is willing to face it with him or her. Erikson says he was alerted to this connection by the patient's 'facial and tonal expression' when he told of the horrible dream face. It reminded him of 'critical moments during his treatment' when Erikson's necessary absences had led to apprehension 'that I might disapprove of him or disappear in anger', and by times when 'he was obviously not quite sure I was "all there" ' (p. 63). Erikson approaches this possible connection with caution. 'The psychotherapist should not force his way into the meanings of his patient's dream images', but 'does well to raise discreetly the masks of the various dream persons to see whether he can find his own face or person or role represented' (p. 63).

Erikson is aware of the effect of his physical presence on patients' imaginations. 'My often unruly white hair surrounding a reddish face easily enters my patients' imaginative productions, either in the form of a benevolent Santa Claus or that of a threatening ogre' (p. 63). In this case it is a faceless face surrounded by horrible writhing snakes. This empty face is among other things a desperate challenge and accusation to the therapist – of facelessness. Once again there is dread and fear linked to the yearning 'to break through to a provider of identity' (p. 66). It is a communication that says something like 'if I never know when you think of yourself rather than attending to me . . . *how can I have what I need most – a coherent personality, an identity, a face?'* (p. 64).

Such a communication requires a personal and a therapist's response. It is another moment of decision and action. To Erikson it was important that 'my communication should include an explicit statement of my emotional response to the dream-report'. As he reviewed with the patient some of his thinking, he told him

> without rancor, but not without some honest indignation, that my response to his account included a feeling of being attacked . . . He had worried me, had made me feel pity, had touched me with his memories, and had challenged me to prove, all at once, the goodness of mothers, the immortality of grandfathers, my own perfection, and God's grace.
>
> (Erikson 1964: 72)

In some such way the therapist acknowledges the deep want expressed by the patient, expressing at the same time his or her own incapacity to fulfil all such demands, and his compassionate sense of the patient's pain and a willingness not to run away from it. 'A sense of mutuality and reality was thus restored, reinforced by the fact that while accepting his transferences as meaningful, I had refused to be drawn into them' (p. 75). He could also show that in the dream the young man had confronted his anger in the image of the Gorgon which, 'neither of us being a hero, we could yet slay together' (p. 75).

This 'specimen' of a case is a valuable illustration of the nature, uses and limitations of interpretation in psychotherapy. It demonstrates the importance of the mutuality of patient and therapist; of a practical balance between intuition and theoretical frameworks; of the therapist's alertness to and ability to express her or his own feelings with appropriate timing; of the responsibility for taking risks and decisions. Erikson recognizes a wide variation in the uses of interpretation according to the temperament of the therapist and the needs of the client. 'Therapists of different temperament . . . and various persuasions differ as to what constitutes an interpretation: an impersonal and authoritative explanation, a warm and personal suggestion, an expansive sermon or a sparse encouragement to go on and see what comes up next' (p. 72).

This case illustrates a comprehensive awareness of the significance of the therapist's response to the patient, including those unconscious communications and interactions which have been explored under the general label of 'countertransference'. Although he does not use this term, Erikson distinguishes a variety of responses and interactions, distinctions which are essential if the therapist is not to fall into easy assumptions or into confusion about different aspects of the relationship with the client.

First are those responses of the therapist which can blind her or him to what is happening and trigger off defensive or destructive reactions. 'Repressed emotions easily hide themselves in the therapist's most stubborn blind spots' (p. 73). This aspect includes the therapist's motivations and the personal meanings of the therapeutic role. As an example Erikson points to the potential distraction from his ability to focus on the client's needs, which comes from this case being a part of his research project into identity diffusion. Such an involvement does not necessarily divert from the listening to the patient, but it may. As Erikson puts it, 'a research minded clinician – and one with literary ambitions, at that – must always take care lest his patients become footnotes to his favourite topic' (p. 64).

Second, there are the unconscious communications and emotional and behavioural responses to the patient that provide creative opportunities both for understanding and for making explicit the themes that are a problem to the patient. The interpretation and use of this 'countertransference' evidence was already being developed by therapists such as Searles (1965), who knew and admired Erikson's work. Erikson's feelings of being attacked and challenged in the above case are examples of this. He emphasizes that this evidence includes responses such as indignation which involve strong feelings combined with moral or ethical judgement. Any psychotherapist 'who throws out his ethical sentiments with his irrational moral anger, deprives himself of a principal tool of his clinical perception' (p. 73). The problem is how to distinguish the two: 'indignation, admitted and scrutinized for flaws of sulkiness or self-indulgence, is . . . an important tool of therapy and theory' (p. 73).

The third aspect is the insistence that the countertransference responses are balanced by those belonging to the role of the therapist. 'I had played neither mother, grandfather, nor God (this is the hardest), but had offered him my help as defined by my professional status' (p. 75).

Erikson's description evokes the daunting complexity of the therapeutic process, yet he also maintains a sense of the simplicity at its heart. 'A therapeutic interpretation', he summarizes, 'while brief and simple in form, should encompass a *unitary theme* . . . common at the same time to a dominant trend in the patient's relation to the therapist, to a significant portion of his symptomatology, to an important conflict of his childhood, and to corresponding facts of his work and love life.' He adds, however, 'This sounds more complicated than it is. Often a very short and casual remark proves to have encompassed all this' (p. 72).

## Identity confusion

Erikson's work in the 1950s was concerned not only with individual cases but also with a generalized understanding of what cases have in common. The two are connected, because 'what is *unique* to the *individual* case' would not 'stand out without that other concern . . . the study of what is *common* to verifiable *classes* of cases' (Erikson 1964: 80). Such a research focus is the basis of his delineation of the identity crisis of youth in terms of identity and identity confusion (which he originally called the 'syndrome of identity-diffusion'; Erikson 1955a).

The data for this work included, but ranged far wider than, his experience at the Austen Riggs Center. It included regular work at the University of Pittsburgh's Western Psychiatric Institute, where he encountered workers and the children of workers from Pittsburgh's mills and mines. The young people he saw were a generation that was vividly typified in the sullen rebelliousness of James Dean in the film *Rebel without a Cause*. Erikson was also familiar with the work of Dr Benjamin Spock at the Arsenal Health Center and Nursery, where he watched 'how relatively poor mothers – many recent immigrants – handled their children' (Coles 1970: 171).

Erikson was a frequent attendant and speaker at conferences throughout America and now increasingly in Europe and Israel. They included a wide range of audiences. There were conferences of fellow psychotherapists, multidisciplinary conferences run by the World Health Organization or the US Department of Health, Education and Welfare, conferences of academics such as the American Academy of Arts and Sciences. In these venues he met workers of many disciplines as well as some of the eminent thinkers of that time, such as Piaget, Huxley and Lorenz. His formulation of the problems of youth thus had a broad foundation in experience and theory, and demonstrated an ability to explain things in others' terms. Erikson was able to speak a variety of academic and public languages according to the audience. As a writer he was reaching an increasingly wide public. To some extent he was now a public figure speaking as an American to Americans, and as an American to a wider world.

In delineating a 'syndrome of identity confusion' Erikson employs four main concepts: (a) the recurrence of earlier life stages and the reworking of earlier crises; (b) identifications as a preparation for identity; (c) negative identity, as a destructive distortion of the transition to identity but also a normal part of that transition; and (d) totalism as a primitive or deviant form of the wholeness of a healthy identity.

### Recurrence of elements from earlier life stages

The crises of the pre-adolescent life stages, and the qualities and deficits that ensue from them, are reflected in the task of identity formation at adolescence. As already noted, Erikson sees in the confusion over time, 'more or less typical for all adolescents' (procrastination, chronic lateness, difficulty completing work) (1968a: 182), a reflection of that 'mistrust of time' connected to the earliest struggles between trust and mistrust (1968a: 181). Guilt, appearing in the form of a 'denial of ambition as the only possible way of avoiding guilt' (p. 184), reflects the conflicts of the third stage. Work paralysis, which Erikson had himself experienced as an adolescent, is 'the logical sequence of a deep sense of inadequacy of one's general equipment' that relates to the fourth stage (p. 184). In these reflections the young person may be 'malignantly regressed' although the regression may also be self-curative. Thus the choice of a 'self-defeating role' may be the 'only acceptable form of initiative on the way back up' (p. 184). The line between the self-curative and the self-destructive may be hard to distinguish. The identity crisis of youth also includes premature forms or prefigurations of elements of later stages, such as generativity versus stagnation (involving issues of 'leadership' and 'followership'; (p. 187) and integrity versus despair (involving 'confusion of values'; p. 188).

## Identifications

Identifications are seen by Erikson as a key stage between earlier introjection and the formation of identity. Identifications with 'trustworthy representatives of a meaningful hierarchy of roles' (Erikson 1968a: 159) are essential bases for identity. But something else has to happen in the formation of a coherent identity that is more than the sum or the extension of these identifications. The final identity 'includes all significant identifications, but it also alters them to make a unique and reasonably coherent whole' (1968a: 161). What this sudden coherence is and how it comes about remain elusive.

## Negative identity

Negative identity occurs when the adolescent makes that necessary leap from 'identifications' to 'identity' in a way that is primarily negative, a reaction to the seemingly impossible positive identities available. Erikson describes negative identity as 'perversely based on all those identifications and roles which . . . had been presented to them as most undesirable or dangerous and yet also as most real' (1968a: 174). It is characterized by 'scornful and snobbish hostility' towards the roles offered as proper and desirable (p. 172). He provides many examples and variations. He speaks of a young person's 'acid disdain' for almost any aspect of his or her background (1968a: 173). It may be the rejection of everything American or everything foreign or of a particular class or of an ethnic background, particularly for second generation immigrants. (Was Erikson speaking from personal experience of his own teenage children?) A young man of upper class background only feels himself and others to be 'real' among the poor and deprived. The alternative negative identities often have a strong element of fantasy and fabrication. One girl of Middle European descent made for herself an elaborate Scottish background complete with convincing accent. Others again feel 'the necessity of . . . defending a niche of one's own against the excessive ideals' of 'morbidly anxious parents' (p. 175). They may identify with the dangerously real, with the addiction or weakness the parents most fear.

Among the most pernicious forms of negative identity are those where an individual from a minority group takes on the projected 'evil' images of the majority or dominant group. Such are the stereotypes of black identity, such as supposed laziness, uncontrolled sexuality or stupidity. Erikson describes how a 4-year-old black girl painted a picture of herself in white on a white background, a 'playful self-eradication' that could become deadly (1964: 94). Under extreme conditions of deprivation a destructive identity, or even nothingness, can be better than an identity without meaning, or the humiliation of identities that are always beyond reach.

## Totalism

Totalism in youth is a primitive and incomplete form of identity that Erikson distinguishes from *wholeness*. Wholeness is 'a sense of "inner identity"' which is expressed in terms like 'wholehearted, whole mindedness, wholesomeness' (1968a: 80). Wholeness 'emphasizes a sound, organic, progressive mutuality between the diversified functions and parts within an entirety, the boundaries of which are open and fluent' (p. 80). In totalism 'an absolute boundary is emphasized . . . nothing that belongs inside must be left outside, nothing that must be outside can be tolerated inside' (p. 81).

The young person who has recourse to totalism, whether in gangs, in snobbery or in scornful fanaticism, may be seen as failing in wholeness. Yet Erikson says that totalism is not necessarily bad. 'It is an alternate, if more primitive, way of dealing with experience, and thus has . . . certain adjustment and survival value' (1968a: 81). It represents at least a capacity for commitment and loyalty.

The concept of totalism is associated by Erikson with totalitarianism. It derives from his attempt to understand the Germany of his youth and to explain how his German contemporaries could have become so subject to Hitler and Nazism. If there is the potential in totalism for a progression to a higher level there is also the potential for individual and collective malignancy – for 'a futile cycle of evil' (Erikson 1964: 93).

In seeking to understand the appeal of totalitarianism for the young, Erikson considers three main sources: the historical, the social and the psychological. The historical causes are seen in a broad perspective.

> Where historical and technological developments severely encroach on deeply rooted or emerging identities (i.e., agrarian, feudal, patrician) on a large scale, youth feels endangered . . . whereupon it becomes ready to support doctrines offering a total immersion in a synthetic identity (extreme nationalism, racism or class consciousness).
>
> (Erikson 1964: 93)

The destructive effect of social conditions is exemplified in a study Erikson wrote with his son Kai, 'The confirmation of the delinquent' (1957). The judge's punitive response to a young 'delinquent', by misinterpreting what is a symptom of a search for identity as a total defiance of society, helps to confirm the delinquency into a permanent negative identity (Erikson 1987: 622).

Erikson also asks, 'In what way do childhood and youth predispose man for totalitarianism?' (1968a: 75). Here he looks to the life stages and the deficits already discussed. These deficits show all too clearly in 'the diversion to outer enemies of the impotent rage stored up within' (p. 84), in fantasies of total domination and in the dreams of a thousand-year Reich. They show too in the extreme polarization of moral judgements, when the 'totally "good" may learn to become torturers' for the greater glory of God or the state (1968a: 86).

What then enables the individual to emerge with a reasonably whole identity, despite the deficits of childhood and the demands of a rapidly changing and often exploitative society? For Erikson there is in each individual an ability to create a unique identity forged in the crisis of 'identity versus confusion'. This ability is dependent on a degree of trust, initiative and competence developed in childhood, and a degree of affirmation, opportunity and recognition from society. The synthesis of an identity is a unique act, self-curative and self-creative. Understanding how it happens means understanding identity as a positive and normal process rather than a pathological one.

### The nature of positive identity

A positive identity is not easy to define. One of the problems Erikson points out is that we are most aware of our identity when we are about to lose it or when we are 'somewhat surprised to make its acquaintance' (1968a: 165). It is the ordinary everyday sense of being who I am that is so elusive. Nevertheless, it is possible to recognize as common experience an assured if surprised knowing who I am. As Erikson puts it, 'An optimal sense of identity . . . is experienced as a sense of psychosocial well-being. Its most obvious concomitants are a feeling of being at home in one's body, a sense of "knowing where one is going", and an inner assurance of anticipated recognition from those who count' (1968a: 165).

To explore this further Erikson turned to descriptions of experiences of crises of identity in the autobiographical writings of 'extraordinary (and extraordinarily self-perceptive) individuals' (1968a: 155). In 'The problem of ego identity' (1956a) he chooses two such individuals: George Bernard Shaw and the pioneer of modern psychology, William James. They make a strong contrast. Shaw is a manipulator of his own masks, adjusting to many roles, yet determined that he alone shall be in charge of the manipulations. James is a retiring, ruminating explorer of himself, of ideas and other people. What they had in common was a struggle to find their identity through a difficult and prolonged adolescence.

In a letter to his wife, William James speaks of a moment when he 'felt himself most deeply and intensely active and alive' (Erikson 1968a: 19). He identifies particularly in this experience an 'element of active tension, of holding my own . . . and trusting outward things to perform their part so as to make it a full harmony, but without any *guaranty* that they will'. Three elements stand out here. First is the 'active tension'; this is no passive experience but one in which the individual is an agent. Second, the experience results in a sense of harmony with outward things. But, third, this harmony does not depend as much on outward things playing their part as on the individual's trust. It is a trust that can survive without the reassurance of external things.

Shaw's account, written when he was 70, describes the attempts of an extraordinary young man to find his place in ordinary society. He was, he says, 'extremely disagreeable and undesirable . . . not at all reticent of diabolical opinion . . . suffering . . . from simple cowardice and . . . horribly ashamed of it' (Erikson 1968a: 142). He experimented with a series of negative identities, 'the snob', the 'noise maker', the 'diabolical one'. His emergence from the crisis seems to have come from a realization that

> Whether it be that I was born mad or a little too sane, my kingdom was not of this world; I was at home only in the realm of my imagination, and at my ease only with the mighty dead. Therefore, I had to become an actor and create for myself a fantastic personality . . . adaptable to the various parts I had to play as author, journalist, orator, politician, committee man, man of the world, and so forth.
>
> (Erikson 1968a: 149)

Nevertheless, his successful identity depended, in Erikson's view, on another factor – that of finding an ideology. In Shaw's words, 'I was drawn into the Socialist revival of the early eighties, among Englishmen intensely serious and burning with indignation at the very real and very fundamental evils that affected all the world' (Erikson 1968a: 188). From this sentence Erikson identifies the essential features of an ideology as a world view, taken seriously and providing an ethical basis to which an individual can be committed with others. An ideology of some kind, he claims, is essential to identity formation. 'Without some such *ideological commitment*, however implicit in a "way of life", youth suffers a *confusion of values*' (p. 188).

While Erikson is insistent on the indispensability of an ideology as a container, a catalyst and guardian of youthful identity, he is aware of its dangers and the danger of being misunderstood in using the word. Ideology has a 'bad name' (p. 190), associated as it is with the propaganda of totalitarian states, the fundamentalism of theocracies, the special pleading of politicians and the manipulations of the media. Ideology in popular use has come to mean a set of ideas that rationalize, excuse or cover up an underlying reality. Erikson is not saying that ideologies are necessarily benign, but that they are a necessary foundation for identity. They provide, as for Shaw, a sense of seriousness, a world image, a basis for ethical judgement and an orientation beyond himself in society, without which he would have been left in isolation with the self-disgust of the cynic.

These descriptions of extraordinary individuals are one source of insight into the formation of identity. Erikson was concerned also 'to be able to trace its development through the life histories of "ordinary" individuals' (1968a: 155). Here he draws on 'general impressions from daily life, on guidance work with mildly disturbed young people, and on my participation in one of the rare "longitudinal" studies' (p. 155). He refers to the Child Guidance Study at the University of California.

'Adolescence', Erikson says, 'is not an affliction but a normative experience' (p. 163). He distinguishes the normative from the neurotic and the psychotic.

> Neurotic and psychotic crises are defined by a certain self-perpetuating propensity, by an increasing waste of defensive energy, and by a deepened psychosocial isolation; while normative crises are relatively more reversible, or better, traversable, and are characterized by an abundance of available energy . . . in the searching and playful engagement of the new opportunities and associations.
>
> (Erikson 1968a: 163)

The ability of the individual to surmount such crises through 'playful, if daring, experimentation', and in spite of confusion and suffering, is central to Erikson's view of the healthy development of identity. The 'adolescent's leaning out over any number of precipices' is a vital 'experimentation with experiences' (p. 164). Erikson is nowhere more impassioned than in his insistence on the self-curative essence of youthful identity formation and his indignation when this is responded to with 'fatal seriousness by overeager or neurotic adults' (p. 164).

As an example of self-curative action in the formation of identity, Erikson tells the story of Jill. The story illustrates 'countless observations in everyday life, where the resourcefulness of young people proves itself when conditions are right' (p. 131). Erikson had known Jill 'before puberty, when she was rather obese . . . was a tomboy and bitterly envious of her brothers'. She also 'had an air about her . . . which seemed to promise that things would turn out all right' (p. 130). One autumn in her late teens she asked her parents to let her stay on a ranch out west, where she had spent the summer, instead of returning to college. Her parents agreed to this 'moratorium'. That winter 'Jill specialized in taking care of new born colts, and would get up at any time during a winter night to bottle feed the most needy animals' (p. 131). She returned home having acquired 'a certain satisfaction within herself, as well as astonished recognition from the cowboys'. In learning to feed needy young mouths, 'she had found . . . an opportunity to do actively and for others what she had always yearned to have done for her'. That she 'did it all in jeans . . . brought recognition "from man to man" as well as from man to woman'. It brought a 'confirmation of her optimism' and a feeling 'that something could be done that felt like her' yet was also 'useful and worth while' (p. 131).

This story encapsulates Erikson's view of the adolescent's predicament: the dependence on already developed qualities and on the right conditions, but also on the individual's ability to find and hold on to what she knows is right for her. He also points here to the way the adolescent looks back as well as forward, utilizing 'a traditional way of life' (p. 130) for dealing with the remnants of negative identity. Similarly, Shaw had relied upon the 'mighty dead' in traversing his negative identities.

## Personal and social identifications

During the 1950s Erikson's professional life in his clinical and research work, as well as his public participation through conferences and writing, had a particular focus on youth. Such a preoccupation has a personal meaning related to his current life stage and concerns. The stage of 'generativity versus stagnation' includes the task of sustaining creativity and generativity in the face of stagnation and of developing a sense of care, both for one's own work and for those who share in it and those who are to inherit it. As in all crises, this involves a return to earlier struggles and a reworking of their themes at a new level. For Erikson this reworking took the particular form of a reworking of the crises of adolescence.

At a level of personal relationships his interest in and empathy with American youth may derive much of its power from his experience as a parent observing and involved in his own children's transition to adulthood in this decade. The story of Jill could well be the story of his daughter. Whether or not this is so, there is a personal quality to his writing here which belongs to a parental as much as a clinical viewpoint, evoking feelings of watchful anxiety, pride, protectiveness and relief. These are feelings which belong to a parent in the stage of both holding on to and letting go of parenthood, as the adolescent is holding on to and letting go of childhood. This experience at the ending of parenthood often involves a reawakening of the feelings of one's own adolescence, whether they are denied, as in the parent who 'has forgotten what it feels like to be young', or seen in the overinvolvement of the parent who tries to be a teenager. The parent's difficult task in relation to the adolescent is both to recognize and to contain such feelings from a standpoint of maturity and care.

Erikson identifies with the young person in his or her search for identity in a world that appears confused, alien, powerful and unconcerned, but which promises opportunities and the possibility of recognition and belonging. There is an affinity in the precariousness of belonging between the adolescent and the immigrant which Erikson noted in 'Identity and uprootedness in our time' (Erikson 1968a: 83).

In the stories of the young people with which he illustrates his ideas may be seen glimpses of the themes of Erikson's own experience. I suspect there is in Erikson himself a counterpart to the theological student and his fear of facelessness. Like the student, Erikson felt a mission to save and heal; like him, he had an absent father and a relegated nostalgic longing for a time and place where life was slower, surer, more whole; and as with the student there was a sense of the impotence of that childhood order to sustain identity in a changed world. There is a counterpart to the young George Bernard Shaw in the acquisition of the ability to adapt to a variety of roles and the need for an explicit expression of a serious ethical world order. There is a counterpart to the adolescent Jill, whose optimistic confidence in herself enabled her to find in a traditional way of life outside her family the self-affirmation she needed. So Erikson had sought a meaningful identity, first as the wandering artist and then in the psychoanalytic world of Vienna.

Erikson identifies with the way in which young people's identity is threatened by the divisions and confusions in American society: the contradictions inherent in the American dream of unlimited progress and opportunity and the contrast with the realities of poverty, exclusion and exploitation. His insights are based on personal experience as well as observation of young people. Like them he is searching for a reliable ethical standpoint, an ideology that can confront and survive society's confusion of values. Such confusion, with no counterbalance in secure or more whole identities, can lead, as in Nazism, to the subversion of totalism into totalitarianism and the projection of negative identities into vicious anti-Semitism. The experience of the loyalty investigations showed that there was the same potential for equally dangerous totalism and negative projections in the United States.

If Erikson identifies with the difficulties and problems of youth, he also turns to youth with a sense of optimism and an almost messianic hope for the future, not just of each individual but for society.

> It is the young who, by their responses and actions, tell the old whether life as presented to them has some vital promise, and it is the young who carry in them the power to confirm those who confirm them, to renew and regenerate, to disavow what is rotten, to reform and rebel.
>
> (Erikson 1968a: 258)

There is also the hope that in working through and balancing the crisis of identity and identity confusion, there may emerge adults capable of sustaining the task of generativity, of creating and caring for a new generation.

Erikson thus invests his hope for the future in the new generation, but at the same time he is aware that American society is confused and fragmented in the face of change and could not be relied on as a 'provider of identity'. This may be one reason why in the fifites his studies also took him away from America to revisit his personal and cultural roots in Germany and to re-examine his professional roots in the work of Freud and the world of Vienna. These revisitings and their outcome are examined in the next chapter.

# The 1950s: return to Freud, Luther and Germany

Between 1954 and 1956 Erikson published three significant papers on Freud. The first of these was 'The dream specimen of psychoanalysis' (1954a), based on some lectures to the American Psychoanalytic Association in 1949. It consists of a comprehensive and somewhat technical formulation of psychoanalytic work with dreams. Within this Erikson inserts a genuinely original and challenging reinterpretation of Freud's own dream of Irma in *The Interpretation of Dreams* (1900).

What Erikson proposes and demonstrates is a new balance between the latent, hidden content of the dream, connecting it to the 'infantile wish' and its associated conflicts, and the manifest 'dream structure' which 'reflects significant trends in the dreamer's total situation' (1987: 278).

The interpretation of this dream of Irma was central to Freud's self-analysis. He tells his friend Fliess of a fantasy of a tablet which would adorn his summer home: 'In this house, on July 24th 1895, the Mystery of the Dream unveiled itself to Dr Sigmund Freud' (quoted in Erikson 1987: 239). Erikson points out that the date is that of the Irma dream. The people in the dream are Irma (a patient), Freud and three other doctors. The dream events include a medical inspection of Irma's throat, a variety of nonsensical and contradictory diagnoses and suggestions of inappropriate treatments, including an injection. What became clear to Freud, with a mixture of shock and excitement, was that the whole meaning fell into place when he accepted the wish behind it. 'The content of the dream is thus the fulfillment of a wish' (quoted in Erikson 1987: 244). In this case it was his wish to be innocent of Irma's illness, and to put the blame in whatever way he could on the other three doctors and the patient herself. Half-humorously, Freud sums it up in the story of the man who was accused by a neighbour of returning a kettle in a damaged condition. 'In the first place, he said, he had returned the kettle undamaged; in the second place, it already had holes in it when he borrowed it; and in the third place, he had never borrowed it at all . . . If only one of these three lines of defense is recognized as valid, the man must be acquitted' (quoted in Erikson 1987: 244). Acquittal, by whatever means, is the latent wish of the dream.

Erikson recognizes the magnitude of Freud's discovery 'that dreams do really possess a meaning, and are by no means the expression of a disintegrated cerebral activity, as the writers on this subject would have us believe' (quoted in Erikson 1987: 245). He appreciates the freshness and honesty with which he records it. But Erikson says that because the discovery of the latent wish so excited and shocked Freud and his world, his followers subsequently hurried to 'crack its manifest appearance as if it were a useless shell and to hasten to discard this shell in favour of what seems to be the more worthwhile core' (1987: 247). Yet without this manifest aspect the dream loses not only half its meaning but half its value to the dreamer's life, that part which connects him or her to the present.

Erikson therefore sets the dream in the context of Freud's current concerns in the expanding circles of his personal, professional, social and political situations. 'The dreamer of the Irma dream was a 39-year-old doctor, a specialist in neurology in the city of Vienna. He was a Jewish citizen of a Catholic monarchy, once the Holy Roman Empire of German Nationality and now swayed both by liberalism and by increasing anti-Semitism' (Erikson 1987: 240). He indicates the personal context: 'His family had grown rapidly; in fact, his wife at the time was again pregnant' (p. 240). The personal and social concerns are interwoven with the professional context of his ambitions 'within an academic milieu which seemed to restrict his opportunities because he was a Jew; at an age when he seemed to notice with alarm the first signs of ageing, and, in fact, of disease; burdened with the responsibility of a fast growing family' (p. 241).

In all this Erikson identifies Freud's central concern and dilemma:

> A medical scientist is faced with a decision of whether to employ his brilliance, as he had shown he could, in the service of conventional practice and research, or to accept the task of substantiating in himself and of communicating to the world a new insight, namely, that man is unconscious of the best and worst in himself.
>
> (Erikson 1987: 241)

The fears and doubts, judgements, apprehensions, ambitions and frustrations of this predicament are as vital to the meaning of the dream as are the links that connect it to the strata of infantile fears. 'Like good surveyors, we must be at home on the geological surface as well as in the descending shafts' (p. 246). The dream points the way not only back to the past but also forward to the future.

Dreams, then, in this reinterpretation, 'not only fulfill naked wishes of sexual license, of unlimited dominance and of unrestricted destructiveness', they also have a purpose in relation to the present total situation: 'to lift the dreamer's isolation, appease his conscience and preserve his identity' (p. 278). In Erikson's view 'the Irma dream and its associations clearly reflect a crisis in the life of a creative man of middle age' (p. 274).

In this description of Freud's predicament there are parallels with Erikson's own personal and professional concerns at this time. Like Freud, Erikson is concerned with his relation to his contemporaries and how far he can or should go in challenging current orthodoxy and risking ostracism. This might explain a puzzling element in this particular paper, the wrapping up of Erikson's controversial views on Freud in a highly technical format with its claims to exhaustiveness and its cataloguing lists. Erikson seems to be trying out his ideas with a protective covering for his analytic colleagues, uncertain of the response of that 'compact majority' which is represented for Freud in the Irma dream by the three doctors.

At the end of the article Erikson suggests that the image of Irma's throat, her oral cavity, is a symbol not so much of her sexuality as of the feminine image of Fate who challenges the hero to his task, but who holds the power to grant or withhold its accomplishment. In a passage that has a visionary quality, he declares that the creative individual's 'cycle of moods and attitudes' permits him 'at the height of consummation to identify with father, mother and newborn child all in one; to represent his father's potency, his mother's fertility and his own reborn ideal identity' (Erikson 1987: 273). But the hero must return to face the consequences of his deeds in the responses of mankind who 'participate with pity and terror, with ambivalent admiration and ill concealed abhorrence, in the hubris of creative men' (p. 273). It is as though Erikson were rehearsing for himself, through the admiring and horrified watching of his master Freud, all the horrors as well as the sublime achievement which are involved in such hubris. It is a theme which he is to pursue through the lives of Luther and of Gandhi.

The second major publication on Freud was a book review (1955b) of Freud's letters to Wilhelm Fliess (Freud 1954). These letters trace the course of a close personal and intellectual relationship between the two men through the very years during which Freud began to work on his new ideas of psychology and practice. Throughout this period Fliess was the confidant of Freud's hopes and fears, the intellectual sounding board for his ideas and his emotional support. Ernest Jones used the letters in his biography (1953) to show Freud's vulnerability and humanity. Erikson sees the relationship differently, as 'mutual lionization' (1975a: 56), and as an idealizing 'transference' (p. 57) through which Freud was able to take his steps into the unknown. The letters chronicle the personal struggle this involved, with Freud dependent on Fliess until he found the assurance he needed within himself; and how, with some ruthlessness, Freud reversed his idealization into hostility and scorn  as the accompaniment to the assertion of his independence and confidence in his creative powers. Erikson notes that Freud himself hints at the transference nature of the relationship as a reason for ending it (p. 78). Erikson points to that 'bipolarization which many creative men need in order to have the courage of their own originality' (p. 56), in which Freud's 'driven Dionysian' is balanced by Fliess's 'Apollonian tower of calm strength' (p. 56). He sees a polarization of feminine and masculine, the balance of which 'was righted' in the 'course of this friendship'. 'Feminine intuition, childlike curiosity and artistic freedom of style were recognized and restored as partners of the masculine "inner tyrant"' (Erikson 1964: 38). These are concepts of which, as Erikson notes, Freud was becoming aware and which he was beginning to use in his new psychotherapy. What Erikson presents is how these interpersonal processes are part of and complementary to that crisis of generativity which has already been outlined in his interpretation of Freud's dream of Irma.

There is also in these polarizations a parallel with Erikson's own struggles to integrate the Dionysian darker side of his inner world, associated most potently with the horrors of a German culture driven mad, and the Apollonian harmony he hoped for in his New World. As we have seen, part of his search lay in an identification with the problems and the hopes of renewal in American youth. Part of it must also lie in facing the source of darkness in its German roots.

The third publication of the mid-1950s is a paper Erikson called 'The first psychoanalyst' (1956b). In content it is primarily a summing up of the two papers already mentioned. Its significance lies not so much in its content as in its context. It was a lecture given to the combined students of Frankfurt and Heidelberg Universities in 1956 to celebrate the hundredth anniversary of Freud's birth.

Erikson is concerned to demonstrate to his audience the magnitude of Freud's achievement in the difference he made to the way of thinking about people and their problems and the equally great transformation in treatment. The hidden workings of the mind had been acknowledged before by philosophers, poets, priests and ordinary people. What Freud claimed was that these workings could be understood and not just wondered at, disapproved of or exalted. The change in treatment of mental and emotional problems was equally radical. Rather than something that is done *to* people by doctors, healers or priests, it was to be something done *with* them. It is a therapy that involves the relationship between patient and therapist. There was nothing particularly new in Erikson saying this about Freud, although it may have been new to the students. The significance lies in the bridge Erikson was making between past and present across the obliterating horrors of Nazism and war.

In so doing he was also making a bridge to his personal past. The most obvious connection is that Frankfurt was his birthplace. On this visit, in which he was the principal speaker, Erikson appears relaxed and confident. Coles (1970) tells the story of how his lecture was introduced by the President of the West German Republic, a white haired old man, Theodor Heuss. Heuss told Erikson that he would feel strange introducing him because, 'I don't think I had any infant sexuality.' Erikson reassured him: 'Presidents don't need that sort of thing' (Coles 1970: 199). Coles tells of another address in Frankfurt to a group of German psychiatrists at which Erikson's eyes filled up with tears. The psychiatrists seem to have thought that his tears were for them. Coles says that Erikson 'could not forget what Germany had done to Europe, to itself, to millions of innocent men, women and children' (p. 262). His tears might also have been for himself.

Erikson later recorded that in speaking to the students at Frankfurt, he experienced another set of feelings. He remembered visiting a family in a small village by the Upper Rhine during his wandering youth, a memory which, he says, 'had been utterly covered by the rubble of cities and the bleached bones of men of my kind in Europe' (Erikson 1972: 9). In the morning, as the family sat down to breakfast the old man, a Protestant pastor, said the Lord's prayer in Luther's German. Erikson had the experience 'as seldom before or after, of a wholeness captured in a few words' (p. 10). It sounds like an experience of coming home, of belonging. He sets this experience alongside that of hearing the Gettysburg Address. In so doing he is recognizing something of the double nature of his identity. His study of the young Luther was another way of reconnecting with his German heritage. It was a way of reconnecting these two sources of identity, and the present with the past.

## Young Man Luther

In 1957 Erikson took a year off from his work at the Austen Riggs Center to write a book on Martin Luther. He explains the origin of the book in the preface. It was planned as a chapter in a book on the 'emotional crises in late adolescence'. But Luther 'proved too bulky to be merely a man of one chapter ... the clinical chapter became a historical book' (1972: 7).

Erikson acknowledges the personal as well as the professional rationale for the subject: 'My choice of subject forces me to deal with problems of faith and problems of Germany, two enigmas which I could have avoided by writing about some other young great man. But it seems I did not wish to avoid them' (p. 9). There is an element of personal identification in Erikson's concern with Luther's problems of identity as they emerge in his struggle for a creative generativity in the middle years.

Erikson presents Luther as a young man going through a crisis of identity, whose fate and genius is to translate that personal crisis in terms of the social, religious and political crisis of a generation. He presents Luther as a troubled, gifted and persistent young man. He is troubled in his relations with his strict and sometimes brutal father and in his search for meaning and identity in the Church as a monk. His rebellion against his father's dismissal of his inner spiritual aspirations is fused with his doubts and fears about the heaven and hell of Christian faith, and his outrage at the cynical use by the Church of its absolute power. In order to resolve this personal dilemma he had to challenge the world he found himself in or be crushed by it.

This personal struggle extended over a prolonged late adolescence of twelve years. It lasted from his entering a monastery against his father's wishes, after an intense experience in a thunderstorm, to the moment when, aged 34, he challenged the authority of the Pope by nailing his 95 theses on a door in Wittenberg. This period is the subject of Erikson's book.

The context is one of transition, or rather a complex overlapping of transitions. The medieval social order was based on feudal privilege and power and dependent social relationships; it was underpinned by a faith in the next world, in heaven and hell, supported by a priesthood claiming an absolute authority and providing a moral framework of good and evil, sin and redemption. This order was increasingly confronted by a new world of secular financial power and of secular authorities claiming independence from religious authority. In the prospering towns and cities, a cultural renaissance blossomed which was absorbed by this world's pleasures and pains rather than those of the next world. The confrontation is complicated by the fact that Luther is not merely representative of the rejection of the absolute authority of the church, but also represents a reaction against the worldliness of the Renaissance and humanism. Luther's reformation is in part a return to face the 'bad conscience' which men and women cannot escape, but must face alone before God without the mediation of priests.

Luther's parents lived in a mining town, part of that increasingly industrialized and mercantile Germany that yet had deep roots in the peasant, agrarian and feudal world. Some of the tensions which were implicit and contained in their world were perhaps unconsciously transmitted to the young Martin Luther. In him they became an irresistible drive towards an explicit formulation in his adolescent struggles with God, the Pope and the devil. The identity he found in himself was not so much a face as a voice, a voice which could penetrate the impassive presence of God and become, in his gifted vernacular oratory, the voice of a new era.

In writing a historical work Erikson faced a number of problems. He was aware of the limitations of his own historical knowledge and training, and he is critical of what he sees as the 'false routes' others have followed. The main danger of the psychological viewpoint is of reductionism, of reducing what must be understood in social, historical, political and spiritual terms to a particular psychological theory. Insights and theories developed from what is said and done between healer and patient must be 'carefully transposed before being applied to the general human condition' (Erikson 1972: 18). He is critical of generalizations from 'fragments of case histories or psychoanalytic interpretations which flutter around in our newspapers and magazines . . . like bats in the daytime' (p. 18).

On the other hand, historians seem equally trapped in their disciplines, without psychological awareness. In particular they 'immerse themselves into the very disguises, rationalizations, and idealizations of the historical process from which it should be their business to separate themselves' (p. 18).

The book is a study not only of Luther but of biographers of Luther. Erikson examines the way in which these biographers, the priest, the Lutheran professor, the psychiatrist of the 'medical-biological' school, the amateur psychoanalyst, see Luther through their own ideological assumptions: 'Each concocts his own Luther' (p. 27). Yet Erikson admits that he too must to some extent invent his own Luther. He also says that all the different ways of viewing a great man's life, the narrow, the broad, the polemical, the hagiographic, 'may be needed to capture the mood of the historical event' (p. 34).

From his own psychological viewpoint Erikson claims the validity of imaginative reconstruction and of trusting intuitive responses to the truth behind myths and legends. A central incident in his reconstruction of Luther's crisis is the story of his 'fit' in the choir, in which he cried out 'Ich bin's nit!' or 'Non sum!' (translated as 'It isn't me!' or 'I am *not*!'). Erikson admits that there is little concrete evidence for this story. He also says that 'the story of the fit in the choir attracted me originally because I suspected that the words "I am *not!*" revealed the fit to be part of a most severe identity crisis' (p. 34). Is he then guilty of seeing myth as fact because it fits his own agenda? Erikson defends himself by saying that we can accept 'half-legend as half-history, provided only that a reported episode does not contradict other well-established facts; persists in having a ring of truth; and yields a meaning consistent with psychological theory' (p. 34). It is persuasive, yet it cannot (but perhaps is not intended to) remove some suspicion that Erikson's version, like others', is affected by implicit assumptions and influenced by personal motivation and by the anticipated audience.

The significance of the study of *Young Man Luther* to the contemporary USA is threefold. First, it is a study of a young man's identity crisis and how he creates something new from the cultural possibilities and problems of his age. In this sense it is a broadly based historical contribution to the study of the 'emotional crises of late adolescence'. Second, Erikson is pointing to specific parallels between Luther's crisis and that of contemporary youth. Luther was responding to an age in which a social and moral framework was disintegrating. For many it no longer provided a convincing ideology; that is, 'a world image convincing enough to support the collective and individual sense of identity' (p. 20). What was forged in the reformation was a new ideology for a new age. Erikson sees the youth of America in a similar predicament, in which the old ideologies have lost their conviction, 'a sudden sense of alienation is widespread' (1964: 204) and youth looks for a new synthesis.

Third, it is that very moral framework which Luther helped to create in the sixteenth century which is now part of the old order that youth is questioning. It was Erikson's view that any new order has to be some kind of fusion of tradition and originality; that young people look back and take what they need from the traditional as well as looking forward to their own ideal vision of tomorrow. Luther's Protestant world image, with its ethic of self-improvement, self-questioning, self-discipline, personal responsibility and labour earning its reward, still has strength and vitality. Like all ideologies it has a negative side. In the Protestant ideologies this is seen in a rigid moralism, a tendency to self-righteousness combined with hypocrisy, a puritan suspicion of joy and a conformist morality that can be stifling of difference. An even darker shadow is cast by elements in Luther's later life: his authoritarianism and his coarse anti-Semitism.

Throughout the United States in the 1950s, and perhaps nowhere more than in Massachusetts, the conflicts between these elements of European and German culture, between Lutheran and Catholic, fundamentalist and rationalist, work-driven and work-disaffected, puritan and high-liver, remained vital and confused. Lutheran Protestantism remains a vital part of the European inheritance which, Erikson claims, 'we have neither completely lived down nor successfully outlived' (1972: 10).

It is worth questioning Erikson's use of the pronoun 'we' in this sentence and considering its meaning if 'I' is substituted. The story of Luther and the Reformation then becomes something which 'I have neither completely lived down nor successfully outlived'. Looked at this way the story of *Young Man Luther* is indeed a story of the 'problems of Germany' for Erikson himself, of the personal meaning for him of his emigration, of his European culture with its cruelty and its disintegration but also its moments of wholeness. The story of Luther makes a bridge between his European and his American worlds.

It also represents a link between the present and the past, between Erikson and the young Erik Homburger. Erikson points out that Luther refers to his early work as 'work in the mud' and that Luther and Freud shared a willingness to 'do the dirty work of their respective ages' (1972: 9). Luther's earthiness often seems like a challenging bid for autonomy against a sense of physical shame. Such feelings, belonging to the stage of the balancing of autonomy against shame and doubt, may have been raised in Erikson as he revisited the land he had left behind him.

Luther's personal story and historical significance have also, I think, a strong resonance for Erikson with that third stage of life in which initiative and purpose are constrained by guilt and a child faces the crisis of conscience, of obedience and disobedience. Erikson pointed out how these issues lie at the heart of 'this Western religious movement which grew out of and subsequently perpetuated an extreme emphasis on the interplay of initiative and guilt' (1972: 257). It also, he says, 'put an exclusive emphasis on the divine Father–Son', while the mother remains a 'counterplayer however shadowy' in the Mother Church (p. 257). But Erikson could also identify with Luther's working out of his father–mother–son relationship. Luther's rebellious challenge to his father and the Pope and his search for a forgiving eternal father is reflected in the young Erik Homburger's search for a father who never knew him, of his relationship with the intruding stepfather, with his healing instruments and with his psychological stepfather, Freud, with *his* healing instruments.

The demons of guilt and the threat of punishment are hushed but never completely subdued and return at times with terrible force to haunt the older Luther as the consequences of his great initiative spin beyond his control or intention. A certain fear of such consequences, the hubris of creative men, may have accompanied Erikson's struggle to move out of the shadow of Freud, 'the first psychoanalyst', as he had physically moved out of reach of his parents and a darkened Germany.

There is one other aspect of the study of Luther that needs consideration. Luther was above all a religious figure and the study of his life therefore raises the problems of applying psychology to religion as much as the problems of applying psychology to history. It involves, as Erikson noted, 'problems of Faith' as well as 'problems of Germany'.

Erikson says that religion 'translates into significant words, images, and codes the exceeding darkness which surrounds man's existence, and the light which pervades it beyond all desert or comprehension' (1972: 19). He also says that religion elaborates on 'what feels profoundly true though it is not demonstrable', while psychology 'endeavours to establish what is demonstrably true' (p. 19). Here he seems to be excluding religious experience from psychological study in a way that contradicts his view of the importance of the subjective in psychological understanding. It is as though psychological understanding can only be based on an objective science, a view which he criticizes in Freud.

He considers Luther's religious experience in terms of ideology and identity. 'Religion will occupy our attention primarily as a source of ideologies for those who seek identities' (p. 19). He also considers faith in developmental terms from the earliest years. It begins with the maternal presence providing the 'basic trust in mutuality' from which comes the optimistic assumption that 'somebody is there' (p. 114). It continues with the significance of the father's presence, which 'provides a sense of otherness against which to develop a sense of self, of autonomy from the maternal matrix' (p. 120). He articulates the elements of the face and the voice into a developmental sequence: 'Next to the recognition bestowed by the gracious face is the affirmation of a guiding voice' (p. 120).

This indicates that a sense of spiritual or existential concern is experienced from the earliest years, and is basic to the development of identity. Yet Erikson views Luther's existential concern with religion from the age of 19 as setting him apart as a *'homo religiosus'* (1972: 254). Erikson is not unaware of or insensitive to religious experience, whether as the affirmation of love or the dark unknown. This experience does not, however, fit easily into his outline of human development. This is an unresolved issue which became a major focus in the next decade when he wrote about the life of Gandhi, another *homo religiosus*. Before we turn to this and other developments in the next decade, however, there is another development to be explored in Erikson's continuing relationship with Freud and psychoanalysis.

## Return to Vienna: Freud's treatment of Dora

In 1959 Erikson returned to Vienna to give a talk to the World Federation of Mental Health on 'Identity and uprootedness in our time' (1964: 83). It has been suggested above that this visit may have been a part of a re-experiencing of his emigration and his German past. It was also a re-visiting of the world of Freud and Vienna and a stimulus to further re-evaluation of Freud's work.

In 1961 he gave a talk to psychoanalytic colleagues in the USA, entitled 'Reality and actuality', in which he re-examined a case of Freud's, that of the patient known as Dora (1964: 166–74). In this re-examination he goes further in criticizing Freud than he ever had before. Freud himself admitted that the treatment was not successful. 'I do not know what kind of help she wanted from me' (quoted by Erikson 1964: 167). Freud implies, however, that the fault was Dora's. Erikson on the contrary concludes that Freud's response to Dora was limited by his eagerness in developing psychological theory and that he was blind to the influence of Dora's involved family relationships on his therapeutic relationship with Dora. It was this that prevented Freud from seeing what Dora wanted, rather than her resistance to treatment, her acting out or unwillingness to change. Erikson also claims that with the benefit of hindsight and Freud's own meticulous account it is possible to see what was going on in this failed therapeutic relationship.

Dora had returned to Freud a year after she had interrupted a treatment that had lasted three months. She was twenty and had come back 'to finish her story and to ask for help once more' (quoted by Erikson 1964: 167). She told Freud that in the interval she had confronted her family with certain 'shady events' denied by them, and had forced them to 'admit their pretenses and their secrets' (Erikson 1964: 167). Freud was angry with her, considering that in confronting her family she had acted out of revenge rather than using the insight which he had helped her acquire. He told her ' "she was not in earnest over her request" for more help' (p. 167).

Dora is presented by Freud as a classic case of hysteria, brought about by an intense conflict between her desire and her repugnance, first at the age of 14 and then again at 16, at the sexual advances of a Mr K, a married man whose children she helped to look after. The situation was complicated by a social context rife with secrets and infidelities. Mrs K, the wife of the would-be seducer Mr K, was in fact the mistress of Dora's father. It was this father who had brought Dora to Freud for treatment, certainly for her hysterical symptoms, but also surely to stop her accusations. The boundaries were extremely muddled. Freud gives the impression of being more concerned for the father's agenda than for the patient's; for example, he says that Mr K's advances to Dora were 'neither tactless nor offensive' (quoted by Erikson 1964: 169). Moreover, the pressures and confusion for Dora were compounded by her being the recipient of the confidences both of Mrs K *and* Mr K, and of another woman who had been seduced by Mr K. In this light the questioning of Dora's sincerity, the accusation of 'acting out' and the brilliant interpretation of the origins of her hysteria, valid though they all might be, were massively beside the point for Dora. What Dora wanted from Freud can be seen in the light of her adolescent search for identity, for which trustworthy adults and a reliable 'truth' were vital. The central theme of the situation is one of broken faith and trust; of 'multiple sexual *infidelity* and *perfidy*' (Erikson 1964: 172). Dora wanted Freud to 'to be "truthful" in the therapeutic relation, that is, to keep faith with her on her terms rather than on those of her father or a seducer' (p. 169). She wanted from Freud what the other significant men in her life had failed to give her. In this Freud failed her too. He did so because he had become doubly trapped: in his own intellectual and professional search for explanations of symptoms and in his collusion with the family dynamics of infidelity. Both had blinded him to Dora's real needs.

Erikson uses this case to illustrate aspects of the young adult's search for identity. The young person has a vital stake in the 'accuracy, veracity, and authenticity, in the fairness, genuineness and reliability of persons, of methods, and of ideas' (1964: 170). The essence of all such preoccupations, he says, is 'the quality of *fidelity*' (p. 171). There is also a personal significance for Erikson, in that he is able to see with some clarity the fallibility of the master, the vulnerability of a man whose intellectual brilliance and ambition can blind him to the real needs of a patient; to see that an insightful healer can be weak and mistaken in his involvement with another human being.

Erikson's debt to and admiration for Freud were such that he would always be something of a parent figure and Erikson was ready to defend him against attacks from others. But there is a change at the end of this decade, a release from idealization, a cutting of ties. He is able to see this giant and distant figure as more real and human than before; and he finds a corresponding release of new ideas and confidence in himself to explore new territory.

## The schedule of virtues

Two new concepts in particular stand out in his addresses to fellow analysts in 1960 and 1961. The first is the concept of human strengths, or virtues as he called them, which add a new dimension to the developmental life stages. Fidelity is the example as seen in the discussion of Dora's case, which corresponds to the stage of the identity crisis. The complete schedule of 'virtues' related to each of the eight stages is: hope, will, purpose, competence, fidelity, love, care and wisdom (Erikson 1964: 115–34). Erikson says that he uses the term virtue, in spite of certain misgivings about the word's associations, because of its original meaning as 'inherent strength' and 'active quality' (p. 113). It is inherent in that it is something which an individual comes to feel belongs to him or her and is recognized as such. It has a persisting and continuous quality – in other words it becomes part of his or her identity. It is active both in the sense that we can observe it in the ' "animated" or "spirited" ' (p. 112) essence of a person and because it is linked to the subjective sense of being an agent with the capacity to act in the world.

A third essential element to the concept of virtue is its positive quality. It is part of Erikson's continuing search to find a way of speaking about human nature in positive rather than negative terms. 'We recognize … affinity between the earliest and deepest mental disturbances and a radical loss of a basic kind of hope … Yet, we are not curious to know what the genetic or dynamic determinants of a state of hope … really are … We truly shy away from any systematic discussion of human strength' (p. 112). He is perhaps expressing his frustration both at others' neglect of the problem and at his own difficulty in grappling with it satisfactorily. Nevertheless, with the schedule of virtues he has taken a further step to finding a language in which to conceptualize that animating quality and state of health 'which cannot be subsumed under the most complete list of negatives' (p. 112).

The fourth defining element of the strengths or virtues is their psychosocial quality, their linking of the individual and the social. 'Virtue in the individual and the spirit of institutions have evolved together, are one and the same strength' (p. 155). Individual qualities and 'virtues' provide strength for the life of the community. Without institutions and traditions which incorporate safeguards and ways of transmitting these virtues, they cannot develop anew in each individual. From this wider perspective, Freud's failure to provide the fidelity, the truthfulness, which Dora wanted from him can be seen as a part of a failure of fidelity in the society of their time. Our sense of outrage may be correspondingly tempered with understanding and compassion for each of its actors.

## The concept of historical actuality

The second major development in Erikson's thinking at this time is his distinction between 'psychological reality' and 'historical actuality' (1964: 159). He insists on the difference between the way we perceive and interpret our world and the way we are involved in it. Reality is 'the world of phenomenal experience'; actuality is 'the world of participation' (p. 165). The purpose of psychotherapy encompasses both reality and actuality. A patient may be 'impaired in his testing of reality' or may be 'inactivated in actuality' (p. 175). In the first case the aim of therapy is 'a minimum of distortion' in the way the individual perceives the world. In the second the therapeutic aim is 'a minimum of defensive maneuvering and a maximum of mutual activation' (p. 165). The danger in therapy lies in focusing on one aspect to the exclusion of the other. This is illustrated by Freud and Dora. In his eagerness to interpret her psychological 'reality', he missed the 'actuality' of her active involvement in her own life and social context and also the 'actuality' of his own involvement with her and her family.

Erikson's concern is partly with the tendency of the psychoanalytic thinking of his time, as in the work of Hartmann (1965), to separate the inner world from the outer world. The term 'outer world', Erikson says, 'represents the Cartesian straitjacket we have imposed on our model of man' (p. 163). To 'undo this straitjacket' (p. 164) is the primary purpose of the distinction between reality and actuality.

The distinction is relevant also to the question of how far and in what ways psychological study and therapeutic insight may be applied to historical and political decision-making. Psychoanalysis has its own actuality, its 'drive for power and the need for a sharp if seemingly unbloody weapon' (p. 212), that lies behind or around its perceptual frameworks and therapeutic activities. Yet, 'by its tradition and nature allied with the doctrines of rational enlightenment and personal freedom', psychoanalysis may 'share [with the methods of liberalism] a relative over-estimation of the value of mere awareness of "reality" and a neglect of the nature of political leverage' (p. 210). In other words, psychotherapists may easily blunder about in a world they do not understand. The first step in bridging the gap must be a recognition of the differences of perspective of each other's realities and actualities. Neither politician nor psychotherapist can do their job properly without an awareness of the other's way of looking at things and the actual context of the other's life.

The concept of actuality does not have the vernacular bite of the concept of identity and has not become so influential or widely known. It is nevertheless in my view a concept of equal importance. It greatly widens the possibilities and at the same time recognizes the limitations of psychotherapy. It provides a bridge for the mutual understanding and interplay of psychotherapy and politics. For Erikson it represented a personal clarification of his separation from Freud and a confidence to continue his personal and professional journey in his own way. It is a culmination of his personal re-evaluation of his German past and his dependence on Freud; and it represents a moving on from his fruitful absorption in the adolescence of America, which was also to some extent a reworking of his own. In the next decade, the 1960s (and his sixties), Erikson turns his attention to the nature of adulthood, the search for an ethical basis for individual and social action, and a search for those patterns in society which can vivify rather than frustrate individual fulfilment. These are the 'generative' issues and themes to which we turn next.

# C H A P T E R  **8**

---

# The 1960s: the search for Gandhi's truth

Erikson's appointment to a professorship at Harvard in 1960 marked a significant change in his life. The award of an honorary MA was his first academic qualification; but more importantly it marked a transition in his relationship to youth from one based on the role of therapist to one primarily as teacher.

At Harvard he taught a course on the human life cycle which was open to a variety of students in the social sciences. He led a seminar studying the lives of 'great' historical figures from St Augustine to Simone Weill and Malcolm X (Coles 1970: 266). He enjoyed lecturing and his lectures were popular events. He refers warmly to the students and the way they teased and challenged him, calling his life study 'from bust to dust' or pointing out how he had progressed from the study of the adolescent Luther to the middle-aged Mahatma. Friedman interviewed several of the students on these courses. He concludes that Erikson 'reaffirmed their hopes and idealism, understood their sense of disorientation, and assured them that they would eventually find themselves' (1999: 319).

In another way Erikson was more than ever involved in the life of youth. His books had become widely known and were part of the inspiration of the young civil rights campaigners seeking liberation for themselves and others in the early sixties. Coles saw *Childhood and Society* among books on a table while visiting students jailed in Alabama for campaigning against school segregation. He recalls that a black student called Erikson's book 'real good!' (1970: xii). Coles saw this book in a number of 'Southern freedom houses and Appalachian "outposts"'. He comments that 'though not all doctors understood what Erikson was getting at, at least thousands of students did' (1970: xiv). For Coles himself Erikson's writings provided a vital link with the young activists among whom he worked.

Yet, paradoxically, it was at this time that Erikson turned his main focus of attention to another part of the world and a man whose life was already history, Mahatma Gandhi. It may be that he felt that this new generation could take care of its own crises and future without his advocacy. Or it may be that he needed to withdraw to a distance in order to find out where he stood in relation to the new activism and the America of which it was part. It may have been part of a continuing need to move on to new horizons and find new perspectives. Erikson himself commented ten years later: 'I interrupted both my practice and teaching of psychoanalysis in order to do historical studies.' He felt that 'future practitioners . . . had to learn to become historically self-conscious'. It was part of his growing preoccupation with 'historical relativity' (Erikson 1975b: 55). The move is symbolically illustrated by his absence in India during the civil rights marches led by Martin Luther King in 1964. 'In trying to trace Gandhi's activities in the city of Ahmedabad in 1918, I missed ongoing – and, in fact, on-marching – history in Selma, U.S.A.' (Erikson 1987: 481).

During the 1960s Erikson developed certain concepts which focus on what he saw as the greatest problems in the relation between individual and society. The concept of *mutuality* provides a way of linking ethics, as a guide to social action, with psychological understanding. The concept of *pseudo-speciation* formulates what has been a basic flaw in all human societies and raises the question of how this flaw might be linked to individual psychology, and possible alternatives. The third concept of *ritualization* provides a model of creatively renewed patterns in society through which individual autonomy can be reconciled with the pressures of society.

Each of these concepts is closely linked with and developed through Erikson's study of Gandhi. Two other issues are relevant to this study. The first is the nature and validity of Erikson's psycho-historical method as a means of combining psychological and historical disciplines. The second is Erikson's interest in Gandhi as a person and as a leader.

## The events at Ahmedabad

As with the study of Martin Luther, Erikson's interest in the life of Gandhi began in a small way, expanding into a major preoccupation. In 1962 Erikson visited the city of Ahmedabad in India to speak in a seminar in which he compared his ideas on the stages in the 'human life cycle' with the life stages in Hindu tradition. He had been interested in Gandhi in his youth, through Romain Rolland's (1924) biography of the man who 'stirred three hundred million people to revolt, who has shaken the British Empire' (Erikson 1970a: 32). He remembered that it was in this city of Ahmedabad in 1918 that Gandhi had led a strike of millworkers against their employers. In the United States Erikson had met the sons of a leading millowner and they had encouraged him to come to India. In Ahmedabad he met the millowner himself, Ambalal Sarabhai, and his sister Anasuya Sarabhai, who had supported Gandhi against her brother. He talked with other witnesses and partners in Gandhi's campaigns. He visited the ashram on the banks of the Sabhamarti river where Gandhi lived during the strike and held meetings.

As he gave his talk and found himself very politely challenged on his Western view of life by his Indian hosts, his mind kept turning to the events of 1918 and their witnesses. 'Now that I knew the scene, the strike of 1918 seemed to me to have not only a certain dramatic and psychoanalytic interest but also had a crucial importance in history' (Erikson 1970a: 45). In the next six years he visited Ahmedabad at least three times and in 1969 *Gandhi's Truth. On the Origins of Militant Non-violence* was published.

Erikson saw in this period of Gandhi's life the kind of crisis about which he had been writing. 'I came to suspect, then, that that strike and that fast represented a demonstrable crisis in the middle age of a great man' (p. 47). Gandhi faced difficult decisions about the sort of political leadership required of him, and what he might require of his followers. Through the mass confrontation of the strike and the personal individual action of the fast, Gandhi was to find his own way in a situation of which, in spite of all uncertainties, he seemed the master.

Within a year of the end of the strike Gandhi was to become the leader in the first campaign of civil disobedience to the British Raj. However, for Erikson Gandhi's significance goes beyond that struggle.

> When I came to Ahmedabad, it had become clear to me (for I had just come from the disarmament conference of the American Academy of Arts and Sciences) that man as a species can no longer afford any more to cultivate illusions either about his own 'nature' ... or about those 'pseudo-species' he calls enemies – not while inventing and manufacturing arsenals of global destruction ... Gandhi seems to be the only man who has visualized *and* demonstrated an over-all alternative.
>
> (Erikson 1970a: 51)

### Gandhi's Truth: the evidence of witnesses

The book is in four parts. The first part begins with an account of the author's interest and involvement in the life of Gandhi and the events of 1918 in Ahmedabad. Erikson meets surviving witnesses and explores with them their memories of Gandhi, whether as followers or opponents; what he meant to them then and through their lives; and how each of them became a part of the life history of the Mahatma and of a whole people.

Erikson carefully considers the problems of the use of evidence in 'On the nature of psycho-historical evidence: in search of Gandhi' (1968b). In this contribution to the integration of psychological and historical disciplines, Erikson insists that such evidence must be viewed from psychological, historical and sociological perspectives. The reviewer of such evidence, as Erikson puts it, 'would have to fathom – in one intuitive configuration of thought ... – the complementarity of at least four conditions under which a record emerges' (1975a: 136). These conditions are:

1 For the individual:
   (a) the recorder's circumstances at the moment of making the record;
   (b) the recorder's context in terms of the sequence of his or her life history.

2 For the community:
(a) the conditions of the moment;
(b) the context in the perspective of the community's development.

Erikson applies this general guide to all records of events, whether of witnesses, leaders or followers. He is sensitive to these 'dimensions' as they affect and condition the way the writer perceives these accounts. Basically Erikson is saying that a coherent psycho-historical account must integrate both the individual and the social context in terms of both the present conditions and the developmental process in time.

An essential witness is Gandhi himself, through his autobiography written several years later (1927). Erikson is concerned to sift this evidence, to look behind the words to its meaning at the time it was written, and its meaning in terms of Gandhi's life. He is also concerned with the context of the community in which the words were written and to whom they were addressed.

## Gandhi's life history

In Part II Erikson tells the story of Gandhi's life up to the events of the strike, asking what it was that made this man so special and what patterns and themes in his life emerged from his experience as a child. He identifies as recurrent themes Gandhi's struggle with his sexuality; his relationship with his father, as an authority that he wished to challenge without destroying the bond between them; his search for rules of life to which he could commit himself in the manner of his mother. These rules had to contain his demons, not only of sexuality but also of an intense ambition and energy: his 'mighty drivenness, an intense and yet flexible energy, a shocking originality, and a capacity to impose on his time what most concerns him' (Erikson 1970a: 395). Erikson sums up the themes as 'a deep conflict between phallicism and saintliness, between paternal power and maternal care' (p. 401).

The young Gandhi left India for England, where he found a first 'professional identity', that of a 'barrister English style' (p. 396), while struggling to maintain a sense of being Indian through his vegetarianism and sexual asceticism. In South Africa Gandhi encountered the humiliation of the arrogant assumption of superiority of the dominant Europeans, which in England had been more politely disguised. Gandhi recognized the weakness and fear underlying the arrogance and realized his own strength with the successful improvisation of personal civil disobedience. He also discovered his power to inspire and lead others.

Returning to India in 1915, he spent the next three years watching, travelling and experiencing the desperate poverty and apathy of the people of his country. This confirmed his view of the stultifying effects of British rule. Such views were not new to him. While in South Africa he had joined the movement for Home Rule among leading Indians with his own particular views. 'Home Rule', he wrote in 1909, 'equals Self Rule and Self Rule equals Self-Control. Only he who is master of himself can be master of his "house", and only a people in command of itself can command respect and freedom'

(Erikson 1970a: 217). With this motto he was to 'formulate a new conscience of action', one which was basically non-violent and which 'blesses him who uses it and him against whom it is used' (p. 225).

### The 'personal word'

Now more than half way through the book, Erikson sets out to tell the story of the events of 1918. Before he can start, however, he addresses Gandhi in a 'personal word'. In a text written as a personal letter direct to Gandhi, Erikson confronts Gandhi with those parts of his story which in some way seem to him to ring false.

In his autobiography Gandhi had in fact anticipated just such interpretations of his words with a mixture of sarcasm and modesty. 'If some busybody were to cross-examine me on the chapters already written, he could probably shed much more light on them, and if it were a hostile critic's cross-examination, he might flatter himself for having shown up . . . the hollowness of many of my pretensions' (quoted in Erikson 1970a: 230). Erikson is warned but not stopped by this comment. All the more he feels the need to address Gandhi directly as though Gandhi were able to reply and reassure him. He is appealing for forgiveness from the great man for challenging what he senses to be a point of pain and vulnerability but at the same time wanting permission to carry on because such an undertaking is in accordance with Gandhi's own principles and search for truth.

Gandhi seemed to acknowledge the pain when he said that such anticipated or real criticisms had almost brought him to the point of no longer writing the autobiography. Erikson responds that he too has felt unable to 'continue writing *this* book because I seemed to sense the presence of a kind of untruth in the very protestation of truth; of something unclean when all the words spelt out an unreal purity; and above all, of displaced violence where non-violence was the professed issue' (1970a: 231).

Erikson details three elements of Gandhi's autobiography which cause him such disquiet. The first is in Gandhi's account of his relationship with his wife Kasturba. Gandhi excluded a sexual relationship with her from early middle age. When she refused to be taught to read by him, he excluded her, vindictively as Erikson sees it, from discussing decisions with him. Kasturba was, Gandhi acknowledged, perhaps the one person who could stand up to him (Fischer 1997: 85). Gandhi claimed that their continence 'knit us together as never before'. He was devastated when she died. 'Her passing has left a vacuum which will never be filled . . . We lived together for 63 years' (Fischer 1997: 491). Erikson did not wish to deny the love and closeness of their relationship. What disturbed him was that Gandhi seemed to be denying the possibility of that mutuality in a sexual relationship which he wanted to promote in political relationships. 'For the future it is important to affirm unequivocally that what you call Satyagraha [truth force] must not remain restricted to ascetic men and women who believe they can overcome violence only by sexual self-disarmament' (Erikson 1970a: 234).

Sexual moralism also appears in an incident in South Africa when he cut off the hair of young girls, who were in his care, in order to 'sterilize the sinner's eye' (quoted in Erikson 1970a: 238). The sinners were young men who made fun of the girls when they went to bathe. In his autobiography Gandhi does not seem to realize the injustice of making the girls suffer for the so-called sins of the young men. Erikson finds a false note in Gandhi's claim that this hurt him more than the girls. 'Too long . . . has man excused his cruelty to others with the claim that he does not spare himself' (p. 234).

The third element which disturbs Erikson is Gandhi's attitude to his eldest son Harilal, who defied and rejected the almost impossibly elevated behaviour which Gandhi expected from all his family. Erikson sees Harilal as in a double bind: condemned for not telling his father the truth, but knowing that the truth would be unacceptable.

Erikson believes that for Gandhi's own principles to succeed it is necessary to add psychological insight to religious principle; to replace what he calls 'moralistic terrorism' with psychological truth.

> For we now have detailed insights into our inner ambiguities . . . and only an additional leverage of truth based on self-knowledge promises to give us freedom . . . whereas in the past, moralistic terrorism succeeded only in driving our worst proclivities underground, to remain there until riotous conditions of uncertainty or chaos would permit them to emerge redoubled.
>
> (Erikson 1970a: 234–5)

In addressing his confrontation directly to Gandhi, Erikson clearly has a personal involvement. It is a recognizable pattern of Erikson's to challenge the feet of clay of the masters he has sought out as models of virtue and as guides: Freud, Luther and later Thomas Jefferson. In claiming the right to criticize Gandhi openly he is perhaps speaking for Harilal as a substitute son. He is appealing to this most compassionate and saintly of all possible fathers, in the name of Gandhi's own phrase 'truth force', to sanction such criticism and to respond with a blessing.

## The strike and the fast

With the air thus cleared, Erikson moves on to describe the course of the strike. At stake was the unacceptable poverty of the millworkers, the despotic power of the millowners and the principle of arbitration. It was in support of this principle that Gandhi led the workers to strike and also undertook his first hunger strike. For Gandhi the means must always be consistent with the ends. His flexibility and improvisation, combined with strict adherence to principle, enabled him to be original and surprising, and to end with honour in spite of compromise. The events in Ahmedabad led to a system of arbitration which survived successfully until Erikson's time. They also provided for Gandhi a way of creating and testing out a form of political leadership. In this workers' strike can be seen a form of civil disobedience by which the many can exercise their power non-violently against the few in whose hands economic and political power is concentrated. In the fast – this was the first of Gandhi's seventeen politically motivated fasts – he found a means of justifying his leadership to his followers.

At the end of the Great War, Indians expected some reward for their part in it. Their hopes were disappointed by the determination of the British to maintain their hold on power. Tension and protest increased. In 1919 General Dyer gave orders for the shooting down of hundreds of unarmed protesters in the square in Amritsar in the cold-blooded belief that intimidation was essential to British rule. In 1920 the All India Congress appointed Gandhi as its official leader of the independence movement. He was 'the "only one available" for the political job of anchoring the independence movement in the spirit of the Indian masses' (Erikson 1970a: 392). Gandhi had found his way to combine spiritual principle with political leadership.

## The leverage of truth

In his 'personal word' Erikson criticized Gandhi for a lack of psychological insight in his autobiography. He claims nevertheless that there is a fundamental affinity between Gandhi's Satyagraha ('truth force') and psychotherapeutic insight. Both operate through relationship, the one personal, the other political. Erikson terms this affinity the 'leverage of truth' (1970a: 393). In Part IV of his study Erikson examines the ways in which psychological truth as he sees it may be linked and compared with Satyagraha. While insight may in some ways be able to reveal hidden or conflicting elements in Satyagraha, it may be immeasurably extended by the 'actuality' of Gandhi's lived truth.

Through this examination Erikson develops the three key concepts noted earlier: of mutuality; of pseudo-species and the alternative possibilities of an inclusive human identity; and of ritualization as a creative means of integrating individual and society.

### Mutuality and the golden rule

The golden rule as a guide to behaviour is known in its most popular form as 'do as you would be done by'. Erikson distinguishes a variety of forms of this rule in religions and philosophies, from those which rely on a 'minimum of egotistic prudence' to those which 'demand a maximum of altruistic sympathy' (1964: 221). He quotes the injunction to humanity in the Upanishads to 'see all beings as his own self and his own self in all beings'; the Christian, 'Love thy neighbour as thyself'; Kant's 'moral imperative' and Lincoln's 'simple political creed: "As I would not be slave, I would not be master"' (p. 221).

Erikson sets these principles in a developmental framework both individual (ontogenetic) and evolutionary (phylogenetic). On the individual level he defines three stages. The first is the establishment of moral rules in childhood. The child in this *moralistic* stage 'somehow must learn the boundaries marked by "don'ts"' (p. 223). The rules are established by 'outer threats of abandonment, punishment and public exposure, or a threatening inner sense of guilt, of shame or of isolation'. In either case, 'it is the threat that counts' (p. 221).

In adolescence a world image is based on the 'ability to perceive ideas and to assent to ideals' (p. 225). Erikson called this the *ideological* stage. It still presents a black and white view of the world, which involves exclusion and condemnation of others who are not committed to the same ideals or world view.

Finally, the 'ethical sense of the young adult ... encompasses and goes beyond moral restraint and ideal vision, while insisting on concrete commitment to those intimate relationships and work associations by which man can hope to share a lifetime of productivity and competence' (p. 226). This involvement in existing social, economic and family structures makes ethical development possible but also makes it difficult. What Erikson is describing in this *ethical* stage is a potential for ethical action, recognized, if inadequately practised, by most people.

Mutuality belongs to this ethical stage of development; it is an ethical version of the golden rule. In order to define it Erikson turns back, perhaps paradoxically, to the earliest stage of human development: the relationship between the primary carer and the newborn infant. This relationship involves a mutuality which is fundamental for human survival and for the later development of an explicit ethical sense. It is a relationship of 'divided function' in which each partner recognizes the other as essential to their well-being and growth, while taking a path that increases and nurtures the separate identity of the other.

So Erikson reaches his developmental version of the golden rule as the principle of mutuality. 'It is best to do to another what will strengthen him – that is, what will develop his best potentials even as it develops your own.' Mutuality 'strengthens the doer even as it strengthens the other' (Erikson 1964: 233).

Erikson extends this formulation to two further relationships. The first is that of man and woman. Mutuality involves an equality of respect and an enhancement of each other's uniqueness and difference. 'A partner's potency and potentialities are activated even as he activates the other's potency and potentialities' (p. 234). Each sex 'enhances the uniqueness of the other' (p. 236).

Second, Erikson believes that the principle of mutuality applies to the therapeutic relationship. Here again there is an apparent inequality between the 'knower and the known, helper and sufferer, practitioner of life and victim of disease and death' (1964: 236). Such inequality brings possibilities of abuse as well as of mutuality. In mutuality an essential recognition is that the patient is as important to the healer as the healer is to the patient. 'Each specialty and each technique ... permits the medical man to develop as a practitioner, and as a person, even as the patient is cured as a patient, and as a person. For a real cure transcends the transitory state of patienthood' (p. 236).

Erikson wrote his lecture 'The golden rule and the cycle of life' (1963) soon after he had begun his study of Gandhi. He concludes it by making the link between mutuality and Gandhi's political principles. Gandhi's own version of the golden rule, announced to his followers under the babul tree in the ashram in Ahmedabad, was this: 'That line of action is alone justice which does not harm either party to a dispute' (Erikson 1964: 239). Gandhi made it clear that by harm he meant not only physical violence or economic exploitation but also 'social indignity, loss of self esteem, and latent vengeance' (p. 239). Erikson saw in Gandhi's life the explicit application of mutuality to social and political action. The events at Ahmedabad in 1918 were the crisis through which Gandhi found the strength and the means for the practical application of this principle.

### Pseudo-speciation

The concept of pseudo-speciation arose from Erikson's contact with the ethologist Konrad Lorenz and biologist Julian Huxley in a symposium in London in 1966. Lorenz attributed the term to Erikson, though he made his own use of it. He saw human beings as the odd ones out in the natural world by their lack of inhibition about killing members of their own species. 'Pseudo-speciation suppresses the instinctive mechanisms normally preventing the killing of fellow members of the species.' This, Lorenz says bluntly, 'is the cause of war' (quoted in Erikson 1987: 327).

Erikson defines pseudo-speciation in terms of both the evolution of human beings in societies and the psychological development of the individual. In evolutionary terms he defines it thus:

> Instead of a consciousness of being the one species he is, man has, as far back as we know, imagined his tribe or nation, his caste or his class, and, yes, even his religion to be a superior species, a claim which he has always reinforced with systematic distortions of history and reality – sometimes poetic and sometimes heroic and often just vain.
>
> (Erikson 1987: 498)

In individual development pseudo-speciation is bound to the development of identity. 'Our sense of identity coincides with our pseudo-specieshood to such an extent that a danger to one is a threat to the other' (p. 499). It is a product of that development through moral and ideological stages outlined above, part of the 'malignant potentials of man's slow maturation' (Erikson 1964: 226). The individual's precariously developing sense of identity is reinforced by the formation of a conscience that splits perceptions into positive and negative and reinforces these perceptions with all the primal rage and fear which conscience has been developed to contain.

Erikson sees possible positive aspects in the formation of pseudo-species. 'Each pseudo-species . . . has made special moral and ritual demands on itself which indeed resulted in a degree of brotherly love among those involved in the assumed superiority.' Unfortunately, 'the ensuing righteousness has also served to sanction the exclusion of the other "species", often to the extent of their annihilation' (1987: 499).

Speaking to students at Cape Town University, at a time when they were demonstrating against the government's imposition of racial discrimination in the university, Erikson (1968c) gave an impassioned exposition on the theme of pseudo-species. However, he warns his audience: 'In case you are now already lustily berating your favourite adversary and *his* self-serving prejudices, I must warn you that insight demands . . . the recognition of the fact that a human propensity, such as has just been described is shared in some more or less subtle form by all of us' (1975a: 176). The propensity identified in pseudo-speciation is 'to bolster one's own sense of inner mastery by bunching together and prejudging whole classes of people' (p. 175).

Erikson recognizes that his use of the term 'pseudo' may in turn be judgemental. He justifies it by pointing to those characteristic elements in pseudo-speciation of 'systematic distortions of history and reality' for which 'I cannot find any more polite term than *pseudo*' (1987: 499). When the 'self-idealization' of the group becomes 'defensive and exclusive', 'existing knowledge is denied, insight prevented, and possible alternatives ignored' (Erikson 1975a: 177). ' "Pseudo" means that somebody is trying, with all the semi-sincerity of propaganda, to put something over on himself as well as on others' (Erikson 1970a: 432).

His judgement is fuelled by a belief that mankind can and has to choose and that there are alternatives to pseudo-speciation. Gandhi demonstrated the possibilities inherent in an inclusive human ethic and a rejection of exclusivity whether of caste or creed. The terrible violence that followed partition in India and Gandhi's own death at the hands of a religious fanatic illustrate the intractability and violence inherent in pseudo-speciation.

In an essay written in 1972, Erikson attempts to draw the balance between the positive and negative prospects for human evolution. On the positive side is the capacity demonstrated in history to transcend smaller identities with larger ones, although there has often been an element of force in this. Nevertheless, 'man' has shown the ability to include 'in his sense of human dignity other "pseudo-species" which he once considered contemptible if not expendable'. 'Man' now enjoys 'a cultural homogeneity that he was once mortally afraid of' (Erikson 1987: 518). On the other hand, the growth of these bigger and wider identities – nations, creeds, empires, markets – has not reduced the propensity to pseudo-speciation, as the twentieth century bears witness. Erikson also notes that there are limits to and dangers in the integration into wider identities. Such wider identities may threaten an 'identity extinction', fears of which can 'drive men to violent attempts at seeking archaic safety in reactionary pseudo-species formation' (p. 518). Moreover, the development of technology, which makes a sense of common specieshood possible, has also made possible the concentration of power and provided 'diabolically perfected means of annihilation' (p. 518).

Erikson draws hope from our natural heritage, which demonstrates a potentiality for instinctive peacefulness and restraint of aggression. What is specific to human development is the capacity for creative thinking and the use of 'playful imagination' (p. 328). Imagination may provide the basis for the distortions of reality in the myths of God-given superiority characteristic of pseudo-species. It also provides the means for self-transformations which can transcend these exclusive and destructive identities.

These potentialities in human cultural creativity, which are balanced against the possibilities of atavistic regression, are the subject of Erikson's third major conceptual contribution in this period: the formation of psychosocial patterns which he called 'ritualization'.

*Ritualization*

Erikson's concept of ritualization is linked to the concepts of mutuality and pseudo-speciation. Ritualization is the social manifestation of mutuality and the container for impulses of love and hate which find their moralistic expression in pseudo-species.

The term first appeared in a paper – 'The ontogeny of ritualization in man' (1966a) – which Erikson presented to the London Symposium, already mentioned as the source of the concept of pseudo-speciation. He distinguishes what he means by ritualization from the ritualized behaviour of animals, from the adult rites and rituals studied by anthropologists and from the pathological 'private rituals' of the psychiatric patient (1987: 576). He postulates that ritualization in man consists of 'an agreed-upon interplay between at least two persons who repeat it at meaningful intervals and in recurring contexts' and that it must have 'adaptive value for both participants'. Ritualization is used by Erikson to describe this process of interplay in human behaviour and also the social patterns or forms (ritualizations) in which the process finds expression. Ritualization can help us to see 'new connexions between seemingly distant phenomena, such as human infancy and man's institutions' (p. 576). It is a continuation of Erikson's attempt to provide a conceptual structure for the exploration of non-pathological, 'normal' interactions of individuals in society and at the same time a means of distinguishing the creative or 'adaptive' from the pathological.

Erikson gives substance to his 'speculations' by tracing the development of ritualization through a modified version of his stages of the life cycle. In the first stage it is seen in the forms created in the interplay between carer and infant: the greeting ritual, the hide and seek game, the naming games and many others. From these earliest interplays comes a 'numinous' sense of being present and recognized in the world. In the stage of 'early childhood', through family rituals at meals and bedtimes, ritualization provides the repeated recognizable social patterns for the discrimination of 'bad' and 'good'; of what feels right and feels wrong; of sanction, punishment and reward. These ritualizations form the basis of the later 'judiciary rituals' of the adult (Erikson 1987: 584). Ritualization facilitates the encounter with wider society and the material environment, with traffic, fire, the notion of 'mine' and 'yours', of 'please' and 'thank you'. It is characteristic of these ritualizations that while they are in some ways universally recognizable they are also capable of almost infinitely subtle and minute variations and invention from family to family and group to group. The feelings attached to them persist through life. They are also a source of confusion in later judgements, so that even adults with a highly developed ethical sense carry over what 'feels right and wrong' from these earliest times (for example, in the way a person eats) into judgements about the goodness and badness of a person.

The next stage of childhood, which Erikson here calls the play age, is vital for the development of creativity in social forms as well as for the formation of a sense of individual identity. 'This age offers the child a micro-reality in which he can escape adult ritualization and prepare his own, reliving, correcting and recreating past experiences, and anticipating future roles with the spontaneity and repetitiveness which characterize all ritualization' (1987: 586). Such are the formal yet creative patterns of imaginative play, of dreams, of often told stories. They form the foundation for the expressive forms through which, in the media of a culture, the traumas and triumphs of the wider world are presented and by which they are framed.

From the 'school age' Erikson emphasizes the formal elements involved in a wider social context. In this stage 'play is transformed into work, game into cooperation, and the freedom of the imagination into the duty to perform with full attention all the minute details which are necessary to do a task and to do it "right"' (p. 587). Such ritualization can be seen in school rules, in tests and examinations.

Ritualization in adolescence centres on the issues of readiness to join or withdraw from the technology of the age and to commit or exclude oneself from a range of social groupings from peer group to nation. Such are the ritualizations of youth and pop culture, of the experiencing of danger and technical mastery, of the ritualized use of drugs and the experimentations with the emotional and interpersonal experience of sexuality. They may involve 'certain *irreversible commitments* to one's pseudo-species' but also ways in which the new generation may 'demarcate their generation as . . . different both from the adult haves and the infantile have-nots'.

> Much of youthful 'demonstration' in private is . . . a dramatization (sometimes mocking, sometimes riotous) of the estrangement of youth from the impersonality of mass production, the vagueness of confessed values and the intangibility of the prospects for either an individualized or a truly communal existence.
>
> (Erikson 1987: 588)

In adult ritualization Erikson emphasizes the generational cycle. Dominant rituals of adulthood are concerned with adults' role as 'ritualizers of their children's lives'. In marriage and in anniversary ceremonies and the more recent growth of Mother's Day and Father's Day, for example, may be seen a means to 'sanction the adult'. 'For his mature needs include the need to be periodically reinforced in his role of ritualizer', a role which, in the generational stage, includes 'parental and instructive, productive, creative, and curative endeavours' (p. 590).

Ritualization provides the means of reconciling conflicting needs within and demands without. It is based on the 'reciprocal needs of two quite unequal organisms' (p. 578). Ritualization is the container for the reconciliation of opposites which Erikson lists as follows: it is 'a highly *personal* matter', yet *'group-bound'*. It provides 'a sense both of *oneness* and of *distinctiveness*. It is *playful*, and yet *formalized*, and this in *details* as well as in the *whole* procedure. Becoming *familiar* through repetition, it yet brings the *surprise* of recognition.' Underlying all these opposites Erikson sees the *'overcoming of ambivalence* as well as of ambiguity' as 'one of the prime functions of ritualization' (p. 578).

| Stages | A<br>Psychosexual stages and modes | B<br>Psychosocial crises | C<br>Radius of significant relations | D<br>Basic strengths | E<br>Core-pathology Basic Antipathies | F<br>Related principles of social order | G<br>Binding ritualizations | H<br>Ritualism |
|---|---|---|---|---|---|---|---|---|
| I Infancy | Oral-respiratory, sensory-kinaesthetic (incorporative modes) | Basic trust v. basic mistrust | Maternal person | Hope | Withdrawal | Cosmic order | Numinous | Idolism |
| II Early childhood | Anal-urethral, muscular (retentive-eliminative) | Autonomy v. shame, doubt | Parental persons | Will | Compulsion | 'Law and order' | Judicious | Legalism |
| III Play age | Infantile-genital, locomotor (intrusive, inclusive) | Initiative v. guilt | Basic family | Purpose | Inhibition | Ideal prototypes | Dramatic | Moralism |
| IV School age | 'Latency' | Industry v. inferiority | 'Neighbourhood', school | Competence | Inertia | Technological order | Formal (technical) | Formalism |
| V Adolescence | Puberty | Identity v. identity confusion | Peer groups and outgroups; models of leadership | Fidelity | Repudiation | Ideological worldview | Ideological | Totalism |
| VI Young adulthood | Genitality | Intimacy v. isolation | Partners in friendship, sex, competition, cooperation | Love | Exclusivity | Patterns of cooperation and competition | Affiliative | Elitism |
| VII Adulthood | (Procreativity) | Generativity v. stagnation | Divided labour and shared household | Care | Rejectivity | Currents of education and tradition | Generational | Authoritism |
| VIII Old age | (Generalization of sensual modes) | Integrity v. despair | 'Mankind' 'My kind' | Wisdom | Disdain | Wisdom | Philosophical | Dogmatism |

*Figure 3*  The life cycle 3. (From Erikson 1985: 32–3.)

In one of his last works (1985), Erikson sketches the ways in which at every stage the positive creative function of ritualization may be debased into what he called 'ritualism'. This is 'ritual-like behaviour marked by stereotypic repetition and illusory pretenses that obliterate the integrative value of communal organization' (Erikson 1985: 46). Thus the numinous 'easily degenerates into idolatry' (p. 46), the judicious into legalism. The 'ritualism' corresponding to each subsequent stage is suggested in the summary chart (pp. 32–3) reproduced in Figure 3.

Erikson sees in the patterns of ritualization and their debased forms a crucial focus for understanding such diverse phenomena as child's play, youth culture, black power, political institutions and posturing, and the social contexts of therapy. He also sees in the health of a family's, group's or nation's capacity for ritualization a crucial element in humanity's future. These social bonds which people have created through ritualization are threatened with disintegration and sterilization. What is at stake is not only the ritualizations of the past but the very ability to ritualize.

Erikson points to three particular areas of danger: (a) the inability to integrate the capacity for ritualization with the technology of production and communication of the age; (b) the dependency of psychosocial identities on affirmation by ritualizations that are locked into the reality-distorting aggression of pseudo-speciation; (c) 'A deep and worldwide disturbance' in the 'central area of ritualized interplay between the generations' (1987: 323). Gandhi highlighted the first problem with his promotion of simpler, less impersonal means of production, such as the spinning wheel, without pointing to a means of integrating this with modern technology. In the face of the second danger Gandhi imagined and courageously tested new non-violent forms for the resolution of conflict. However fragile these creations may seem against the destructiveness and violence of pseudo-speciation in the twentieth century, they remain an inspiration and a way forward. Gandhi, Erikson wrote, 'may have created a ritualization through which men, equipped with both realism and spiritual strength, can face each other with a mutual confidence analogous to the instinctive safety built into the animals' pacific rituals' (1970a: 433).

While taking these further steps in his conceptual journey through the study of Gandhi's life, Erikson was also involved in the unfolding history of the 1960s in America. These events highlighted the third area of danger noted above, that of the 'interplay between the generations'. They included new demands for liberation, the apparent submergence and disappointment of many of these demands, and new challenges to authority which could not but include Erikson himself. How these affected him and how he responded to them form the subject of the next chapter.

# Dilemmas of liberation

It is no coincidence that Erikson's presentations of his study of Gandhi and the ideas involved in it took place in London, India and Cape Town as well as in the USA. It was part of his search for a wider perspective, both cultural and historical, from which to view the unresolved questions of psychosocial development. Towards the end of the decade, however, events in the USA began to involve him personally in a way they had not done before. The year 1968 marks a historical turning point, with the assassinations of Robert Kennedy and Martin Luther King and the failure of the liberal aspirations of student activists after Nixon's Republican victory. The choice seemed to be increasingly between an impotent liberalism and a more militant activism. Erikson's dilemma was that his ideas could be seen by disappointed activists as a collusion to support established society rather than an inspiration to liberation. The events of 1968 meant that Erikson had to ask himself: which side am I on?

There were four main aspects in the search for liberation during these years: racial discrimination and the struggle for integration; student protest at entrenched authority; women's liberation; and the opposition to the Vietnam War and the nuclear arms race. The ideas examined in Chapter 8 had to be applied to unfolding events which presented problems for Erikson that were personal as well as theoretical.

## Problems of race

As far back as 1946, Erikson had analysed the predicament of the American black population in terms of identity, imposed negative identities and racial caricatures. He described the poignant but damaging collusions by which the exploited take on the negative projections of the exploiters. In 1964, in the light of the growing civil rights campaigns, he confessed that 'a lack of familiarity with the problem of negro youth' was a 'marked deficiency in my life and work' (Erikson 1987: 644). By 1966, when he wrote 'The concept of identity in race relations', he had made up for some of this by reading widely in the black American literature.

In this essay he focuses on the black response to economic and social prejudice but also on the involvement of young white students seeking their own identity in the cause of desegregation. Erikson considers the possible identities which North American society offers to black youth. It is hard, he says, to find a way between those identities which are 'too wide' and those which are 'too narrow' (1968a: 316). The widest is that of humanity. Such an identity may represent 'a genuine transcendence of the pseudospecies mentality'; but it 'tends to take all specificity out of "human" relations' (p. 316).

Other potential identities cramp by their narrowness, yet provide elements that may individually be transformed into viable identities. There are identifications related to technical skill (provided that society does not exclude so many black people from employment); to a new middle class (which may create new barriers if only a few are successful); to an African identity; to a religious identity which may link, as for black Muslims, to a wider post-colonial identity.

In Erikson's writing on race there is a mingling of hope and uneasiness. His outrage at the dominant exploiters' resistance to change is mixed with disappointment at the response of the exploited and of those who try to 'help' them. In spite of what had been achieved, Erikson reflects a frustration at the lack of 'realism, solidarity and conviction which welds together a functioning radical opposition' (1968a: 310). He is disturbed by the militancy which sees the way forward only through violence and the dependence of new black identity on reverse projections and pseudo-speciation, even as he tries to understand it by engaging in dialogue with Huey Newton, the young leader of the Black Panthers (Erikson 1975b).

## Women's liberation and the inner space

Erikson's work in the 1930s on children's imaginations through 'play constructions' had convinced him that girls and boys tended to use space differently and that this difference was connected to a 'difference in the ground plan of the human body' (Erikson 1975a: 231). In the sixties he described the relationship between men and women as an example of the mutuality of divided function, in which each contributes to the unfolding potential of the other. However, such divided function may involve elements of inequality and there is a narrow line between recognizing difference and justifying inequalities of established power.

The development of feminism and women's liberation led to renewed focus on these issues. Friedman describes the development of a 'groundswell of hostile feminist criticism' to Erikson's work (1999: 423–5). In 1963 Erikson contributed a paper to a conference on 'The Woman in America' which he called 'The inner and outer space'. He responded to criticisms of this in 'Once more the inner space' (1975a: 225). Criticism was mainly based on the rejection of his view that the ground plan of the body should in any way determine the social function and political rights of individuals. Kate Millet charged that 'Erikson's whole theory is built on psychoanalysts' persistent error in mistaking learned behaviour for biology' (quoted in Erikson 1975a: 228). Erikson replies that this criticism distorts his viewpoint. He does not say that biology determines function in society but insists that psychosocial identity results from an interaction of three elements: the psychological, the social and the biological. Each of these is autonomous in the sense that they do not determine each other; but neither can any one of these elements be excluded from consideration in understanding the individual or society.

Erikson claims that his view of women's specific experience of inner space shifts the psychoanalytic view from Freud's emphasis on the lack of a penis to the positive possession of creative power. He also insists that he is asserting the autonomy of each individual in the psychological aspects of development. There is a degree of choice which is not determined by either nature or nurture. The individual matters, and cannot be reduced to biology or sociology.

Erikson confesses, however, that his personal experience of women as 'the son and brother, husband and father to women' must be subjective (1975a: 226). 'The special polarity of the erotic encounter and of lifelong love is so close to the secret of life that only poets would attempt to find words for it' (p. 226). He acknowledges that his 'slogan-like title' of 'The inner and outer space' may be seen as crude labelling of men as penetrators and women as enclosers. Wherever 'a category of others turns into a bunch of "them", there is already something very wrong' (p. 226). The truth is always more complex. He points to the importance of inner and outer space in both men and women and to a contemporary search for 'that inner space which we all share' (p. 247).

Erikson acknowledges and deplores the social reality of male dominance with its 'age-old stance of armed militancy plus righteousness' (p. 246). However, he points to the danger of a feminist response which adopts just those attitudes of militancy and righteousness and which relegates others to an inferior or less than human 'pseudo-species'.

Erikson also claims that in women's liberation, along with rejection of male domination and the 'attempt to raise consciousness', there is a 'determination to repress the awareness of unconscious motivation' (1975a: 227). 'It is the idea of being unconsciously possessed by one's body', he suggests, 'rather than owning it by choice and using it with deliberation, which causes much of the most pervasive anger' (p. 227). There is a temptation to deny the existence of what may not be available to control. This has led to the 're-repression of much that has so far been . . . widely half understood and that, more fully understood . . . could help importantly in true liberation' (p. 227).

Suggestions of blind spots in awareness of unconscious motivation, however, may apply to all participants in this debate. Feminists may well sense that some of Erikson's tone and language, whatever his conscious intentions and liberal principles, betray unconscious condescension and a context of male assumptions. For example, Erikson admits that it was 'imprudent' to say that both sexes 'learn readily to *imitate* the spatial mode of the other sex'

(1975a: 233). He agrees that what he *should* have said is that both sexes learn to 'make use of, to share and sometimes to imitate, the configurations most typical of the other sex'. Nevertheless, a psychoanalyst knows that slips often indicate the presence of unconscious assumptions. Later readers cannot easily escape a feeling of a male-dominated context when confronted with Erikson's consistent use of the word 'man' and male pronouns for both male and female experience.

The issues raised by the biological and social differences of men and women are both vital and unresolved. Erikson was aware that in his world 'birth control' and 'arms control' were 'stirring up both the male and the female self-images'. It was his view that such a world needed to find ways to combine these images 'in a more all-human identity' (p. 245). He believed, nevertheless, that the world could not evolve 'except through an equal involvement of women and their special modes of experience in the over-all planning and governing so far monopolized by men' (p. 247).

## The protest of youth

I have already noted that while Erikson's writings were being read as an inspiration to American youth, Erikson seemed to be distancing himself from youthful explorations and crises. In 1962 he wrote an article on 'Youth: fidelity and diversity' (Erikson 1968a: 232). This summed up his ideas on adolescence as a time for finding an identity out of role confusion, and of balancing the explorations of diversity with a commitment to society, involving what he called the vital strength of fidelity. In this essay he emphasizes that such fidelity is not an absolute good but has to be balanced by diversity. 'Fidelity without a sense of diversity can become an obsession and a bore; diversity without a sense of fidelity, an empty relativism' (p. 245).

By the late 1960s the climate had changed. The issue now was not so much how youth should respond to the tasks of joining society but how society should respond to the active challenge of its youth. On the one hand there were the civil rights marches, the occupation of campus buildings, the defiance of the draft; on the other a variety of responses from new legislation to the shooting of students by the National Guard. The painting of slogans and taunting of professors even reached the hallowed lawns of Harvard. It was, as Erikson put it, a situation of 'revolutionary potential' in which he and fellow academics 'found ourselves, at a given stage of our own life cycle and career, as involved witnesses' (1975a: 194).

Erikson's professional response was his 'Reflections on the dissent of contemporary youth' (which was published as 'Reflections on the revolt of humanist youth' in 1975), given to an audience of academics at a conference topically entitled 'The Embattled University' in 1969 (1975a: 193). His aim is to 'define certain progressive and retrogressive group phenomena' and to find a way of discriminating what is creative from what is not. He makes clear that he is not saying that retrogressive is necessarily bad and progressive good. Just as retrogression in the individual may be, as Peter Blos put it, 'regression in the service of development' (Erikson 1975a: 194), so in society group retrogressions may be in the service of social transformation and may provide 'the imagery and the energy necessary for a radical reorientation' (p. 194).

Moreover, not all protest is retrogressive. He cites as progressive the Gandhian model – 'anticolonial and non-violent' (p. 201) – and the 'ethical' leadership of the statement of Michael Ferber, one of the leaders of the anti-draft ceremony in Boston in October 1967, entitled 'A time to say no' (p. 208).

Much contemporary youthful activity, however, did appear to Erikson as 'retrogressive'. He distinguishes four main positions of contemporary youthful response, the first three of which are at odds with society and challenge it; the fourth is one which adapts and conforms. Erikson relates each of these responses to a specific stage of psychosocial development.

The *pre-moral* position 'denies the separation from paradise' (Erikson 1975a: 207). It is the 'totalization of the first developmental position', that of 'trusting love' (p. 209). It can be seen in the phenomenon of 'Hippiedom'. Its danger is the 'repression of a necessary minimum of mistrust', which may lead to exploitation by 'microbes, drug pushers, and publicists' (p. 210).

The second position is the *amoral* position, which Erikson describes as 'totalistic rebellion', associated with the second developmental stage of autonomy versus shame and doubt. These dissenters 'may sport shamelessness, obedience may become defiance, and self-doubt, contempt of others' (p. 211). The black-leathered bikers are an example of this position.

A third group Erikson calls *anti-authoritarian* or *hypermoralistic*. For these young protesters any authority is seen and denounced as persecutory. Erikson associates this response with the third developmental stage of initiative versus guilt. It is the age of moralism. These protesters possess the same strident tone which, Erikson says, parents are sometimes embarrassed to recognize as their own, when they hear their children direct it at each other (p. 214).

A fourth position is one of conformity rather than protest. It is the response of a vast majority who cultivate a '*moral pragmatism*' (p. 216). It is associated with the crisis of the school age between competence and inferiority. For these members of society 'what works is good'. The element of retrogression lies in the possibility of an 'all too early, all too exclusive emphasis on the adjustment to the dominant modes of production and success' (p. 216). In this position 'the identity of the competent workman organized with his co-workers in units of economic and political power provides an identity so grounded in tradition and language that the humanist youth may well envy it' (p. 217). Yet in this position there is also a lingering sense of inferiority, as if something were missing: the lost paradise claimed by the hippie, for which material goods and career status cannot be a total substitute.

In this analysis of youthful protest, in spite of its coherence and insights there is a sense of disillusion and weariness and a loss of confidence in youth as the source of renewal in society. 'Youth', he says, 'finds itself between an older generation that has not been able to make integrated sense of the ethical ideal it bestowed on youth ... and an adolescence lacking in ideological integration.' He notes the danger of 'emotional exhaustion' in radical undertakings among young revolutionaries. 'Psychoanalytic insight will have a role to fulfil in the critique of wasteful aspects of cultural and historical change – waste which youth as a generation and mankind as a whole can ill afford' (p. 194). But while it can watch and comment, there is doubt as to what effect this may have. For this depends on 'political factors, including the availability of emergent leadership' (p. 194).

When Erikson turns to the responses of those in authority, professors like himself, he reflects not just pessimism and doubt but also shock. 'As we perceived that much of youth deeply mistrusted us, we were shocked to note that we mistrusted ourselves and each other.' This loss of trust is accompanied by a personal weariness: 'we were overcome by a new sense of awe before such blatant eternal youthfulness or by a re-doubled fatigue which told us that nothing ever really came of youthful utopias' (p. 218).

He describes and seems to identify with the uncertain response of the older generation, 'exposed to a dangerous doubt as to when to be "permissive" and where to "draw the line" . . . What was at stake, then, was the authenticity of either our strictness or our permissiveness' (p. 218). The older generation were challenged to prove 'that our indignation was more than a retrogression to unreconstructed moralism; that our permissiveness was really more than a forced suspension of our indignation' (p. 219).

Such thoughts lead to an anguished reappraisal of 'deals' made in the past. 'In enjoying academic and professional freedom under the protection of and with massive grants from the "establishment", what deals had we made unknowingly or quite knowingly, and with what questionable profit?' (p. 219). For Erikson himself there was the experience of having his ideas rejected, superseded or misapplied. 'Some militants . . . even refused to concede a need for identity' (p. 220). The reason for this, he notes, is that 'to them the very concept was only another attempt to force youth into overdefined roles prescribed by the establishment' (p. 220). He concedes that there is some truth in this. 'Even the most carefully verified observation will prove to have been subject to the ideological polarizations of their historical period.' He makes the point clear that 'this certainly has been the case with psycho-analytical theories, including that of identity' (p. 220). Erikson is here reflecting the impulse to deconstruct, to reveal the secret deals and relative context of all thought and of rationality itself which lies behind the thought of so much of the next thirty years. It is an issue which will be considered further in assessing Erikson's relevance in the continuing postmodern debate.

In reflecting on his experience of these events as an involved witness or 'very participant observer' (p. 199), Erikson felt that it was 'of great import-ance that we should apply what insight we have to our relationship to our own youth' (p. 219). It was a relationship which concerned, as he had noted, the 'stage of life cycle and career' of each witness. Erikson had described the generative stage of life as mainly one in which the task is to care for what has been created in the face of potential stagnation. However, it seems to me that Erikson is here expressing a psychosocial crisis in which the issue is one of letting go as much as taking care. It might be seen as a post-generative or second generative stage.

For parents there is a stage of life which involves letting go of their 'children' so that they can take responsibility for their own lives. Erikson is describing a wider social process in which the older generation has to stand back and watch as the younger generation makes its mistakes; seizes or hides from its opportunities; creates, denies or is denied its place in the world – and so changes that world. It involves the frustration of seeing ideas and principles rejected, ignored, turned on their heads or used in a way that had never been intended. At the same time, older people cannot avoid responsibility for the part they have had in forming the lives of the younger, even as they no longer control what they do with them.

It is a time in which the thoughtful adult is forced to reflect on those deals once made and the coherence of his or her own life as power passes to others. It is a time for reappraisal and for the recognition, as Erikson puts it, that what mattered to young people was not 'our professional stature' or our ' "success" in the world', but 'our inner authority as adults' (1975a: 219).

## Professional and personal criticisms

It is no coincidence that it was at this time that Erikson's work was coming under critical scrutiny and that this involved not only professional but personal criticism. It was perhaps inevitable that as Erikson became established as a public figure in the USA and beyond his ideas should come under challenge. Criticism came first from those whose liberation Erikson supported, but who saw in his liberalism, whether as students, ethnic minorities or feminists, a subtle and patronizing attempt to maintain the status quo. Where in the fifties Erikson had been 'bunched together' with communists and left-wing professors, he now found himself bunched with all forms of authority in what he called the 'revolt of the dependent' (Erikson 1975a: 202).

Although his views diverged in many ways from those of mainstream psychoanalysts such as Hartmann and Peter Blos, he had always kept on good terms with them. He had a way of disarming criticism by anticipating it. He resisted efforts to fit him into the mainstream of psychoanalytic ego psychology by his friend David Rapaport, maintaining an idiosyncratic detachment from the psychoanalytic milieu.

In the early seventies there was criticism on a more personal basis which has been noted when considering Erikson's change of name. These criticisms followed Erikson's publication of an autobiographical essay (1975a: 17). Berman (1975) accused Erikson of 'disguising a Jewish past' (Roazen 1976: 95). Roazen concluded that Berman's 'accusation of evasiveness seems justified' (1976: 95), and called Erikson's change of name an 'act of repudiation' of his stepfather and his mother. These criticisms point to conflicts in Erikson's life which may indeed have been too painful to acknowledge directly and may, as has been suggested earlier, be connected to his identification with the American self-made man, and his ambivalence towards his stepfather. Wright noted how Erikson revised what he had called his 'ambivalent identification' with his stepfather to a later version of 'strong identification' (Wright 1982:

5). It is hard to say whether such a change is evidence, as Wright sees it, of Erikson's 'reliving, reviewing and revising' of the past (p. 6) or, as Roazen says, part of the way Erikson 'camouflaged the testing of his own rock bottom that went to make up his adult sense of self' (1976: 94). Perhaps it is both.

What must have hurt Erikson most was the charge of dishonesty set against his commitment to ethical behaviour. Erikson's evasion, says Roazen, is 'particularly disappointing in one who writes in such an ethically high-minded fashion' (p. 96). There is an echo here of Gandhi's anxiety of how critics might use his autobiography to show up 'the hollowness of many of my pretensions' (Erikson 1970a: 230). High-mindedness, as Erikson might have seen it, involves a continuation of the adolescent struggle for ideological commitment in the face of uncertainty. It is connected too to Erikson's lifelong conflict between roots and restlessness, which perhaps has, after all, a Jewish significance.

These issues take on a new emphasis as the mature individual seeks a new basis for a secure but undogmatic integrity in old age. It is an integrity that, as Erikson observed, must rest no longer on an identity linked to status or achievements but on 'inner authority' (1975a: 219). In Erikson's response to youthful and feminist critics and to the personal criticism of colleagues and rivals, there may have been flickers of that despair at the heart of the self which he had identified in the crisis of old age – integrity versus despair. In this anticipated crisis both his own reappraisal of the deals in his life and the critical challenges of others play their part. The final balance of this crisis in Erikson's life is considered in the last chapter of this book. But whatever disturbing sense of despair may have been present in his life at this time, there is a new sense of inner authority conveyed in two sets of lectures delivered during the mid-1970s.

## Play and politics: a critique of American society

In 1972 and 1973 Erikson explored the relationship of childhood develop-ment to politics in two series of lectures. Both present a critique of American society and in particular its basis in the ideology of the self-made man. It is a theme, as alluded to above, which Erikson was exploring in his own life as well as in his view of the society to which he was committed.

The Godkin lectures of 1972 were published as *Toys and Reasons* (Erikson 1978a). They develop an 'improbable theme' which 'struck me as elemental'; this is the relationship between 'childhood play and the political imagina-tion' (p. 11). His aim is to 'clarify the relationship of play to reality in different stages of life and in various compartments of human existence, including, eventually, the politics of everyday life and at least approaching "real" politics' (p. 28).

Childhood is linked to politics through the 'development of playful imag-ination'. This has the essential quality of 'playfulness' which 'is placed in the service of an inner ordering of experience and of the ritualizations of everyday life'. Such ritualizations involve 'shared visions' and so 'introduce the growing individual into functioning institutions' (p. 167).

Erikson had been impressed by the accuracy with which the play constructions of 11- and 12-year-olds in the 1930s Berkeley studies had expressed unfolding themes of individual lives as recorded in later years. He describes one such individual to illustrate the significance of playful imagination. The play constructions at 12 of a black boy represented cages which contained 'wild animals watched over by uniformed figures and dogs' (Erikson 1978a: 38). Thirty years later Erikson met this boy as a man. He had made a 'special name for himself' because of his ability to 'guide groups of black teenagers about to get involved in destructive (and self-destructive) activity'. He explained his ability thus: 'These boys . . . feel that I have it in me to be violent myself. But they also know that I have my anger well in hand' (p. 39). Erikson comments that here is a continuation and a fulfilment of a theme of 'wildness contained and yet also transcended by discipline and self-expression'. Set in a wider perspective, 'historical developments and a new political vision had permitted this man to go beyond the early solution of smiling compliance: he had become aware of his anger and yet also learned to employ it in social action' (p. 39). So individual themes, imaginatively expressed, become the basis of a 'shared vision'. Biology, individual psychology and society have each contributed to an outcome where a continuing 'playfulness' underlies, if it cannot ensure, 'a promise kept beyond prediction' (p. 39).

By contrast, Erikson describes what happens when 'playfulness' is lost and the shared visions become 'shared nightmares' (1978a: 157). He gives as his example of the subversion of playfulness and the breakdown of ritualization the events at My Lai in the Vietnam War in 1970. As reported in the account of Seymour Hersh, the lieutenant's order to 'Waste them' led to the massacre of over 400 men, women and children (p. 164). One soldier put it: 'The people didn't know what they were dying for and the guys didn't know why they were shooting them' (p. 164). It was 'a rage without any familiar pattern' (p. 162). Erikson calls it a 'catastrophic de-ritualization' of the 'instinctive impulse to spare children' (p. 164).

In Erikson's view this event was not a freak occurrence. The success of the black social worker in transcending an oppressed childhood and the My Lai massacres must both be seen as the outcome of the 'American dream' (1978a: 155). Both the shared visions and the shared nightmares evolve out of the specific dreams and beliefs, forming events, achievements and promises, illusions and delusions that have unfolded in American history. The material prosperity of North American society ensures that both the visions and the nightmares have vital significance not only for America but for all the inhabitants of the planet.

## The Jefferson Lectures: *Dimensions of a New Identity*

Erikson explored this theme further in his Jefferson Lectures (1974). The first part of the book is an appreciative, even adulatory, survey of the life, character and sayings of Thomas Jefferson, one of the greatest of the Founding Fathers, prime author of the Declaration of Independence and an individual model upon which the post-colonial United States of America was founded and prospered. Both in himself and in his words Jefferson incorporated the post-colonial identity of the self-made man in a self-made society. 'It is part of the American character', Jefferson wrote, 'to consider nothing as desperate; to surmount any difficulty by resolution and continuance. Remote from all other aid we are obliged to invent and to execute; to find means within ourselves and not to lean on others' (Erikson 1974: 70). Jefferson was by any standards a humane man. He was Protean in the sense that he could apply himself with confidence to any role or the completion of any task he set about. His trust in the material success that would attend due labour was tempered by a genuine wish to use power without seeking it for its own sake. A framework of transcendent values in his religion gave boundaries and perspectives to his humanist aspirations.

As Erikson expounds Jefferson's virtues it might seem that in this shared vision of the self-reliant and self-confident individual lies a 'new identity' which can be transmitted to the world as a basis for the prosperity and liberation of all. His title *Dimensions of a New Identity* might indeed seem to promise such a design. If so, Erikson is perhaps preparing his audience, like a skilled preacher, for an answer which they did not expect.

Erikson says that this 'new identity' of the self-made man, founded in the image of Jefferson and American history, is not flawless and never was. Erikson identifies two particular elements which, while they may have helped to contribute to the successes of the land of opportunity, also led to My Lai. The first is that the Jeffersonian model depended on the exclusion of those it found expedient to consider inferior and on the idealization of the dominant white skinned person, particularly the male. Jefferson himself firmly believed in the necessity of slavery, though he was troubled by and aware of its effects not only on the slaves but on their masters, of whom he was one. He also believed in the apotheosis of the white male. Jefferson, says Erikson, 'needed for his new consciousness the certainty that white is beautiful, and that the nobility of emotion he saw in the white face guaranteed both moral power and restraint in the usurpation of power' (1974: 113). In spite of the humane intentions of Jefferson and many like him, the dangers of exploitation in such illusions were manifested in the dispossession and extermination of native peoples and the subjugations of slavery, supported by the myth of racial superiority and backed by the legal and illegal abuse of power. The deal offered was to 'become one of us' or perish, and even that deal could be arbitrarily applied or withdrawn. For Erikson such a deal had resonances in his Jewish ancestry as well as in the common American experience of the immigrant.

The second flaw to which Erikson draws attention is the belief in unlimited material expansion. In Jefferson this belief was balanced by the values he found in the Bible, and so it is for millions of Americans. Yet such values are often held with a moralistic self-righteousness that only serves to intensify the first flaw of exclusive pseudo-speciation. For others the seduction of material success achieved through scientific inventiveness, confidence in action and persuasive selling of products has eroded the power of transcendent values to restrain or question the right to expand and dominate.

Erikson is telling his American public that the identity being offered to the world in the name of liberty is fatally flawed. The rest of the world must not be allowed to become the playground for the self-made man's 'obsession with the game of unlimited expansion' (Erikson 1974: 119). Nor must it be threatened with a deal that you must give up your identity and become like us, or be eliminated.

Is it not possible, nevertheless, to find ways of removing or transforming the flaws so that this 'new identity' with all its promise and achievements can yet be a standard bearer for a liberated world? Erikson declines even to consider what such a transformed 'new identity' might be. He suggests that with such flaws at the heart of the self-made ideology what is needed is heart-searching rather than renewed plans to liberate others.

It is here that Erikson sees psychotherapy in general and psychoanalysis in particular as having a contribution to make. It can provide an ethical rather than a moralistic basis for heart-searching. It is concerned with both insight and conscience; it presents a way of acknowledging and dealing with guilt that does not rely on self-punishment, blaming others or denial. He believes that the search for insight in its modern forms which Freud initiated, and which others have developed in a diversity of ways in the twentieth century, have an inherent playfulness and mutuality essential to a benign transformation of social forms. It is, however, crucial that this contribution includes awareness of its own flaws, a continuing heart-searching of its own conscience.

Erikson's critique of the self-made individual in American society reflects his own struggle to recognize the deals he himself made, particularly as an immigrant. In his meeting with Huey Newton he tried to explain what coming to America had meant to him:

> I will never forget the moment when our ship first sighted that coldly competitive skyline of New York. The sight more or less puts you in a state of survivorship . . . in the sense of having to accept, without looking back too much, the fact of your survival . . . All this at first narrows your perceptiveness and, I'm afraid, your capacity to empathize with the struggling masses, until you have gained a foothold and a self-definition as American.
>
> (Erikson 1975b: 67)

The struggle to make it in the land of opportunity is the basis for an identity as a self-made man. It is also the basis for a narrowed perception of the struggles of others that can divide and exclude. Acknowledging his part in this is also Erikson's way of trying to bridge the divide.

The next chapter is a critical review of Erikson's work and influence. The two following chapters consider the relevance of Erikson's ideas in the contemporary world. The final chapter returns to Erikson's own life history in its final stage and the summing up and completion, still necessarily incomplete, of his life and work.

# Critical review of work and influence

In this chapter Erikson's work is evaluated in the light of criticisms and his responses to them. The influence of his writings and professional activity in the second half of the twentieth century can then be assessed.

## Criticism of Erikson's work

Criticism is a way to reach a more complete picture of Erikson and his work. There are four main areas of criticism to be considered. The first concerns Erikson's idealism: that he avoids negative aspects of life and confuses what is with what he would like, or thinks ought to happen. The second area concerns the social and political implications of his work. His ideas have been said to support and justify an unjust status quo; alternatively, his work is seen as part of an undermining of traditional culture and values. The third area of criticism is that his work is distorted by the assumptions of his own gender and culture. The fourth area is his method and style: a lack of rigour in his thinking, and vagueness and ambiguity in his style.

### Is Erikson an idealist?

The charge of idealism is forcefully put by Paul Roazen (1976). Roazen appreciates Erikson for his humanity, original and comprehensive concepts and vision, but claims that his work is distorted by his idealism. He claims that Erikson's optimistic view of human nature ignores its darker side, in that he 'takes for granted a natural harmony of human needs' (Roazen 1976: 158), by contrast with Freud's assumption of the ineradicable conflict both within the individual and between individual and society. As another critic, Kovel, has put it, Erikson lacks a 'sense of evil' (1988: 75). Second, Roazen (1976) sees Erikson's idealism as ignoring the basic conflicts in society: 'Supposed advances in human culture are more illusory than Erikson would care to admit' (p. 165). Contending conceptions of the good life, says Roazen, 'have been the stuff of all known history' (p. 156). Erikson's ethics are utopian and do not 'involve a confrontation with divergent goals' (p. 162). A third aspect of the charge of idealism is that Erikson confuses values with objective reality, what ought to be with what is. As Wrightsman (1994: 81) puts it, 'desirable values are rife in his theories'.

How far are these criticisms justified? Erikson's generally optimistic view of people and society can be seen as an antidote to the emphasis on the pathological in psychoanalysis. His affirmative view of human potential is a warning not to label unsocial behaviour as pathological. I have demonstrated that Erikson does not ignore the darker side of human nature or of society. Nevertheless, there is in Erikson's work a presumption of the positive over the negative as natural and normative. Very rarely does Erikson face us with a struggle that ends in defeat or despair.

It is less just to accuse Erikson of ignoring the role of conflict in human development. His stages are very much dialectical, involving a crisis of conflict and struggle. Erikson does not exclude the role of conflict from his vision of wider identities but points out the dangers and reactions which such wider identities may provoke. The question is not whether or not conflict exists but how it is managed. Erikson distinguishes between the ethical level at which it is managed by dialogue and mutuality, and the levels of ideology, moralism and primitive violence. He does not claim that these levels can be eliminated or that even on an ethical level there will be no conflicts. But on the ethical level they become the stuff of growth and learning.

As far as the confusion of values and reality is concerned, the issues that values involve cannot be resolved, as Hartmann (1960) tried to do, following Freud, by positing a value-free science of psychology. As Erikson says, 'what is called material reality at a given historical time may still, on the whole, be dependent as much on what we *wish* to have true as on what we *know* to be true' (1975b: 55). Erikson's recognition and exploration of the involvement, and indeed the indispensability, of values in therapy, in individual develop-ment and in social structure is one of his major contributions, in spite of the problems it leaves unresolved.

### Social and political implications

Does Erikson justify an unjust society? Roazen links Erikson's idealism to 'social conservatism' (1976: 171). 'The troubling question is whether or not, for all the attractive features of Erikson's ethical position, he has not served in the end to reinforce the status quo' (p. 171), because 'desiring something in the future need say little about the likelihood of its ever coming to pass' (p. 170).

A writer who makes similar criticisms with greater force and venom is Kovel (1988). Writing from a Marxist intellectual viewpoint, Kovel candidly admits to an almost physical antipathy to Erikson. He feels 'suffocated when reading Erikson' (p. 28) and expresses his disgust in phrases such as 'the cheap perfume of identity' (p. 73). Like Roazen he accuses Erikson of idealism – 'he spares himself critical reflection by keeping his eye on the heavens' (p. 74) – and of confusing values with analysis – 'a hodgepodge between the way it is and the way it ought to be' (p. 72). But his main criticism is of the political implications of Erikson's ideas, which depend 'on explanations which remain fixed – for all the transcendent rhetoric – to the values of the established order' (p. 77). It is a lack of a political explanation of human suffering and conflict and a lack of commitment to political change which is at the root of Kovel's criticism. For him Erikson's 'pontification about ethics' shows 'moral confusion and political backwardness imposed ... by the identity concept' (p. 78). Kovel cites Erikson's account of the millworkers' strike in *Gandhi's Truth* to demonstrate that 'Erikson chooses, as he must, the side of property' (p. 78). What Erikson 'doesn't like to explore' is 'sex and power – real power, the economic and political kind' (p. 74). So Erikson must align himself inevitably with the unjust and exploitative status quo.

Kovel's and Erikson's premises and approach to life are so far apart that disagreement seems inevitable and mutual understanding impossible. Yet there is a kind of surprising closeness in this antagonism. In spite of all his criticism Kovel writes one of the most succinct appreciations of Erikson's work, apparently without sarcasm. Erikson is:

> the one who has done the most to bridge psychoanalysis and the rest of human science ... Virtually single-handedly, Erikson has launched the problematic and promising field of psychohistory ... There is no holding back from taking a stand, none of the hothouse aura that has come to surround psychoanalysis ... He sees himself as having a mission to bring the truth-telling discipline of psychoanalysis directly into grips with the reality of events ... and he has done this, on the whole, with great subtlety and breadth of mind.
>
> (Kovel 1988: 68)

Kovel complains that Erikson has become a 'sacred cow' (p. 68), rarely subjected to critical investigation. The personal nature of his criticism and the ambivalent mixture of appreciation, insight and rejection suggest that Erikson may have been for Kovel a parental figure who must be overthrown, as Freud was for Erikson. Kovel's criticisms evoke insights, as in his description of Erikson's 'rhapsodies over identity' as 'rising away from something seen but unbearable' (p. 74). He is suggesting that Erikson's weakness is a deep reluctance to face fully the negative side of life and the possibility of evil. Kovel says what others dared not say, sensing aspects of Erikson's hidden psychological vulnerability and its connection to his weaknesses as a thinker. Kovel at the same time both appreciates and tries to demolish Erikson's strengths.

Is Erikson then socially and politically conservative? It is true that he is never comfortable with activism or politically committed to radicalism, though he tries to communicate with and understand those who are (1975b). On the other hand, he is not a conservative in the sense of opposing change, for he clearly advocated change and growth through conflict both in the individual and in society. Nor is it true that he is tied to and unable to speak against established views, whether psychoanalytic orthodoxy or the 'American dream'. Kovel's charge that Erikson 'gives up on what has to be the central problem of critical psychohistory: negation within the established order' (1988: 76) does not hold up. Erikson condemned and cogently exposed the delusions and manipulations of power, not just in academic writings but to gatherings of senators and church leaders. This did not perhaps come easily either by temperament or to the immigrant who was initially dependent on his new homeland. The growth of his confidence to take a stand is part of the story of his life this book has tried to follow.

There is nevertheless a conservative element in his emphasis on the import-ance of continuity to identity, and of the dependence of individuals on social structures. Some of his most original ideas have an almost provocatively old-fashioned flavour, as in his use of the term 'virtues' for personality strengths. Nevertheless, Erikson's recognition of the creative as well as the limiting potential in the social environment and people's shared worlds may actually be a more realistic basis for change than revolutionary struggle for political power. Choosing between Erikson and Kovel may be a matter of temperament, but it is not a choice between reaction and radical change. Nor is it a choice between a contemplative and an active approach to life. In Erikson there is a continuing tension and dialogue between action and con-templation, inner and outer worlds, change and continuity, political and spiritual aspirations. This tension is inherent in his life stages and in the lives of all the major figures he studied: Luther, Gandhi and Jefferson (see Bellah 1978: 63). What these criticisms help to bring out is the complex nature of Erikson's personality and ideas, as a pioneer who values tradition and an original thinker who prefers convergence and continuity to controversy and confrontation.

In addition to this criticism from the political left, Erikson is implicated in criticism of psychotherapy from the right. Lasch (1975) in particular articulated an attack on psychotherapy and counselling as undermining the traditional structures of society. For Lasch, institutionalized therapy is a self-serving professional activity which creates the needs and dependencies that it claims to cure. Thus it destroys traditional values as well as support systems.

Lasch's argument merges with the socialist analysis, in seeing this profes-sionalism as colluding with an elitist monopoly of power and resources. This criticism has troubled many therapists. It is still a substantial criticism when, as Pilgrim (1997) points out, resources, attention and care in psychotherapeutic services in the NHS in Britain are deployed in reverse relation to people's needs.

It is a problem which Erikson certainly takes seriously. Throughout his career, from his arrival in Boston, he attempted to balance work in privileged environments, as at Austen Riggs, with working with the deprived and the exploited. He acknowledges the force of the criticism when he speaks of his need to recognize the 'deals' (1975a: 219) made by those who worked in the privileged enviroment of universities such as Harvard.

Lasch has a wide conceptual view of social problems but he does not seem to have a very real picture of how therapists think and work, or the degree to which self-criticism, from Freud onwards, is an inherent element in psychotherapy. There is a crucial difference between those who see the practice of psychotherapy as irredeemably self-serving, and those who see it as *potentially* exploitative but not necessarily so. Thus for critics such as Masson (1992: 7) a 'good therapist' is 'not very likely'. For Pilgrim (1992: 241), what is required is 'an honest acceptance that therapists are potential abusers'. Erikson is certainly aware of this possibility in psychotherapy. Like Luther's examination of conscience, psychotherapy makes the demand (postulated, according to Erikson, by Freud) 'that one take an especially honest look at one's honesty' (1972: 246). This is a debate that lies at the heart of the place of psychotherapy and counselling in society.

## The developmental stages

Criticisms of Erikson's developmental stage model fall into three categories. First, there are those who accept the general outline but question its details, such as the particular characterizations of each stage, the attribution of a particular crisis to a particular stage, the order in which the stages occur and the need for substages and for overlap between the stages. Among these critics many have evolved new schemes on the basis of Erikson's and others' work and these are considered in more detail later in this chapter, when Erikson's influence and developments arising from Erikson's scheme are assessed. Second, there are those who propose radically different developmental concepts. Jung, for example, focused attention, like Erikson, on the adult years. In Jung's view, however, the earlier and later years have rather different purposes, whereas each of Erikson's is a preparation for the next. Transpersonal schemes such as those of Ken Wilber (1996) describe a series of developments or levels of the self, which an individual may or may not attain. This contrasts with Erikson's life cycle, where the biological and social as well as the psychological or spiritual levels provide integrated challenges which all must face in some way.

A third group challenges the validity of any kind of developmental scheme as an adequate way of making sense of human behaviour. Wrightsman describes Erikson as a leading stage theorist (1994: 59) and compares this approach with other paradigms of human life. For example, in the 'dialectical' approach 'contending needs create a state of constant tension in the individual' throughout life (p. 151). In the dialectical approach 'no significant issues are ever put to rest' (p. 150). As Wrightsman acknowledges, however, Erikson's scheme allows for a dialectical element in his continuation and reworking of themes from earlier stages throughout life. The dialectical view can lead to a celebration of life as conflict and defiance rather than as leading to integration and acceptance. Those devastated by the death of a child may find it hard to find meaning in life in terms of a succession of stages which find their fulfilment only when the series is complete.

Not everyone accepts the need for a developmental scheme such as Erikson's in making sense of their life. Nevertheless, some consideration of development and growth, and some narrative element, seems indispensable to the student of human nature and society, linked as they are to the seasonal cycles of growth and decay. Erikson's scheme is remarkable for the way in which all the stages of human life are linked by the underlying concepts of crisis, identity formation and human strengths. His scheme also embraces the integration of individual and society and subjective and objective phenomena. Erikson's achievement was to draw developmental psychology away from the psychoanalytic emphasis on childhood sexuality without losing the insights which Freud had initiated.

### Gender assumptions in Erikson's work

Criticisms of Erikson as imposing a biological determinism on women's development have already been discussed. It has been noted how his use of the male pronoun gives a male bias to his descriptions of experience. His work has also been criticized for its use of exclusively male figures in his psychohistorical studies, which form a testing ground for his psychosocial theories. A former student of Erikson's, Carol Gilligan (1982), claimed that the stages of the life cycle were based on male experience and that a separate development chart for women would be helpful (Friedman 1999: 426). The positive way in which he insists on the need for women in world affairs (1968a: 261–2) can still be seen as conveying stereotypes of women as carers and nurturers that may collude with entrenched male dominance and men's assumptions about themselves as 'natural' leaders, decision takers and initiators. In Roazen's view 'Erikson has too readily accepted traditional Western male–female stereotypes' (1976: 146). Erikson acknowledges that his suggestion that 'women may yet contribute something specifically feminine to so-far masculine fields' is seen by many women as 'only a new form of discrimination' (Evans 1964: 46). His reply is that 'we have no right to foreclose the matter by assuming that women once truly emancipated and fully competent may *not* have some new directions to offer. As a man living in the nuclear age, I can only hope they do' (Evans 1964: 46).

The debate about gender difference is far from concluded. The relative importance and influence of biological, cultural, political and psychological factors and their interaction with personal development and social structures is likely to remain a matter of controversy and research. It cannot be resolved by the attempt to reduce the problems to any one level. Erikson's insistence on this and on the significance of the ground plan of the body in psychological development must remain an essential element in this continuing debate. At the same time, the feminist challenge to patriarchal or statist attitudes appearing as universal assumptions, and to the way in which power structures are moulded by these assumptions, is also essential to the debate.

### The social and personal relativity of the concept of identity

Criticism of the concept of identity goes back, as I noted in Chapter 9, to the late 1960s when students and activists rejected what seemed to be a concept too closely allied to existing oppressive power structures. For some liberation lay in an intense intellectual effort to uncover the deeper structures that lie behind all thinking and from which values and knowledge are derived. Particularly in France, which had shared revolutionary aspirations with the United States and suffered deep disappointments, thinkers such as Derrida and Foucault deconstructed systems of ideas with a mixture of philosophical and historical analysis. This has never been without its furious critics, who maintain the necessity of a universal standard of value and objectivity. In England, sociologists such as Hall used these ideas to uncover the assumptions behind racism and cultural bias. Nevertheless, Hall (1996: 16) has said that identity, however questionable the concept may be, remains 'a matter of considerable political significance'.

If postmodernists criticize Erikson's concept of identity as deriving from his social context, others see the concept as deriving from his personal experience. Wrightsman has pointed to Erikson as a particularly clear example of a thinker whose 'concepts derive from their own experiences' (1992: 60). His preoccupation with identity is linked to a confusion of identities experienced in early life and throughout his childhood. Does this invalidate Erikson's theories? Wrightsman thinks not, for a number of reasons. It is valuable to have the variety of viewpoints which such experience produces. 'Subjectivity', he says, is 'virtually inevitable' in the study of human experience (p. 58). In assessing the value of a theory people judge it against their own experience and this, not its subjective origins, is the measure of its worth. Another view is put forward by Wright, who sees Erikson's work 'to solve his own crisis' of identity as 'lifting his patienthood to a universal level' (1982: xii).

Erikson's work can be seen on three levels. At one level his ideas can be seen as an expression of his own psychology. At another level they are significant formulations of the problems and confusions of his age and culture, if at the same time limited by them. At yet another level they are explorations of fundamental concerns of common humanity.

A further criterion for assessing the value of subjectively based theories is how far the individual is conscious of his or her assumptions and can articulate them. Erikson throughout his life sought to widen his views by experiencing different social contexts and by testing out his assumptions in Sioux reservations, in student seminars, in discussion with politicians or representatives of other cultural traditions. His change of direction in 1960 was taken specifically because he felt the need both in himself and in those aspiring to be psychotherapists to become more 'historically self-conscious' (Erikson 1975b: 55).

### Criticisms of method and style

Richard Stevens says of Erikson, 'while there is no doubt about the vigour of Erikson's work, questions can be raised about its rigour'. He is 'sometimes prone to dogmatic pronouncements entirely unsupported by argument or evidence' (1983: 111). Roazen says that 'he does not adequately distinguish between a subjective feeling and an objective condition' (1976: 138). Others include Erikson among those whose work is valueless because it cannot be 'operationalized' to take the form of a verifiable hypothesis (Gellner 1992: 47), although, as will be noted, much practical study has in fact flowed from Erikson's work.

Stevens recalls how in an interview Erikson accepted criticism of his lack of clarity with 'disarming frankness'. 'I've read it over and over again that people felt something, found it very good and found it very convincing and afterwards they didn't quite know what I had said. So my readers have to be warned here' (Stevens 1983: 112). It is true that Erikson is sometimes vague or inconsistent in his definitions, such as in his use of 'actuality' and 'reality' and 'ego-identity'. Erikson sometimes confuses logical categories, as when he says that '*purpose* is the *courage* to . . . pursue valued goals' (1964: 122; italics added). It is true that his theories are not always backed by evidence. Sometimes this is when he is involved in working across disciplines, as in what Wrightsman (1994: 105) calls the 'highly questionable "fact"' of Luther's 'fit' in the choir. There is also sometimes an arbitrariness about his choice of pivotal concepts in his stages: shame, doubt, industriousness and inadequacy. These concepts become fixed in a scheme and take on a solidity which is more apparent than real. On the other hand, a closer look at these concepts often reveals surprising depths and consistency. Erikson is usually careful to state when he is speaking speculatively. Inconsistency has been noted earlier in the values Erikson attaches to the negative aspects of the crises, i.e. mistrust, doubt, despair. It is not clear whether these are essentially destructive or valuable balancing counterparts to their corresponding positive qualities.

Stevens defends Erikson on the grounds of what he is trying to do. 'The problem of validity (in the sense of assessing whether an interpretation is correct or not) arises because it may not be an *appropriate* criterion to apply to the kind of task in which he is engaged' (1983: 113). 'Such intractable problems arise because psychoanalysis involves the study of *meaning*' (p. 113). Meaning is explored through language and there is an inevitable element of ambiguity in any words used to explore it. 'A core feature of language is an inherent ambiguity' (p. 114).

Giddens points out that Erikson's concept of ego-identity 'has at least four connotations' and comments that 'none of these single uses . . . is particularly lucid' (1984: 60). In discussing this criticism, Craib defends Erikson's vagueness: 'Conceptual clarity is not always desirable if we are trying to grasp a difficult reality. It serves only to avoid problematic reality' (1998: 66). Craib instead sees Erikson's fault in that 'he oversimplifies the notion of ego-identity'. This is the danger of any conceptual model – that the concept is taken for the reality. Erikson was aware of this but even so could not always avoid it.

It is not easy to distinguish between justifiable or inspired poetic subtlety in the use of language and intellectual sloppiness. Ambiguities can be used to explore the depths and ambivalence existing in a relationship, a feeling or a meaning, or the paradoxical nature of life itself. Erikson certainly uses words in this way. However, it is possible to look for intellectual rigour without accepting all the claims of positivist science. Erikson made a sustained exposition of his method, which he summarized as 'disciplined subjectivity' (1964: 53), although this has been criticized for vagueness of definition (Strozier 1976). The future of a genuine 'disciplined subjectivity' in qualitative research vitally depends on the ability to establish its own kind of rigour.

Erikson's conceptual configurations do more than explore and reflect ambiguities of meaning. They seek to recognize and connect, in a coherent pattern, different levels of meaning and interpretation: the biological, the psychological, the social (including the political), the ethical and the spiritual. Some at least of Erikson's lapses may be attributed to what Pilgrim calls the sheer 'hard work' of such an enterprise. 'Multilevelled, multifactorial reasoning is extremely difficult to maintain' (1997: 110). Such work is essential in coming to grips with the complexities of our world. Conceptual complexities can sometimes obscure reality. They can also sometimes lead to glimpses of a surprising simplicity.

## Erikson's influence

There are three main areas of Erikson's influence that require critical consideration: first, developmental psychology; second, his influence on the development of psychotherapeutic and counselling theory and practice; third, interdisciplinary studies and the application of psychodynamic ideas to other disciplines in the study of human life in society.

### *Developmental psychology*

Erikson's developmental scheme is generally acknowledged as one of the most influential in the twentieth century. Kovel's summary is typical of many in crediting Erikson with 'achieving in the course of his career the first really systematic elaboration of a developmental point of view about human phenomena' (1988: 68).

Erikson's scheme is remarkable for the way all the stages of human life are linked and included in a coherent scheme through the concepts of crisis, identity formation and human strengths. His concepts integrate individual and social development, taking into account both subjective and objective phenomena. Erikson's achievement was to extend developmental psychology from the psychoanalytic emphasis on childhood sexuality and the pathology of the inner world, to a truly psychosocial development.

This influence can be noted in two ways: a broad influence of the developmental concepts such as identity and crisis, and specific stimulation in each of the eight stages he outlined. The popular use of the term 'identity crisis' illustrates a difficulty in evaluating Erikson's broader influence. It is applied on an almost daily basis to pop stars and politicians, to political parties and nations, to cricket clubs and professional groups. It appears in academic discourse, often without acknowledgement, and in popular journalism. Its use may not bear great resemblance to Erikson's use of it. Yet it is a term, like Adler's 'inferiority complex', which somehow resonates with social consciousness at a deep level. Its wide use fifty years after Erikson first used it indicates a significant if diffuse influence.

Erikson's influence has been direct, if widely spread, on many specific stages of developmental psychology. A bibliography for 1982–92 (Schwartz 1998), listing works directly or indirectly focused on Erikson, includes work on all Erikson's stages of development. The largest number of references are to the adolescent stage of identity formation, but other research and discussion areas include studies of the problems of disabled people, female identity, mid-career crisis, computers in education, stages of educational development, drama, ageing, infertility, play and insomnia. There is hardly an issue or area of human activity that has not been influenced by his ideas. It is worth noting some specific influences that stand out for each of the stages.

*Infancy and early years*

In the two decades that followed the publication of *Childhood and Society* there was intense research into and study of the development of infants and young children, including work by Mahler, Bruner and Stern. This was paralleled in Britain by the work of Bowlby and Winnicott.

The connection between Stern and Erikson is particularly interesting. Stern's radically new way of looking at infant development rejects most of the psychoanalytic framework (1985). In some ways Stern is the antithesis of Erikson. Where Erikson seeks the widest possible perspective, Stern focuses intently on one specific age. Where Erikson relies on configuration and illustration, Stern organizes detailed research projects. Yet they have much in common. Both attempt to combine a subjective and objective understanding of human development. Both emphasize the interpersonal. Stern's view of successive stages in the development of the self is very similar to Erikson's epigenetic succession. Like Erikson, Stern allows for the recurrence of earlier themes in later stages. Stern's identification of the central importance for the developing self of the senses of agency, continuity in time, physical cohesion and intentionality overlaps strongly with Erikson's description of identity formation as the ability 'to experience oneself as something that has continuity and sameness, and to act accordingly' (1965: 37). In demonstrating the practical functioning of intersubjectivity in empirical research, Stern provides a valuable grounding for Erikson's concept of the mutuality of mother and child.

*Adolescence*

This stage shows Erikson's greatest influence, at least as registered by published work. Studies taking Erikson as their basic paradigm include those of learning situations, the emotional problems of students, problems of and the interaction between intimacy and identity, moral development in adolescence, and juvenile crime and alienation. The work of Marcia (1966), for example, is noted (Clarke Stewart *et al.* 1985: 617) for its 'intriguing findings about college students' feelings of commitment and crisis in regard to religion, politics, and work'. Lowe has commented that 'until Erikson formulated his concept of identity, psychologists had found it extremely difficult ... to understand the psychological preoccupations of adolescents' (1972: 152). Though Lowe writes in a British context, this is equally true of America.

*Adulthood and old age*

Wrightsman states that in the area of adult development 'Erikson's stage theory has served as a foundation for systematic thinking about personality development in adulthood' (1994: 110). He also claims that more recent theories show the influence of Erikson and that the systematic writings of Havighurst (1972), Gould (1978) and Levinson (1978) on adult development are 'laboratories of Erikson's ideas' (p. 110).

Typically Erikson's influence extends not simply to stimulating the study of each stage in detail but also to a wider perspective, through the comparison of life stages in different cultures and centuries. Thus the work he edited and inspired on *Adulthood* (1978b) contains studies of the nature and meaning of adulthood in Confucian, Christian and Islamic thought, nineteenth-century Russia and India and contemporary Japan and America.

Finally, the basic paradigm of Erikson's life cycle has contributed significantly to the developing study of old age. In *Vital Involvement in Old Age* (1989), Erikson and his wife, Joan, both in their eighties, cooperated with a younger colleague in the detailed study of now elderly participants in the Californian study begun fifty years before. Their findings not only substantiate this period as one with its own tasks and crises and ways of dealing with them, but also at the same time demonstrate how earlier themes are taken up once more in this final stage of life.

## Erikson's influence in Britain

Erikson's influence on developmental psychology is less evident in Britain than in the United States. Perhaps this is because of the domination of the work of Bowlby and Winnicott, who, like Erikson and Stern, emphasize the significance of the parent–child relationship in developing trust as the basis of autonomy. The work of Winnicott, of Klein and her followers, as well as of Anna Freud and the Hampstead Clinic, focuses, like Erikson's, on the significance of play for development and on its therapeutic potential. The object relations school developed concepts for individual development in terms of the interdependence of self and other. Bion, Menzies Lyth and others in the Tavistock Institute have made crucial extensions of Freudian and Kleinian concepts to the psychology of small groups and organizations. Nevertheless, what these developments sometimes lack is Erikson's sense of the impact of the wider social framework on individual development, the continuing interdependence of society and the individual throughout the life cycle, and the corresponding emphasis on crises and tasks specific to adolescence and adulthood.

The influence of Erikson's work seems to have slipped quietly into Britain through the need of expanding counselling organizations such as RELATE (formerly the National Marriage Guidance Council) and the Westminster Pastoral Foundation to train counsellors. In addition to their existing life experience and social skills these mature students needed some grounding in developmental psychology. Erikson's life cycle approach, combining psychodynamic concepts with life experience, has been particularly appropriate for such training. It is not surprising therefore that training courses for counsellors have included works which use Erikson's developmental framework, such as those of Lowe (1972) and Jacobs (1985, 1998). This developmental framework has also become part of eclectic and specifically person-centred counselling courses as well as those more psychodynamically based. In the early 1980s Erikson was seen by Stevens (1983) as an important link between the psychodynamic insights of psychoanalysis (seen as a search for meaning) and the humanistic search for self-fulfilment in the human potential movement.

In the second edition of *The Presenting Past* (1998), Jacobs has shifted the emphasis from developmental stages to developmental themes. He develops a model that still owes much to Erikson, but introduces a 'cyclical element into progression instead of the linear model', so that 'personal development might be seen as more like a spiral staircase' (Jacobs 1998: 13). In so doing he brings out Erikson's notion of the recurrence at each stage of issues from earlier stages. Jacobs had in his earlier edition (1985) developed the idea, inherent in Erikson's configuration, of adolescence as a 'watershed'. Following Laufer's (1974) division of adolescence into three periods, Jacobs suggested that 'each period of adolescence looks backwards as well as forwards, like a true watershed' (pp. 14–15). Now he prefers to see each 'age' as continuing all the elements of the other 'ages', and, like adolescence, pointing both backwards to earlier issues and forwards to (what Erikson appears to suggest are) later issues. The influence of Erikson's developmental psychology in Britain may particularly be seen in therapeutic work with adolescents and students (for example, Rogers 1993; Klinefelter 1994), and in discussions of ageing and ageism (Craig 1998; Gorsuch 1998).

### Erikson's influence on the development of counselling and psychotherapy

Erikson's contribution cannot be grasped in terms of a particular practice or single concept, but through its comprehensive vision of what psychotherapy is about, as well as its possibilities and dangers. His work is both a part of and a significant contribution to the gradual change in the nature of psychotherapy in the USA, which has its parallel in Europe and elsewhere. It is a change from an activity which bases itself on a medical model as a science, applying verifiable knowledge, to one which is 'hermeneutic' as Stevens defines it: 'a capacity to elicit meaning and offer insights into many aspects of individual and cultural life' (1983: 108). It is equally importantly a change from an emphasis on the inner world of the individual to an interpersonal perspective.

Writers and critics have disagreed in where they place Erikson in the history of psychotherapy. Bateman and Holmes (1995: 40) include him among the neo-Freudians, such as Horney and Fromm, who broke away from the orthodoxy of the time. Frosh (1987: 88) includes him among the ego psychologists led by Hartmann. This ambiguity is not surprising, as Erikson challenged the 'scientific' orthodoxy of the 1940s and 1950s and at the same time retained basic psychoanalytic principles. As Kovel describes it, Erikson's is a 'humane approach, so free of psychoanalytic reductionism yet so demonstrably enmeshed in Freudian thought' (1988: 68). Erikson himself saw the split as between 'last century's preoccupation with the economics of energy and this century's emphasis on complementarity and relativity' (1985: 21). Stevens says that Erikson 'does not attempt a fundamental restatement of psychoanalytical propositions but his contribution is rather to enrich, clarify and extend it by introducing new significant considerations' (1983: 108). In my view this is accurate but underestimates the significance for psycho-therapy in what Stevens also called Erikson's 'truly *integrative* analysis' (1983: 108). Three main elements contribute to this integration: an emphasis on relationship, an awareness of social and cultural context and an insistence on the ethical foundations of psychotherapy.

One consequence of the change from a scientific to a hermeneutic basis is that the therapist becomes a fallible individual instead of the expert. Typical of Erikson's practice was the informality of his sessions, his hesitancy in making interpretations and his readiness to share his own feelings with his patients. His theory of mutuality underlined the mutual respect involved in complementary functions of the helper and the helped. Erikson's emphasis on the interpersonal in the therapeutic relationship is integrated with his recognition of the interpersonal aspects of human development and the formation of psychosocial identity.

An example of Erikson's influence on the way psychotherapy has developed is recorded in the writings of Searles (1965), who developed the positive use of the unconscious communications of transference and countertransference. Referring to 'the invaluable work of Erikson concerning identity crises and other aspects of the struggle for identity', he speaks of its 'beauty and percep-tiveness' and how it has had 'so great an impact upon our thinking in recent years' (p. 648). Erikson's presence, along with others such as Searles, can be perceived as advancing into new interpersonal territory in the therapeutic relationship. His influence does not consist in ideas that are simply followed, but as a stimulus and a framework for new perceptions.

Awareness of the clinical significance of the client's social and historical context was an essential part of Erikson's therapeutic approach. Erikson shifts attention in clinical 'casework' to include changes in social context and the future as well as the present and the past. This is shown by many examples in his discussion of 'ego pathology and historical change' (1968a: 53–70). As he sums up, 'A large-scale decrease of mental discomfort can be envisaged only by equal clinical attention to conditions as well as to cases, to the emerging design for the future as well as to the fixation on the past' (p. 69).

The influence of this aspect of Erikson's approach on the work of other therapists and counsellors is hard to assess. The mainstream psychodynamic world, whether Freudian, Kleinian or Jungian, remained focused on the inner world, notwithstanding the developments into social engagement of the Tavistock Institute (Trist and Murray 1990) and the influence in the public services of Winnicott and Bowlby. New horizons have been opened up by the humanist and person-centred therapists, such as Maslow and Rogers, that celebrate individual human potential and by transpersonal therapies that celebrate human spirituality. But, despite 'personal power' having the potential for radical transformation of society from within (Kearney 1996), these movements have emphasized the separation of the individual from society. Group therapy and organizational consultancy have provided vital steps towards a full recognition of social context. In the late 1970s and early

1980s writers such as Scott Peck (1990) began to address directly the prob-lems of how to transfer psychoanalytic insights from the therapeutic milieu to society as a whole. Not until the 1990s has the interaction of the personal and the political been taken up in mainstream therapy. These issues are considered in the contemporary context in Chapter 11.

Erikson's influence is seen most directly in what appear to be the marginal areas of human society; for example, in the work of the Grinbergs on migra-tion (1989), a situation in which the element of cultural alienation is most acute. It is perhaps through Erikson's concern with those marginalized by gender, race, disablement, youth, age or minority culture, and their return to claim their cultural space, that his clinical approach makes its strongest contribution. Erikson's influence is acknowledged by therapists developing an 'intercultural therapy' (Littlewood 1992: 6). These practitioners challenge the cultural assumptions of counsellors and psychotherapists and insist on the need for greater cultural self-awareness. They have helped to make therapy a little less sure of itself, rather more aware of what it assumes and does not know, and of the way power structures are entangled with the urge to know and to help. It is argued in Chapter 11 that the issues concerning the conflicts and discontinuities of cultural identity, experienced most acutely by the immi-grant and the refugee, but manifest also in large-scale conflict and violence throughout the world, are increasingly relevant to human development.

Erikson held that the problems of the individual cannot be separated off from the problems of society, and that this is true for therapist as well as for clients, and so too for the therapeutic relationship between them. He insisted on the place of ethical commitment and 'fidelity' in the formation of a healthy psychosocial identity, of knowing 'who I am'. He saw this commit-ment both as part of personal growth and as linking the individual to society. This view is part of his developmental perspective and of direct relevance to work in the therapeutic relationship. It also contributes to the continuing search for an ethical basis for psychotherapists' and counsellors' professional activity. His vision of a liberal conscience, reasonably free from the irrational compulsions of moralism, is part of the contribution which depth psychology can make to individual fulfilment in a saner world.

## Interdisciplinary influence

Erikson's persistent aim was to bridge the gaps between psychoanalysis and other established disciplines. His influence was felt not only through his writ-ings, but also through his personal contacts and discussions with individuals from many disciplines, cultural traditions and spheres of activity. There are four main areas for consideration: history, sociology, political science and religion.

### Psychohistory and the history of childhood
As we have seen, Erikson's radical critic, Kovel, states that 'virtually single-handedly, Erikson has launched the problematic and promising field of psychohistory' (1988: 68). In their review of psychobiographical studies,

Crosby and Crosby (1981) conclude that 'Erikson is generally considered to be the most effective exponent of psychohistory' (Wrightsman 1994: 99). Thompson (1996) states that 'although Erikson's work was severely criticized by some historians, it was welcomed by others, who found in his eight stages an accessible paradigm for applying psychoanalytic theory'. As an example she cites Demos's work (1970), which found the Eriksonian coupling of autonomy and shame 'strikingly relevant to Puritan culture'.

Wrightsman says that Erikson's approach to psychohistory has the 'virtue of being comprehensive and lifespan oriented' (1994: 81). Equally important is Erikson's insistence (1968b) on an awareness of the life context of all witnesses, including the writer. As Wrightsman (1994: 109) notes, Erikson states that 'psychobiographers must be "reasonably clear about" the stages and conditions of their own lives when they involve themselves in the historical lives of others'.

Erikson's influence has been particularly felt in the study of the history of childhood. Erikson was acutely aware of the neglect of childhood by most historians. He called this 'a universal blind spot in the makers and interpreters of history: they ignore the fateful function of childhood in the fabric of society' (1965: 393). Since he wrote this, considerable data have been amassed, although it is an area clouded with speculation, linked perhaps with the deep emotions attaching to these early years. On the one hand, the history of childhood is seen in the work of De Mause (1974) as a catalogue of horrors from which society is gradually emerging. On the other hand, in Ariès's (1962) view, the modern world is destroying the balanced communal framework of childhood in earlier times and driving modern children into the ever more isolated world of the nuclear family.

Hunt (1972) is a historian who uses Erikson's developmental scheme to interpret the bizarre childhood world of the future Louis XIII in early seventeenth-century France. He concludes that 'the second Eriksonian stage [autonomy versus shame] has been the most pertinent to the study of childhood in the old regime' (p. 191). However, he finds no evidence for a sense of adult 'care' as described in Erikson's stage of generativity. He concludes that '"generativity" is a cultural artefact' (p. 26). Another historian, Dunn, in his study of childhood in Imperial Russia, concludes that 'the second psychosocial stage of Erikson's model is of most value to historians' (1974: 395).

*Sociology and social psychology*
Sociology and social psychology are the fields that most overlap with psychology in terms of subject matter, as Erikson's term 'psychosocial development' indicates, although perhaps for this very reason the disciplines strive to keep separate. It is hard to distinguish Erikson's influence from that of others, but three examples may illustrate the extent of his influence.

The first is the focus in sociology on the concept of identity. 'Sociology', says Craib (1998: 1), 'seems to have a lot to say about identity.' Hall states that 'there has been a veritable discursive explosion in recent years around the concept of identity' (1996: 1). Some sociologists have attempted to reduce personal identity to a function of social forces or to deny its existence altogether. Yet Hall concludes that this concept cannot be dispensed with, pointing as it does to some of the most intractable and challenging human dilemmas. The image he provides of the 'suturing of the psychic and the discursive' vividly evokes the effort, the pain, the danger and the skilfulness involved in these issues (p. 16). Erikson has, of course, no copyright on the term identity. Yet at the heart of the sociologists' debates seems to be a concern with how to deploy the exploration of sociological observations in a way that does not exclude subjective experience. Behind these searchings can be sensed a continuation of the work which Erikson's concept of psychosocial identity pioneered.

Some sociologists have made renewed attempts to bring psychoanalytic concepts to bear on social phenomena. The sociologist whose work seems nearest in spirit to Erikson is Richards in his explorations of popular phenomena such as football and pop music in *Disciplines of Delight* (1994). Richards describes these activities as situations in which individuals can experience an affirming sense of belonging, through the containment of their ambivalent feelings about authority. 'Despite the constraint and disappointment necessarily involved in this, the reconciliation with authority which it brings is vital for the containment of feelings about loss, destructiveness and death with which we are all continually struggling' (p. 162). Richards uses psychodynamic concepts from Bion and Klein. Yet the social forms of the 'disciplines' that can contain such feelings have strong similarities to Erikson's ritualization. Richards's emphasis on containing ambivalence echoes Erikson's list of the 'opposites which appear to be reconciled' in ritualizations (1987: 578; see also Chapter 8, p. 105), and Erikson's view that 'the overcoming of ambivalence as well as of ambiguity is one of the prime functions of ritualization' (p. 578). Perhaps the greatest similarity is in the emphasis on the positive and creative aspects of Richards's 'disciplines' and Erikson's 'ritualization'.

A third area of exploration is in the sociology of material possessions. The work of Kamptner (1991), noted by Dittmar (1992), draws on Erikson's model of identity and the life cycle to explain changes in 'favourite possessions as markers of age, sex and culture', and notes how 'Erikson's three adult identity phases . . . appear reflected in how the adults described their attachment to possessions' (Dittmar 1992: 115).

*Politics and psychology*
In *Toys and Reasons* Erikson takes as his 'improbable theme' the 'relationship of childhood play to political imagination' (1978a: 11). He aims to link the inner life of the individual to the crises of social institutions. 'The psychoanalytic assessment of political reality' can help us to 'recognize that combination of inner defenses and communal deals which is inherent in the distribution of power' (1978a: 174). He claims that this theme 'can be made more comprehensible only by interdisciplinary work' (1978a: 11).

Erikson's ideas on the interdependence of the psychological issues of the leader and the led have been the prototype for a number of studies; for example, 'The leader and the led: a dyadic relationship' (Moses 1990a) and the work of a group of writers linking the psychological issues of Presidents and the electorate in the USA (Offerman-Zuckerberg 1991). The autobiography of President Sadat of Egypt, *In Search of Identity* (1993), illustrates Erikson's theme of how a politician both experiences and manipulates an idealized identification with 'his' people.

The concept of pseudo-speciation has had both theoretical and practical influence. The theoretical can be seen in Volkan's work *The Need to Have Enemies and Allies* (1988). Volkan and others, including diplomats and psychoanalysts, were also involved in a series of practical initiatives which became known as 'unofficial' or 'Track Two' diplomacy (Montville 1991). Erikson's influence in the practical applications of conflict resolution is noted by Volkan. He describes a series of US–Soviet relations seminars in the 1980s, which, he says, 'derived much of their vigor from the presence of the pre-eminent psychoanalyst, Erik H. Erikson and his wife Joan' (Volkan 1988: xvii). Unfortunately, we have no details of what the Eriksons actually did at these meetings.

Alongside the pathology of pseudo-speciation is Erikson's insistence on the possibility, in spite of dangers and limitations, of an inclusive human identity. Indeed he sees it as a necessity for human survival. Such ideas have influenced writers like Oliner (1991) in his study of altruism among those who aided the persecuted against the dominant ideology in Nazi Germany. Oliner concludes that an important element was an ability to identify with a common humanity rather than with an identity defined by what it hates as much as by what it loves.

*Psychodynamics and religion*
Erikson's studies of Luther and Gandhi stimulated both criticism and enthusiasm not only among historians but also among religious thinkers. Wright sees in Erikson 'a prophet for our period of history who needs to be read and understood' (1982: xi). He values Erikson for his integration of scientific and artistic viewpoints and for finding transcendent meanings in a secular world. 'What makes Erikson so significant is his interdisciplinary approach' (p. xiii). Fowler (1981) is another writer who uses a developmental model that combines ideas of Piaget, Kohlberg and Erikson.

In *Living Illusions* (1993; 2nd edn 2000), Jacobs has developed a view of faith in which styles of belief are associated with dominant life themes. For example, 'unquestioning, simple faith can be associated with early trust and dependency issues' (Jacobs 1998: 90). Other beliefs 'tend to mirror issues around authority'. Yet other 'styles of belief include more universalistic ways of thinking', which find parallels in 'themes about cooperation, wider social concern, and deeper self-exploration' (p. 90). Jacobs builds on Erikson's developmental model to develop his own concepts in which life stages are linked to lifetime themes.

Erikson's sensitivity to religious feeling is balanced by scepticism and criticism of its institutional and dogmatic forms. Nevertheless, he provides a basis for a better understanding of the creative possibilities of formalized religion with its heritage of ritual, imagery, mystical experience and its variety of communal forms. One of Erikson's last works was a study of the sayings of Jesus in 'The Galilean sayings and the sense of "I"' (1981). Erikson is searching for a spiritual connection at the core of individual identity. Nevertheless, he never committed himself to any one religion, preferring to 'live on the shadowy borderline of the denominational ambiguities . . . into which I seem to have been born' (Friedman 1999: 43). His work acknowledges a place within psychodynamic thinking for an awareness of an individual spiritual search which infuses many humanist and transpersonal approaches to therapy, such as can be found expressed in ways as diverse as Scott Peck's (1978) emphasis on spiritual growth, Gunzburg's (1997) application of Martin Buber's concept of I/Thou relationships, Wilber's (1996) comprehensive spiritual ecology and Symington's re-evaluation of psychoanalysis and religion (1994). Erikson's work contributes to such a redirection of psychotherapeutic theory and practice away from the dismissive attitude of Freud and towards what Samuels (1993: 11) has called the 'resacralization of the culture'.

From this brief survey of Erikson's influence, there is an overall impression of his pervasive presence in the cultural landscape of the second half of the twentieth century, articulating an accessible and relevant aspect of psychotherapeutic thought. In a world uncertain of itself, with expanding resources that seem to be outstripped by the problems they engender, Erikson's conceptual configurations offer no certainties. They are a significant contribution to ways of encountering and understanding the uncertainties, and to ways of finding a realistic commitment to individuals and society through an ethically based psychotherapy and counselling. His presence is a continuing creative force. In the next two chapters some specific aspects of this potential are described: first, in relation to the identity and place in society of counselling and psychotherapy; second, in the contribution that psychotherapeutic thought and practice can make towards a better understanding and management of some social and political problems.

# Personal and cultural identity in contemporary counselling and psychotherapy

This chapter illustrates the application and development of Erikson's concepts to three areas of contemporary concern in psychotherapy and counselling: first, the influence of cultural difference and identity in the therapeutic relationship and process; second, the significance for individual counsellors and psychotherapists of their occupational identity; third, problems involved in the collective identity of counsellors and psychotherapists and in their relation to society.

## Personal and cultural identity in the therapeutic relationship

In the early years of psychotherapy, therapists were mostly too preoccupied with problems within their own culture to be able to stand outside it. The inadequacies of this are increasingly apparent in the face of the political exploitation of one culture by another, the overlapping of cultures and cultural values and the rate of transition within existing cultures. The problem increasingly faced is how to live with different or changing cultural identities and values. Counsellors and psychotherapists can no longer afford to be blind to these changes or to the exploitative power structures of the social context and the mechanisms of stereotyping and prejudice.

These are problems which Erikson began to recognize from his work with the Sioux, and he concluded that practitioners had to learn to become 'historically self-conscious' (1975b: 55). Since then many have worked to develop approaches to counselling and psychotherapy which recognize how personal and cultural issues are interwoven and how cultural differences and similarities may be reflected in the therapeutic relationship. Such an approach is the 'intercultural therapy' of the Nafsiyat Centre founded in London in 1983 (Kareem and Littlewood 1992).

The intercultural aspects of counselling and psychotherapy have been explored at four main levels in the USA and later, as Littlewood (1992: 5) points out, in Britain. The first level focuses on differences of culture as sources of miscommunication and misunderstanding. The work of Pedersen and Ivey develops 'culture-centred counseling' which 'presumes that all counseling, to some extent, is multicultural' (1993: viii). Detailed differences in communication between various cultural groups in the USA have been analysed (Sue and Sue 1990); for example, in the use of gaze, level of voice and acceptance of silences. Lago and Thompson (1996) point out how these differences are like an iceberg. There is a visible tip of public characteristics, such as dress and communal festivals, but the much larger invisible part embodies attitudes, styles of communication and values (p. 51). These differences, as Littlewood says, are 'personal impediments which we may bring, unrecognised, to such [therapeutic] encounters' (1992: 11). Similarities are also important, as they provide a basis for empathy; but they may also be a source of unconscious collusion.

The second level focuses on the interrelation of cultural groups in terms of power. It involves the experience of relationships between rulers and ruled, majorities and minorities, between all who participate in the exercise of power and opportunity in a society and those who are excluded by discrimination on whatever grounds. These relationships drastically and pervasively affect individual lives through both past history and present context. The cultural is in this sense political. These experiences of power differences may also be reflected in the therapeutic relationship; for example, in unconscious repetitions of relationships of victim, persecutor and rescuer or the transference of idealized or denigrated aspects of self. In Erikson's words, 'the analyst is woven into the patient's unconscious life plan' (1968a: 66). He gives the example of how in the 1950s a European analyst might be idealized as representing a 'more homogeneous past' or alternatively might be 'resisted as the brainy enemy of a potentially successful American identity' (p. 66). Kareem (1992) held that an intercultural approach recognizes these power relationships and aims to 'create a form of therapeutic relationship between the therapist and patient where both can explore each other's transference and assumptions'. It is an approach that 'attempts to dilute the power relationship which inevitably exists between the "help-giver" and the "help-receiver"' (p. 16).

A third focus explores the way in which cultural differences are connected to the personal development of the individual. Erikson summed up this developmental connection when he wrote how the 'polarity Big–Small' is 'the first in the inventory of existential oppositions such as Male and Female, Ruler and Ruled, Owner and Owned, Light Skin and Dark' (1965: 407). In therapy, interrelated personal and cultural issues may provide a unifying theme that is also expressed through the therapeutic relationship. However, distinguishing between the personal and the cultural can be important because on the one hand cultural patterns may impose an intolerable burden on the individual and on the other hand personal defences may cut an individual off from a vital source of nourishment in their cultural roots.

The fourth level recognizes the way in which all cultures are in transition both in themselves and in relation to each other. Complex changes and fragmentations of identity may produce a sense of alienation but also provide new possibilities. Erikson wrote of the problems of transition in the USA from his clinical experience. He identified prototypic figures, such as the Southern lady, the Prussian officer, the Western pioneer. Such figures were crucial in his patients' struggles to cling to, recover or dispense with forms of identity in the ever-changing culture of the USA, with both its external and its internal migrations (1968: 53–66). The work of feminist writers Bhavnani, Phoenix and others continues to explore the pressures and the possibilities of these 'shifting identities, shifting racisms' in both America and Europe (Bhavnani and Phoenix 1994). The oppressions of the past may be overcome through the formation of new alliances and the creation of new plural identities. The encounter of client and counsellor, of therapist and patient, is itself a part of a wider interaction involving changing cultural differences and changing cultural identities.

Erikson provides a perspective in which these various levels may be integrated and balanced. The two cases which follow illustrate some aspects of this. They are based on my own experiences as a counsellor and are intended as starting points for exploration of the issues raised above.

*Tessa*

> Tessa is the only child of immigrant parents from the Indian subcontinent. During her teens she became involved in drugs and petty theft. After a bad experience with drugs she withdrew into a depressed dependence on her parents, living at home without regular employment. At 28 she was found a place on an arts course and moved into a student hostel. A relationship with another student did not last.
>
> Tessa came to counselling as a student. She had little idea of what she might do to earn a living or her ability to do so, though she coped well enough with the course. She had a dream of setting up an ethnic clothes shop. She felt totally alienated from her parents. Her mother, she felt, had treated her like a doll. Her father was only interested in his business and associating with male members of the family. Tessa said she wished to find a way to be grown up and to feel equal – with someone.

On the basis of these few details there are a great variety of possible approaches to helping Tessa through counselling or psychotherapy. Her early life, what happened in her adolescence, her lack of self-esteem, her current hopes, fears, anger and feelings of loss, a search for her true self and for meaning in her life, for work and for a relationship – all these may be the focus for enabling her to find her way forward.

From whatever perspective Tessa's problems are viewed, they seem to centre on issues of dependence, alienation, and self-confidence. Her clearest and most urgent cry is for 'equality', which she feels has been denied to her. What this means to her and her therapist will be part of the exploration of the therapy. What is explored here is the way in which these issues are both deeply personal and part of her cultural situation and inheritance.

On the first level, a therapist needs to consider cultural differences in language, styles of communication, attitudes and values. How can these differences (or similarities) be recognized and how may they frustrate or promote the therapy? What information might it help to have, or be disastrous not to have? The answer to these questions depends on the cultural background as well as the skill and experience of the therapist. What 'impediments' in working with Tessa might there be, for example, for a white, middle-aged, privately educated, psychodynamically trained man? Or for a woman social worker in her thirties of West Indian origin and with a person-centred orientation? Or for the reader? The above descriptions are, of course, stereotypes, telling us little about the character of the counsellor, who he or she really is or his or her ability to relate with Tessa. Nevertheless, these stereotypes can play a powerful part not only in first impressions, but in more hidden assumptions that may link with the client's, and the therapist's, vulnerabilities.

On the second level, how might these differences, or rather Tessa's and the therapist's perceptions of them, be reflected in the therapeutic relationship? How might Tessa's experience of alienation be expressed in response to the therapist's gender or appearance, or the furnishing of the consulting room? What feelings of dependence and humiliation might be reflected in the control of time and space in the sessions? How can words be found to articulate these feelings and issues and what might be involved in the very act of giving expression to them – and whose words would they be? Tessa's episode of 'petty theft' might be a claim to some ownership – or an expression of defiance. What in the therapeutic relationship can be claimed or owned, or might be perceived as stolen? What might be expressed in a wish to touch or be touched and how could the therapist respond to this? What sort of 'equality' can be achieved so that difference is perceived not as a source of alienation and exploitation but as a possibility of mutuality?

The third level takes up the connection between personal development and the cultural context. How may deficits and strengths in Tessa's experience of the relationship 'big–small', in her development from dependence to autonomy, initiative or competence, have been incorporated in and expressed through the cultural and political experience of her parents; for example, in the experience of arbitrary power, and of the deals made with that power? What 'negative identities' might be involved in the use of drugs or what search for identity suffered defeat in the 'bad experience' following drug use? What real possibilities for generative hope does Tessa have in her present social context? What prototypic figures from the past or from myth might represent a guiding wisdom, or a despairing fantasy?

In Erikson's perspective Tessa's predicament is seen as a crisis which involves the reworking of issues from earlier crises in a new social and personal context. The central crisis for her seems to be that of identity versus identity confusion, closely linked to that of the struggle between isolation and the search for intimacy. Erikson's approach also stresses the importance of anticipating a potential generativity within the social context and access to some form of reliable wisdom that can sustain a personal sense of integrity. It looks forward as well as back, while linking both to the central issues of the present.

The fourth level extends the connection between the personal and the cultural to a perspective of cultural transitions which include both Tessa and her therapist. The complexities of the four levels can be linked by what Erikson called a 'unitary theme', which can be identified by careful 'configurational attention' to personal and cultural experience, to imagery, to the therapist's own responses, to the therapeutic relationship and to the context of the therapy.

The dream of the clothes shop, for example, might represent a fragile thread connecting Tessa to her rejected parents and their culture through experience of colour and aesthetic quality. It might be a way to recover and honour her cultural group's ability to make deals and wealth and to preserve a degree of room for manoeuvre and choice. It may be a means of appropriating for herself as a woman a space where she can meet the invited world on her terms. Or could the 'impossibility' of the dream be a defiant rejection of all these things? It might express the impossible expectations invested in Tessa to redress or repair the past, to solve, without adequate resources, the accumulated problems of isolation and alienation experienced by her parents. In this image may be seen both the positive and negative possibilities in Tessa's crisis.

At the same time the image of the shop may link these developmental and cultural issues with the experience of the issues of power in the therapeutic relationship. The shop may represent the consulting room, raising questions of whose territory this is. What is being exchanged in the therapy, with what degree of mutuality and what imbalance of power? Can a fair bargain be achieved? What may be the relative worth put upon each other's culture, as expressed in the material imagery of clothes, an image relating both to aesthetic value and to intimacy? The image of the clothes shop expresses on the one hand the fear that a fair exchange in the therapeutic relationship may be impossible; on the other hand lies the possibility of an exchange across cultural differences which can enhance each other's identity and provide the basis for a recovered autonomy and trust.

The therapist's task will require an awareness of Tessa's unconscious communications as well as the therapist's own cultural assumptions. It will stretch the ability to listen and to be genuine. Tessa's repeated experience has been of differences as alienation and oppressive inequality. The struggle in the therapeutic relationship will be to experience difference as a mutuality that can restore a sense of identity and agency, of belonging and of being equal.

*Kate*

Kate is the eldest child of a farming couple, whose forebears had worked on the land for generations. When Kate was 5 the farm failed and the family had to move to London, where her father became a building worker. Her mother took a part-time job and joined a strict nonconformist chapel. She died when Kate was 15. Kate did well at school, went to college and became a vet in a small country town. She married and had two children. She left her husband when he became violent. Her father died soon after. Five years after her father's death Kate formed a relationship with a farmer. When this broke up she became severely depressed, with helpless sobbing and anxiety states. She had to take prolonged sickness absence from her work.

She came to counselling, aged 36, wanting to recover her ability to carry on the work she loved and to understand why she felt so devastated and helpless. She had joined a local green group but now felt that their work was pointless. She had a recurring nightmare in which giant bulldozers were scraping the fields into a mountain of rubble. Her feet were stuck in mud. She tried to shout but her voice could not be heard against the sound of the machinery.

As with Tessa, this outline presents problems of the interplay of personal and cultural issues. The core issues for Kate seem to be an uncharacteristic helplessness and in particular a sense of being overpowered and an inability to make herself heard. There may be problems around caring for others and being cared for. There are multiple losses which may not have been adequately mourned. Experiences in her personal relationships appear to be involved in these issues. But these relationships and Kate's perception of them also seem to be related to a cultural transition from a rural to an urban culture, to the impact of technological change and the decline of a rural community.

Personal and cultural experiences converge in the issues of helplessness, loss and the difficulty of care and repair. The image of the vulnerable earth overrun by brutal machinery may express her helplessness in the face of experiences of loss and violence. The image may relate to Kate's experience of loss at the age of 5, an age when new-found physical freedom and initiative struggle with new constraints and with feelings of guilt and the need for reparation. But the despair and the rage expressed in the image may also be part of a helplessness made all the more overwhelming by a transmitted or self-imposed task of repairing her parents' and grandparents' loss of a whole way of life. Failure in this task, whether as a vet or in the relationship with the farmer, may involve guilt and also resentment. Loss and change are not unfamiliar aspects of rural life. The question arises of how the ways of dealing with them, such as migration or the social bonds and values of church or chapel, have failed to provide Kate with the resources needed to cope with her personal and cultural losses.

Her participation in the green movement might represent an idealized but impossible task of repairing a world (internal and external) that seems irreparably damaged. It may also provide Kate with a new basis for belonging in an alliance with people seeking a new relationship with the natural environment.

How might these personal and cultural issues be reflected in the therapeutic relationship? There is likely to be a strong positive attachment to the therapist who listens and cares. Feelings about this attachment are also likely to reflect the split in Kate's perceptions of power and vulnerability. There is something depersonalized in her images of the destructive and the vulnerable. It is perhaps this that will make the relationship with her therapist difficult yet important; a way to seeing the 'good' and the 'bad' in human terms. From this integration can come a recovery of her personal power, a way of seeing the humanity in the figures of her past. The unequal struggle between nature and technology may also be seen as a human one in which personal action is possible against the image of the overpowering machines in the dream.

The development of the therapeutic relationship will be facilitated by the recognition and exploration of real and perceived differences and similarities in manner, life experience and attitudes, and the power differences expressed through the management and control of the sessions. For example, a 'natural' informal manner in the therapist might be seen as vulnerable, and a sign of a need to be cared for, so adding another burden that is resented or about which to feel guilty. A formal, clinical manner might be perceived as powerful but persecuting or 'bulldozing'. Her experience of power and vulnerability, expressed in the image of the ravaged countryside, is likely to be connected to her experience of her sexuality. This may be reflected through the difference or similarity of gender in the therapist and re-experienced in some way in the therapeutic relationship.

Perceptions of space in the therapy, literally or metaphorically, may connect with early losses of freedom associated with the family's move away from the countryside. The therapist's awareness of similarities or differences in her or his own personal experience (for example, as a 5-year-old) or cultural identity (for example, in what 'nature' means to him or her) will affect the relationship. Whether or what to disclose of such details will be a matter of sensitive timing and judgement.

Both Kate and Tessa face a unique predicament for which they have sought help through a particular kind of listening and relationship. Their predicaments are uniquely personal, and illustrative of two very different cultural transitions. Though they may feel isolated or alienated, they are not only casualties but vital participants in changes which they share ultimately with all other people on the planet at this time. In the widest sense Tessa and Kate may be seen as confronting the continuing search for ways to live with other people and ways to live in harmony with our natural environment. The therapist or counsellor is also a participant in the confusion and challenges of this search.

Case studies that provide opportunities to explore these particular aspects of therapy can be found in the following. Pedersen and Ivey (1993) give detailed examples of miscommunication and the application of their 'culture centred counseling skills'. Lago and Thompson (1996) include studies of intercultural counselling which have the extra value of being available on video (1989). Kareem and Littlewood include case examples based on experience in Bradford (Bavington 1992), extending their perspective to multidisciplinary work involving psychotherapists with doctors, psychiatrists, probation officers and social workers. This gives an opportunity to explore how the power relations of class, gender and ethnicity may be transmitted and reflected between organizational, professional and personal contexts. Issues of cultural difference are also raised in relation to different psychotherapeutic approaches in Jacobs's study *Jitendra: Lost Connections* (1996a).

## The occupational identity of counsellor and psychotherapist

Counsellors and psychotherapists looking back after practising for some years often seem to see the decision to undertake training as a turning point in their lives. Personal comments include: 'I found a new sense of myself'; 'I never felt I could put my heart into anything until I started counselling'; 'I found a feeling of equality I had never found anywhere else'; 'I found an opportunity for self-expression'; 'I felt I had found a place in society'.

Such comments suggest many of the features which Erikson found characteristic of an identity crisis and its resolution. There is a sense of integration after confusion or alienation. There is a feeling that natural abilities have found a means of expression and that these are valued by society. There is fidelity to a particular set of values, a world view that can make sense of experience.

The question why an individual wants to be a counsellor or psychotherapist is asked of most aspiring applicants for such work. Interviewers for courses are looking for a degree of commitment, natural ability, experience and the meaning and values that the work holds for the individual. They try to assess in what ways the individual may be seeking a way of resolving their own inner conflicts, their awareness of this and what sort of balance there might be between commitment to others and gratification for oneself.

For many, the interest in counselling or psychotherapy may come from a long experience of being the kind of person others naturally talk to when they are troubled. For others it may come from having experienced counselling or psychotherapy themselves at a time of distress or crisis. They know its power personally and wish to 'give something back'. Many have experienced both sides of the relationship.

Becoming a counsellor or psychotherapist may be an extension of skills learnt early in life as the child who harmonizes and reconciles within a family and among peers. Questions arise here whether such skills, valued as they are, may also be part of a defensive pattern of avoiding conflict. For those for whom the need to serve is paramount, there is a question of whether such a need may mask a difficulty in asking for help for oneself. These are questions that should be raised and addressed during assessment and training.

Mutuality is a relationship in which each partner responds to the needs of the other without exploiting those needs. A client comes into counselling at a particular point in his or her life to meet some purpose, need or crisis. It is important to consider what purpose, need or crisis in the life of the counsellor or therapist is being met by the client.

For many counsellors and psychotherapists the crisis that leads them to undertake training occurs well into life rather than as part of adolescence. Often it occurs as the unsatisfactory nature of an initial choice of occupation becomes apparent. The following story is an unpublished memoir which reviews such an identity crisis in terms of Erikson's life stages.

Tony is a social and community worker whose work has included training and working as a counsellor. He begins by considering how earlier life crises have provided the foundation for dealing with later ones. From Erikson's stage 1 he identifies a lasting sense of optimism. 'This has its drawbacks, perhaps making me miss failings and problems which it would be more helpful to spot and deal with. The advantage is that people tend to trust me fairly easily.' From stage 2 he derives a need for others' approval, finding it difficult to 'go it alone' regardless of what others think. From stage 3 'the strong religious component in my upbringing led to a strong sense of responsibility that restricts, but does not stifle, initiative and purpose.'

> The years from 6 to 12 held significant events for me: the death of my father when I was 8 and going to a boarding school for prospective catholic priests when I was 12. These two events shaped a major part of my life. My father's death and my maternal grandmother's death a few months later led to a growing sense of responsibility for my mother's happiness. My becoming a priest fitted my religious upbringing and had family approval.
>
> My identity in my adolescent years was very much tied up with becoming a priest, which inevitably affected the way I dealt with my sexuality as an adolescent. Issues of intimacy during my early adult years were then effectively not addressed, and came out I suspect in a strong sense of duty to others, in compassion and care: all of which found a ready expression in my work as a young priest from age 24.
>
> My energies in the social welfare and community fields were my ways of dealing with the increasingly impossible tensions between my life as a priest and the love for the person who was eventually to become my wife. The commitment to social and community issues was, I guess, my 'generativity – and my work as a social worker now is maybe my way of continuing that.
>
> My decision to leave the priesthood and eventually marry was an experience of great personal integrity for me, and also resolved issues of intimacy – mixing together in a most peculiar way issues from stage 8 and stage 6! Their resolution provided a deep sense of wholeness. It was like getting a reward after years of painful work.

Tony's story is of course unique. Nevertheless, it contains elements which may be representative for many counsellors and psychotherapists. First, there is the way generativity emerges through the long drawn out struggle with his occupational identity. The essentials of this generativity are a feeling of contributing something of value and finding a way of integrating past strengths and weaknesses in the occupation. Second, there is the interplay between issues of identity and those of intimacy. This may be characteristic of an occupation closely concerned with problems of intimacy. Third, there is the 'peculiar way' in which the crisis of integrity versus despair (stage 8) is mixed with that of intimacy versus isolation (stage 6). He is illustrating how the search for ultimate meaning in life and the despair involved in a lack of it are present in the mingled crises of intimacy and identity, and indeed in all the stages from the beginning. Perhaps it is only at the end that we can fully recognize it.

There has been comparatively little written on why people become counsellors or psychotherapists, in spite of its relevance to the work. One exception is an account by ten eminent psychotherapists on the experiences and motivations which led to their choice of work in *On Becoming a Psychotherapist* (Dryden and Spurling 1989). In the penultimate chapter the editors identify some of the threads running through the accounts, including a childhood feeling of isolation or being a stranger, a wish for intimacy or 'yearning to be close' and the development of the capacity for empathy (p. 197). It is a choice of occupation which has at its heart a particular kind of relationship which Dryden and Spurling have called 'detached intimacy' (p. 198).

Another story illustrates and explores these themes in a choice of career as a psychoanalyst. It illustrates Dryden and Spurling's suggestion that the potential psychotherapist is driven (or called) by a desire to understand both others and herself or himself. There is a need to repair and also a confidence that suffering has meaning and repair is possible (Dryden and Spurling 1989: 193–4). The story is told by Allen Wheelis (1959), who in the 1950s was a colleague of Erikson during his time at Austen Riggs.

Like Erikson, Wheelis had begun to question the function and relevance of psychoanalysis in a changing world. Interwoven with his discussion of these issues, Wheelis writes what may be guessed is a largely autobiographical account of how an Alabama doctor's son became a psychoanalyst – and what happened after that. Larry is 19 years old. He has given up studying to be a doctor and is writing a novel which 'was to embody his ideas of love, the most remarkable of which was that physical love brings about the death of spiritual love', ignoring the fact that he had very little experience of either. As he neared the end of the book Larry became unable to sleep and unable to write any more. He became disturbed and ill. In desperation he went to the library to find out more about his insomnia. On the way out he picked up a book by Alfred Adler called *Understanding Human Nature* (1928). Back in his room he read avidly and saw in a flash of insight how his insomnia was a 'symptomatic defense of his self esteem'. 'If he couldn't sleep he couldn't work; if he couldn't work he couldn't finish the novel; if he couldn't finish the novel, then noone would be able to say definitely that it was a failure' (Wheelis 1959: 221). With this insight he fell asleep soundly for the first time for months and in the morning wrote to his mother that he was returning to his studies.

Fifteen years later Larry became a psychoanalyst but it was this particular experience that Wheelis says was 'the principal determinant of the vocational choice of psychoanalysis' (p. 224). The story illustrates the complex blending of issues of identity and intimacy that Tony noted in his story. Wheelis suggests that this connection lies at the heart of much professional psychoanalysis. An example of this can indeed be seen in Erikson's life story, where his decision to become an analyst was closely linked to those vague psychosexual problems for which psychoanalysis seemed the 'treatment of choice'. In the major psychohistorical studies of Luther and Gandhi, Erikson explores how issues of intimacy are mixed with issues of identity and vocational choice.

In Larry's decision to become a psychoanalyst the link lies, according to Wheelis, in the power of insight. Insight is defined by Wheelis as 'the ability to look into obscure aspects of one's personality, to recognize disguised motivations, to integrate what is discovered with various elements of conscious experience, and to utilize one's findings in such a way as to bring about a change in feeling, action, and reaction. It implies a belief that no inner danger is so bad but that knowing about it will be better than not knowing' (p. 211). Insight is experienced as a powerful and reliable means of resolving problems of intimacy. It becomes the basis of an approach to healing and the foundation of a profession. Yet as a resolution of an identity crisis it is also an ideology, a way of explaining the world but one which idealizes the belief as having universal applicability.

Wheelis goes on to describe the disillusion the analyst experiences when he or she finds that the ideal is not as universally applicable as was believed. Powerful as it can be, insight does not resolve all problems. Patients do not always get better. There are failures. Some resist or resent the help offered. 'Cure' may be followed by relapse. Moreover, 'the problems of intimacy may be aggravated by the life-work that was meant to solve it' (p. 245). Some, he says, respond by withdrawing from both hatred and love and 'insulating themselves from their patients'. Or they may 'yield to what appears as love and enter upon a personal relationship with the patient', which 'not only precludes therapy but also violates the moral commitment of an analyst' (p. 246). Wheelis claims that many come to terms with disillusion and 'survive the professional aggravation of their personal conflict. They come to seek other ways of dealing with problems of intimacy, no longer expecting their work to provide a solution (p. 246).' If the crisis of intimacy is resolved in some such way, the crisis of occupational identity may also find a fruitful resolution in a good enough matching of professional skills with non-possessive warmth.

A few years after Wheelis's book, Adolf Guggenbuhl-Craig (1989) made a similar connection between problems of intimacy and the career choice of psychotherapists which he extended to all the 'helping professions'. He describes the dangers in Jungian terms: the archetype of the healer is split so that the healer is always strong and the patient is always weak. The healer who succumbs to the defensive power of this split ignores the shadow of weakness and neediness in himself or herself, seeing it only in the patient. Intimacy and mutuality are sought but precluded. Guggenbuhl-Craig saw the greatest danger when therapists meet their need for intimacy through their patients without exposing themselves to the risks of true friendship. 'There may be other ways than friendship to safeguard him from the psychotherapist's shadow – but I haven't found them yet' (1989: 152).

### The collective identity of counsellors and psychotherapists

There are also issues facing counsellors and psychotherapists as a group. These are not just the dilemmas of the individual writ large. They involve patterns of organization and decision making and ways of dealing with difference, as well as public perceptions, comment and regulation. In spite of divisions and vagueness of boundaries there exists in the minds of both practitioners and the public some kind of collective identity which may be referred to as the 'field' of counselling and psychotherapy.

In his foreword to *Psychotherapy and Its Discontents* (1992), Samuels writes that the field of psychotherapy cannot be defined intellectually, ideologically, functionally or socially. However, he suggests that it *'can* be defined by dispute' (p. xi). *Psychotherapy and Its Discontents* includes criticisms of psychotherapy for its lack of integrity, its ineffectiveness, its elitism, its political evasiveness, its lack of spirituality, its shaky theoretical foundations, its untestability and abuse of its powers. These criticisms with their responses and rebuttals do serve in some way to define the parameters of the 'field' and the issues with which it is engaged.

The field is certainly one in which there are many differences in practice and theory. Another way of defining the field is to bring together leading protagonists of these different practices and visions, as, for example, in collections such as the *Handbook of Individual Therapy* (Dryden 1996a) and *The Future of Counselling and Psychotherapy* (Palmer and Varma 1997). While this presents a creative diversity it deals less comprehensively with the dynamics between the various practices and their relation to society. Others have been working since the 1960s (see Newman and Goldfried 1996) to find ways of integrating the many branches of the field and developing communication between them; for example, in the Society for the Exploration of Psychotherapy Integration.

One undisputed fact is the expansion of counselling and psychotherapy in both practice and public consciousness in recent years. Lago and Thompson (1996) note how this 'spread of interest' is supported by a 'huge increase in literature, training courses and media exposure'. They conclude that 'counselling and psychotherapy has come of age' (pp. 13–14). Coming of age, however, does not necessarily coincide with adulthood or an established identity.

In the divisions, confusions and challenges confronting the field there are a number of identifiable patterns which have parallels with Erikson's concept of the process of identity formation in individuals. An identity crisis in Erikson's definition involves a struggle with confusion, uncertainty and diverse options that leads to a commitment to action on the basis of a more or less explicit set of values and a constructive engagement with society. The transfer of a model or process from an individual to a group can, of course, lead to false assumptions. Nevertheless, similar characteristics and patterns may throw light on the present state of collective development of counselling and psychotherapy. Viewed in terms of Erikson's overall pattern of development, it seems that the field of counselling and psychotherapy at present shows characteristics of the confusion, as well as the creative diversity, of an identity crisis. The field as a whole seems to hover on the brink of constructive engagement.

Three characteristics in particular stand out as comparable to those of the individual crisis of identity: first, the uncertainties of definition, function and purpose; second, the polarization of differences into apparently irreconcilable oppositions; third, the difficulty of finding an agreed common core of values.

### Identity confusion

Perhaps the most obvious illustration of the confusion of identity is the awkward use of the two terms counselling and psychotherapy to define the field – and more, if counselling psychology is added to the list. Writers such as Jacobs (1996b) and Dryden (1996b) find no easy way to distinguish between the two in theory or in practice. Others, such as Naylor Smith (1994: 286), hold that the words express distinct activities but that 'we can learn to respect our differences . . . and learn to work together'. Why then is it so difficult to find a single term? Dryden suggests it is a matter of 'status, money and/or professional identity' (1996b: 17). Kearney (1996: 102) argues that the concept of a professional identity is part of a socialization process that frustrates the aim of finding one's own truth as well as helping others to find theirs. The twin terms may have a defensive function in relation to public perceptions. 'Psychotherapist' may be perceived as a more professional term but with negative associations of the prying expert. 'Counsellor' may be perceived as more client-centred but negatively as the work of volunteers or an easy living, sitting listening to others talk. So I may call myself a counsellor or a psychotherapist according to the anticipated positive or negative perceptions.

The characteristics of confusion and uncertainty in the field of counselling and psychotherapy can be seen in four areas: organization, practice, aims and the relation to the world outside the field. Organizationally there are keen disputes about whether there is or ought to be one profession or several professions, or whether there can only be 'implausible professions' (House and Totton 1997). Representative organizations are wary of each other. There are disputes as to what if any should be the criteria for entry into the field or the justification for or method of restricting it. The practice of counselling and psychotherapy provides a wealth of creative diversity but much uncertainty as to effectiveness and much mutual distrust. There is little progress on appropriate matching of practices to problems or how practices may be integrated. Differences in practice are related to deep divisions over the basic ingredients of training. Underlying these debates are fundamental unresolved questions of purpose. Is the primary purpose the alleviation of symptoms of distress, the remedying of dysfunction or the enabling of a personal or spiritual growth or enlightenment? Finally, the relation of the field to society as a whole is unclear. What part has the field to play in social and political issues? Can and should it have a political orientation? What might be the field's contribution to the understanding of social and political problems? How is the field itself affected by its social and political context? Are restriction of access and discriminatory practice a reflection of, and a contribution to, injustice in society?

It is through the ferment of questions such as these that a way forward is sought. However, the first question to be addressed is whether there is any need for resolving these questions. Is an *identity* needed? Are the debates not a sign of valuable diversity and questioning and a sign of vitality? Can people not find in small groups centred on particular organizations, practices or leaders adequate inspiration and focus for their commitment and abilities?

All the above may well be true. Erikson's approach is to view the problem as the search for a good enough positive balance between commitment to a particular practice and set of values and the acceptance of a degree of creative uncertainty and confusion. There is a necessary and valuable time for dreaming dreams and inner debate; there is also a time for commitment and engagement. Premature engagement may lead to the stifling of vision in social structure. To defer the commitment too long leads to a withering of potential in cynicism, self-absorption and wasted abilities.

### Polarization

One way of distinguishing an avoidance of commitment from an acceptance of difference that can lead to constructive dialogue is the degree of polarization in opposing views. In polarization difference is seen in terms of an exclusive 'either/or'; in dialogue difference is seen in terms of an inclusive balance or 'both/and'. The pattern of polarization is similar to that characterized by Erikson in describing pseudo-species. It involves an idealized myth of the origins of the group and a stereotypic denigration of other groups. An ideology supports the exclusive identity through a rationalized sense of superiority.

Current differences in the field of counselling and psychotherapy may be seen as established either in terms of exclusive pseudo-groups or as an inclusive balance extending along a number of dimensions of difference. There is a dimension of purpose that extends from those who see their primary function as relieving distress to those who see it as a way to personal or spiritual development or enlightenment. Another dimension is concerned with power, from those who see power as residing primarily in the therapist to those who see it primarily in the client. A third dimension extends from those who see the therapy as operating primarily through individuals' thinking to those who emphasize intuitive and emotional functioning. Fourth, there is a dimension of process, from those who see it as dependent on the identification of specific goals and solutions to those who see it as an unfolding process of change mediated by the relationship. There is, fifth, a dimension of cause, from internal to external causation. A sixth dimension concerns the way the work is seen in relation to its social and political framework, from the detached to the fully involved.

While the differences in practice and viewpoint are real, there is often an unnecessary degree of polarization. This might be illustrated between any two of the many approaches to counselling or psychotherapy. The criticisms and rebuttals in *Psychotherapy and Its Discontents* (Dryden and Feltham 1992) lead to an entrenchment of the views of the protagonists rather than a constructive listening to another point of view. Discussions between proponents of psychodynamic and person-centred approaches to counselling often seem to be more about stereotypic conceptions of others' views than a search for mutual understanding. However, closer study shows the differences to be a matter of different emphases in the above range of dimensions rather than exclusive opposites. This can be illustrated by a comparison between rational emotive behavioural therapy (REBT) and person-centred counselling as presented in many books by Albert Ellis and Brian Thorne respectively, but particularly in the chapters each contributed to *The Future of Counselling and Psychotherapy* (Palmer and Varma 1997). These two approaches are often considered opposites in most of the dimensions above. Ellis, for example, claims REBT as 'one of the most didactic forms of therapy' (1997: 4), he focuses on solutions to specific dysfunctions and he puts the primary emphasis on cognition. Thorne, on the other hand, emphasizes the self-healing ability of the client, sees the primary purpose as being to 'minister to the human spirit' (p. 165) and emphasizes intuition and feeling more than thinking.

However, these views do not in fact exclude each other. Ellis acknowledges the aim of REBT as showing clients how to 'help themselves be happier, more self-actualized individuals' (p. 5). Emotional responses and their effects have been specifically included in REBT. The response of the client is certainly not neglected in the relationship. Similarly, Thorne's aims include the relief of distress; he acknowledges the power of the counsellor's empathy; he does not exclude the client's thinking as irrelevant. Both these practitioners include a recognition of both ends of the scale in each dimension. The differences are real but they may be seen as differences of balance in a commonly accepted scale.

Why then does there appear to be so much polarization? The individuals themselves have some responsibility in their attempts to clarify their own specific identity. Even practitioners as respected as these two employ an occasional put down of the other. Ellis's lightly damning comment that '"spiritual" therapies will also remain popular' (1997: 8) is matched by Thorne's 'perhaps there will always be a place for psychological technicians' (p. 165). This is not to say that counsellors should always be nice to each other! Much of the polarization comes from the perceptions of the public or of followers. The temptation is to collude with the fantasy element of these perceptions.

When the polarizations are recognized the differences between these two creative, experienced and committed practitioners can be seen as personal and cultural as much as in theory and practice. The personal differences are expressed in Ellis's irrepressible confidence and enthusiasm for his own methods and Thorne's sensitive awareness and perceptive analysis of his own anxieties. These differences are part of each individual's humanity and strength, contributing in their own way to the field. They may also be seen as reflecting aspects of the cultures, American and British respectively, from which each has sprung.

### Core values: mutuality and attentiveness

An important element in the development of a collective identity in Erikson's concept of an individual identity crisis is commitment to a set of values. Values have inherent worth and are the criteria by which we distinguish 'good' from 'bad'. They are the ethical heart of any enterprise. Problems and complexities arise in the search for values which are genuinely personal, shared with others and recognizable and acceptable to the surrounding society. Much hard thinking has gone into the production of Codes of Ethics and Practice such as those put forward by the British Association for Counselling (BAC). These set out the aims of practice in broad terms and provide for many a 'common frame of reference'. The basic values are described as 'integrity, impartiality, and respect'. Counselling is a 'non-exploitative activity' (BAC 1993). However there are those like House who attack the codes as contrary to the values of counselling and psychotherapy. House sees them as 'externally derived, didactically imposed' (1997: 323), and as a way of avoiding personal responsibility for one's own values. It is the institutional nature of the codes that House criticizes, not the possibility of common values. He suggests that a 'self-generating community of therapeutic practitioners will tend to gravitate towards some kind of commonality of values' (p. 331).

A further problem with such codes as statements of common values is that the claim to be non-exploitative is just the one which public critics most challenge. There is a credibility gap between ethics and practice in public perception, a crisis of trust. Some of this mistrust derives from a belief that what one partner in a relationship gains the other must lose. Erikson's 'golden rule' of mutuality can help here. It describes a relationship as good when it benefits both partners or, in Shakespeare's words, 'blesses him that gives and him that takes'. The aim and possibility of mutuality provides for counselling and psychotherapy a core value and a criteria for distinguishing a relationship that is mutually beneficial from one that is exploitative.

It is also helpful to identify some core characteristics in the diverse practices of counsellors and psychotherapists that are consistent with their values. Such a common element can be found in the art and skills of listening to others or as has been suggested (Pedersen and Ivey 1993: 103) in the multisensory word 'attending' to others. Erikson (1985: 21) described it as '*configurational attention* to the rich interplay of form and meaning' in the experience of others. This attentiveness is congruent with and indeed an essential foundation for mutuality and trust. It is a core characteristic of all approaches to counselling and psychotherapy. The skills of 'active listening' are rightly considered the most essential part of counsellors' and psychotherapists' training and development. Counselling and psychotherapy have been called the talking therapies. They might be equally well termed the listening or attending therapies.

Ernest Jones said that what first inspired him in Freud was that he was a 'man who seemed to listen to his patients' (Evans 1964: 124). Freud's originality lay also in his willingness to listen to himself. Wheelis described the therapist as listening 'with unwavering intent' (1959: 246). Rogers developed the idea of the therapeutic power inherent in such intensely present listening with respect and genuineness. For Erikson it meant looking beyond the therapist's own preconceptions to the 'actuality' of the patient and asking 'What does he or she really want from me?' It has been my own experience of counselling that while success, in so far as it can be presumed, has come in many and surprisingly varied ways, failure seems to have a consistent theme – that of not having listened, or attended, deeply or carefully enough.

## The interaction with society

Attentiveness can be applied not only to clients and to oneself, but also to those outside the field of counselling and psychotherapy, to the society of which this field is a part. These include journalists in the various media and their readers and audiences, those in power, professionals of many kinds, business people, organizations and cultural groups and their representatives. It includes those of various cultures whether within or outside our immediate society. It may include the whole extended human family. It may also include ourselves in so far as we are many of these things as well as counsellors or psychotherapists. What is it that they really want from us? What is it that we really want and have to give? It is a vastly complex question which depends on willingness to enter a dialogue and to attend deeply without prejudgement to others and to ourselves.

In the voices of these others can be heard mixed messages that are difficult to reconcile. The media include material which rubbishes counselling and psychotherapy in one column while recommending it to readers in another part of the paper (Walsh 1997). Counselling for marital relationships is widely recommended and even promoted by government. Counselling and psychotherapy for mental breakdown and emotional distress is an increasing but precarious part of primary health care. A football star's use of counselling produces mirth, scorn and sympathy. Young people are reported to distrust counselling for sexual problems when it is available, yet many seek help. Counselling at work has spread, yet is often too much at odds with the culture of the workplace or organization to be widely used. Counselling help for those suffering from disasters is assumed, though questioned. The relationship between the field of counselling and psychotherapy and society is ambivalent on both sides.

The comparison with an individual identity crisis suggests some pointers to the way forward. It involves an activity requiring a variety of specific skills and a commitment to the values underlying that activity. It involves a recognition of the value of the activity to and by society. It involves negotiation and dialogue about the value of this activity and its limits and potential misuse. At the centre of the work of psychotherapists and counsellors, and of their contribution to society, is a careful attention to others. This is both part of what counsellors and psychotherapists do and the means to finding out how to make it more effective in the wider social context. This attention includes the recognition of polarizations and other defences. The challenge includes the integration of a creative variety of practice with core values, which are nevertheless personal as well as social. These are some of the issues facing counsellors and psychotherapists, both as individuals and collectively, in response to society's ambivalent, uncertain but real expectations.

# CHAPTER 12

# The contribution of counselling and psychotherapy to contemporary social and political issues

Counsellors and psychotherapists engage with social and political issues in a number of ways. First, psychological theories and insights can be applied to the understanding of social and political actions and relationships; second, techniques of therapeutic practice provide models for facilitative interventions in the public sphere; third, there is a vague but significant permeation of ideas and perceptions derived from psychotherapy and counselling in our changing culture; fourth, counsellors and psychotherapists may involve themselves as individuals or in organized groups in political and social processes.

Erikson held that psychotherapy could engage with social and political problems and had a responsibility to do so. This chapter explores how this view and the concepts he developed are relevant to contemporary efforts to relate the world of psychotherapy and counselling to the problems of society.

I noted in Chapter 1 the efforts of Freud and subsequent practitioners and thinkers to apply psychoanalytic theory and psychotherapeutic ideas to social and political problems. At the end of the twentieth century there seems to be a renewed search for ways to understand the connection and make it effective. This movement to apply psychotherapeutic ideas to public life is optimistic that psychotherapy and counselling can not only contribute insights but help to create a new kind of politics. Depth psychology can, in Samuels's view, find fresh ways of 'introducing the subjective factor into political discourse, of making the personal political' (1993: 29). Politicians themselves seem more ready to acknowledge the value of psychotherapeutic ideas, such as Bowlby's attachment theory, as relevant to politics (Kraemer and Roberts 1996). On the other hand, Samuels (1998: 28) also notes that 'the record of psychotherapy in the social responsibility area is actually very bad'. He cites homophobia, the support for fascism and the insistence on the necessity for dual parenting. The involvement of psychotherapists in politics cannot have a worse example than ex-psychiatrist Karadjic, the Bosnian Serb leader and wanted war criminal. Feltham points to the need for 'a recognition within counselling institutions of their own fictions, philosophical oppressions and other "shadows"' (1996: 297).

The present mood is therefore one that combines visionary hopes and a belief that much is possible and necessary with sober reflection on past failures and future obstacles. Not only is there a mountain to climb but there is also the danger of falling.

Erikson struggled with these problems through much of the twentieth century and his work can therefore be helpful and instructive. He clearly believed that psychotherapy could help in the understanding of social issues. At times he sounds optimistic that 'we are firmly approaching the study of society' (1965: 405). He acknowledges, however, that psychological explanations by themselves cannot explain events or behaviour. 'The problem to be elucidated is that of the extent to which man is apt to project on political and economic necessity those fears, apprehensions, and urges which are derived from the arsenal of infant anxiety' (p. 396).

Societies and people must be studied independently and in their interactions. 'Because nations and persons are entirely different systems, then, every infantile and prerational item . . . recognized and named must be studied in its double nature of being a property of each individual life cycle and a property of a communality' (Erikson 1964: 207). It was this interplay between the two 'systems' that Erikson analysed in detail in his psychosocial biographies of Luther and Gandhi.

Psychotherapy as he saw it had developed methods through which understanding and insight could be applied both to individuals and to the 'communality'. Without psychological insight, attempts to understand politics and society are shallow and inadequate.

Erikson's confident assertion that psychological insights can be applied to social and political issues is nevertheless matched and to some extent diluted by an awareness of the difficulties and pitfalls of such an application. The difficulties lie not only in the complexity of problems which require the attention of more than one discipline but in the fallibility of those involved. The twin dangers are reductionism and aggrandizement. 'When men concentrate on an uncharted area of human existence, they aggrandize this area to become the universe' (1965: 404). Such aggrandizement, feeding on a 'naive sense of power', leads the psychotherapist as psychologist to 'play the manipulator of man's will' and to join the exploiters rather than the enlighteners in the 'attempt to make man more exploitable by reducing him to a simpler model of himself' (p. 409).

Even if insights are accurate there is danger in stripping away from people the defences by which they maintain their identity. Erikson fears that the 'drive for tolerance has its diminishing returns: it causes anxiety' (p. 408). When identities are threatened, Erikson warned, men will kill. It is a warning that cannot be ignored in a world of inter-ethnic violence and terrorism.

Erikson experienced how good intentions turn sour in practice. He had seen an enlightened approach to child rearing become a new orthodoxy in which 'a new system of "scientific" superstitions had resulted' (p. 403). He felt sure that the way forward must be through interdisciplinary cooperation, but saw that what often happened was 'a kind of halt-and-blind cooperation in which a social scientist with little psychological vision carries in piggy-back fashion a psychologist who has not learned to move with ease in the public events of this world' (p. 405).

Faced with such doubts about the application of insight, about the ethical reliability of psychotherapists and about the consequences of an incautious stripping away of superstition and the irrational bases from people's identities, Erikson appears to waver. His misgivings seem almost to cancel out his confidence in the possibility of a socially and politically involved psychotherapy.

Yet Erikson continued to work on these issues for thirty years after writing *Childhood and Society*. His response to his doubts is threefold. First, he emphasizes the importance of viewing the relation between individuals and society in an extended historical perspective including a degree of cultural relativity. Second, he insists on the need for a framework of principles which act as a guide through the ethical dangers of grandiosity and the abuse of power. Third, he continues to study the ways in which the work of enlightenment – that is, the uncovering of hidden impulses and feelings, the healing of past hurts, the blending of insight with action – might be transferred into social forms. Such a transformation is the function of 'ritualization', 'a *creative formalization* which helps to avoid both *impulsive* excess and *compulsive* self-restriction' (1978a: 82). In this perspective psychotherapy and counselling can be seen as contributing new forms of communication in society, leading to new patterns of communal behaviour.

Erikson wrote that 'Enlightenment has done the ground work; new forms of communication must cement the foundation; society must provide the structure' (1965: 407). In this sentence Erikson summarizes the three essential elements for an effective application of psychotherapeutic ideas to society and politics. Each element is necessary to the others. Each is considered in what follows.

### The application of insight

Following Wheelis's definition (1959: 211; see Chapter 11, p. 147), insight has three main elements: first, the bringing to light of hidden motivations, meanings and feelings; second, the connecting of unconscious material with existing consciousness; third, a hoped for change in feelings, thought and behaviour.

The potential power this promises is great, but there remains after a hundred years a lack of credibility in its explanations and a lack of confidence in its capacity to effect change. Nevertheless, in spite of misgivings and difficulties it is the continuing view of Erikson and others that psychological insight is an essential link between public affairs and the subjectivity of personal human experience.

One major step towards a practical social psychotherapy was the application of psychodynamic ideas to group situations. T-groups, gestalt groups and encounter groups, which were first developed in the USA, and the group work of Bion and others in the UK, led to extensions of theory and practice that included the dynamics of groups. The application of insight was further extended into the study of organizations, such as the interpretations of Menzies Lyth (1970) of the organizational weaknesses and personal behaviour in hospitals in terms of defence against anxiety, and those of Miller and Rice in terms of dependency and counterdependency (Miller 1993). Stapley (1996: 211) describes the potential of insight in creating an 'organisational holding environment' that echoes Winnicott's (1965) concept of the facilitating environment of the good enough mother.

Psychodynamic concepts have been applied to a wide range of political and international situations; for example, concepts of splitting and projection to explain the rhetoric of US–Soviet relations in the Cold War, in which the conflict is presented as one between good and evil. The study of cults such as that led by Jim Jones in Guyana provides further examples of splitting and group paranoia (Nesci 1991). Psychological concepts of loss and of incompleted mourning have been used to explain the intractability of ethnic and religious conflicts such as those in Northern Ireland, former Yugoslavia and Israel–Palestine. Hidden griefs from trauma and victimization in the past are clung to rather than mourned (Volkan 1990: 218). Processes of loss and mourning are basic to understanding the uprooting experience of refugees and emigrants, with their widespread social and political as well as individual effects (Grinberg and Grinberg 1989). The denigration and dehumanization of an enemy that lead to ethnic cleansing and genocide have been studied by Moses (1990b). The study of terrorism is another important area for psychological explanation (Montville 1990). The connection between totalist ideology and terrorism has been vividly recorded in the experience of hostages such as Brian Keenan (1992). Erikson's concepts, such as pseudo-speciation, negative identity and totalism, and his exploration of the problems of uprootedness remain influential and potentially powerful for further work in these areas.

A crucial area in the understanding of political events is the relationship between leaders and their followers linking, as it does, individual and group psychology. It is here perhaps that Erikson's contribution is greatest. His psychohistorical studies of 'great men' set out to integrate the psychological, the historical and the political.

Erikson's earliest psychohistorical study was of Hitler. Erikson was aware of the danger on the one hand of seeing Hitler as an embodiment of evil, and thus beyond psychological explanation; or on the other hand as diagnosable in terms of mental illness as a 'psychopathic paranoid' or 'overcompensatory sissy'. 'At times', says Erikson, 'he was undoubtedly all of that. But unfortunately he was something over and above it all . . . He knew how to approach the borderline, to appear as if he were going too far, and then to turn back on his breathless audience. Hitler knew how to exploit his own hysteria' (1965: 320).

Erikson's approach is to apply to the understanding of public men and women a widening of his approach to his patients. This process is an extension of the the clinical process of 'configurational attention' (Erikson 1985: 21), which sets aside preconceived formulations or judgements, faces the anxiety of not knowing and ranges through as many levels of experience as possible. At some point, which cannot be hurried, this opening out process begins to focus on a configuration or form. Configuration implies both a pattern, a linking together of the various levels of experience, and the condensation into some image or thought which, like a face, has its own pattern, shape and history.

In the public figure such images link the personal history of the individual with the history of the community of which he or she is part, and with that of the followers. The images provide what Erikson in his clinical work called the unifying theme. Thus in the Hitler study he identifies the split image of the idealized German soldier as 'Watcher on the Rhine', vulnerable only to the stab in the back, linked to the unprotected back parts of the body associated with guilt and shame, and the reviled and denigrated Jew who represents all that the soldier must protect against or deny in himself (1965: 338). Themes and images from the individual life histories of public figures which resonate with the history of the times are explored in Erikson's studies of Gandhi, the religious actualist, and the Protestant Luther.

Erikson's psychohistorical approach provides a matrix for the insightful understanding of the relationship between leaders and led. In our own time the personal and political lives of our leaders are almost obsessively entangled. This is perhaps no coincidence but an indication of the potentially fruitful confusion which exists in society between the personal and the political, of which changes in gender and sexual relationships are a significant element. President Bill Clinton in the late 1990s presented an outstanding example of this. Samuels, in a 'sketch of the erotic leader', says that 'the populace, in its obsession with the sexuality of leaders, is on to something important' (1999: 3). He suggests that the interplay of the sexual and personal with the political can be seen as positive as well as negative. From Erikson's configurational viewpoint the popular epithet for Clinton as the 'come-back kid' provides a rich image that links the child in both leader and follower (outfacing shame with a smirking grin) and an apparently powerful and successful adult identity. The connection with sexuality may, as Samuels suggests, 'bring out and reflect back the healthy self-love' (1999: 4) of the citizen. But behind the smirk may also lie the sadness and pain of an unattainable intimacy, embedded in the culture and its child rearing. The relationship between the follower and the leader may be founded on a collusion to keep hidden what is too painful to be acknowledged, the loss of a capacity for intimate relationship or the fear that the all-powerful may yet fail, and failing be found guilty.

It is important, however, to note Erikson's warning that psychological interpretations of politicians have to consider not only the politician's personal experience and his or her audience's expectations and projections but also the skill, self-awareness, integrity – or their opposites – with which the politician makes use of this experience in the predicaments of the times.

## New forms of communication: the facilitating relationship

The configurational insights of depth psychology may illuminate political as well as personal relationships. However, the application of such insights to political situations in a way that can lead to effective action and change meets a crucial obstacle, an almost impassable chasm. Change in therapy depends on a relationship of trust through which insight is facilitated. Through the therapeutic alliance strength is nurtured to face anxiety and change. The whole culture of political and public life, by contrast, seems to be the opposite of that needed for therapeutic trust. The adversarial nature of politics, economy with the truth, the polarization of feeling and opinion, and journalistic intrusion on privacy create a context of mistrust.

The essence of the problem lies in the nature of the public relationships. Unless insight is communicated within a *facilitating relationship*, it is likely to be rejected as irrelevant or resented as intrusive. When one politician says of another 'there is something of the night about him', it does not require great insight to suspect that the speaker is projecting an aspect of herself. But only within a dialogue of trust can the balance of truth in such an insight be worked out constructively.

Erikson saw the problem but maintained the possibility not only of creating new 'forms of communication' but also of harnessing what was inherent in most cultures towards social conditions of trust. Even among politicians trust is a key issue. There remains in people and in society, perhaps despite experience, a huge reservoir of willingness to trust the leader. The problem is how to find social and political forms or conditions for the channelling of this trust into a mutuality of relationship that can be infused with insight. Erikson saw the extension of these conditions through 'new forms of communication' as a crucial element in the application of psychotherapeutic ideas and practice to social and political issues. Without such conditions insight is impotent.

This extension of the facilitating relationship can be illustrated in three specific areas of social life. The first is that of large organizations, where a key problem is how to maintain a human scale of relationship and agency against the pressures of bureaucracy and competition. The second area is that of conflict and exploitation between groups within a society. A central problem in this area is the dependence of identity on prejudice. The third area is that of international conflict, which, as well as including elements from the first two, highlights the involvement in human society of the use of power and the threat of violence.

In the first two of these areas there is no clear evidence of direct influence of Erikson's work and credit must certainly be given to the original and pioneering work of others in the field. Nevertheless, their developments may usefully be considered in terms of the matrix of insight, forms of communication and social structure provided by Erikson and the principles which he articulated. These are: first, the commitment of the facilitator to *skilful attentiveness* (configurational attention), which can be recognized, accepted and internalized by the participants; second, facilitators and participants are committed to a relationship of non-exploitative *mutuality*; third, these forms of communication provide a bridge between insight and action, reality and actuality, subjective and objective experience, the individual and society. As such they manifest the creative *ritualization* of experience in society, containing and transforming conflict in non-violent ways. These principles are illustrated in the following examples.

### Facilitation of change in large organizations

A leading part in the application of insight to organizations has been played by the Tavistock Institute (Trist and Murray 1990). Its work not only applies psychodynamic insight to organizational situations, as already noted, but aims to transfer the facilitative *relationship* through which it can become effective. Menzies Lyth, for example, called her work 'psychoanalytically orientated institutional consultancy' (1989: 27). The consultant's responsibility is 'in helping insights to develop, freeing thinking about problems . . . and helping [the client] to bear the anxiety and uncertainty of the change process' (1989: 33). Miller describes his work as 'action research' in which there is an interactive relationship between the organization and the consultants (1993). That relationship becomes a means by which unconscious processes in the organization or society can be reflected (Rioch 1979). The therapeutic community provides another situation which aims to provide a facilitating environment for the development of insight.

In the USA, Rogers saw in his facilitated group therapy 'models which are available to be utilized on a larger scale when and if society so wishes' (1980: 204). Rogers gives examples of the potential of group facilitation in creating change throughout an organization. The effect of all these approaches is difficult to determine. Real change seems painfully slow. As Menzies Lyth almost despairingly writes (1989: xi), 'The painful yet little tackled issue is how one can transfer the successful model to the hundreds of other institutions of the same kind . . . There must be a way but we have not found it yet'.

Scott Peck has set out to develop just such a model which can be applied to create change in any form of community (1990). His Community Building Workshops aim to facilitate the creation of a community in which listening to others, accepting change and freeing from stereotypes become the norm rather than the exception. Trained leaders facilitate a process of change that leads from an initial stage, which Scott Peck calls 'pseudo-community', in which there is politeness but little real trust or listening, into a second stage of 'chaos' characterized by fluctuating emotions and struggles for power or attention. If the emotions are contained and find expression, the group moves into a third stage, which Scott Peck calls 'emptiness'. It is an uncomfortable but crucial stage in which the members of the group share the anxiety of giving up previously held positions and accept the discomfort of not knowing. Through listening to each other and allowing trust to emerge the group reaches a deeper sense of sharing and community (1990: 86–106). This process is one which acknowledges the subjective experience of individuals in a facilitated group process that has the formation of community as its goal. Two major problems arise, however, which Scott Peck himself noted. The first is how to sustain the sense of community once the time frame and facilitation of the workshop is removed. The second and perhaps greater difficulty is how to get groups of people who might benefit from the experience, but whose trust in others is lowest, to undertake such an experience in the first place.

Nevertheless, the Foundation for Community Encouragement, founded by Scott Peck and others in 1984 (1990: 331), has trained facilitators and run groups in a wide variety of organizational and group situations, from community groups, city councils, business organizations and churches to work with hostile ethnic groups in Bosnia and with convicted criminals in prisons. There is a British branch of FCE called Community Building in Britain (CBiB).

## Facilitating change between conflicting groups

The facilitation process as a means of resolving conflict between hostile groups has developed in a number of forms termed variously mediation, conciliation or conflict resolution. One example of such work is that of the National Coalition Building Institute (NCBI) developed by Cherie Brown in the USA and brought to the UK in 1985.

NCBI runs 'Welcoming Diversity' and 'Prejudice Reduction' workshops in areas of prejudice and discrimination. The workshops train people to 'take the lead in taking on prejudice and discrimination in their spheres of influence' (Brown 1999: 1). Workshops have been run for youth services, probation services, football stewards, mental health trusts, recruitment agencies, city councils, housing officers, Homestart workers with parents, adult learning workers and solicitors – all of whom may experience the challenge of discrimination on a daily basis.

The form of the workshops is itself a facilitative process which aims to develop the ability to facilitate change in social situations. One of the first elements in the workshops is an experiential exercise which brings out the hidden assumptions, often accompanied by feelings of dislike, fear or hatred, that we attach to those we perceive as belonging to different groups from ourselves. It brings a recognition of the prejudices in each of us. The workshops go on to cover a range of experiential learning, from venting negative feelings and listening to others to the practical management of prejudice and violence.

Other workshops are run by NCBI for groups in conflict. The following is an example. When a planning application for an Afro-Caribbean centre to extend its hours brought objections from local residents, NCBI brought together 40 people, including members of the centre and residents. The first step in changing hostility to negotiation is the provision of a containing framework. 'Feelings were running high from the outset with the first ground rule revealing the level of anxiety: NO violence!' (Brown 1999: 2). It is then possible to begin some kind of dialogue. 'As real concerns were laid out people began to see beyond their previous posturing. Black people were able to explain how important the Centre was to them and white people revealed that they wished to see the Centre continue and prosper.' Negotiation on real conflicts of interest now becomes possible. 'Meeting face to face enabled a tremendous shift . . . the application was revised and permission conditionally given. The most significant change . . . is the increased understanding that has so radically and positively changed the atmosphere' (Brown 1999: 3).

Such activities demonstrate how facilitation can help to replace prejudice with dialogue. The chasm between interpersonal therapy and public conflict situations can be crossed by these 'new forms of communication' which create trust infused with insight.

*Facilitating the non-violent resolution of conflict in international situations*

International conflicts are dominated by the overriding influences of state power and perceived interests of security. The questions to be addressed are whether and how facilitative approaches to conflict can be effective alongside those of force and realpolitik. Erikson was cautious about therapeutic intervention in international affairs. Nevertheless, he maintained that an ethical politics was not only possible but essential if the human species was not to become the victim of its own irrational impulses and fears and of its unrestricted technological achievements.

Erikson personally took part in the development of facilitative workshops during the late 1970s and 1980s, as already noted in Chapter 10 (p. 135). The workshops brought together representatives of groups in conflict, including Russians and Americans, Turks and Cypriots, Israelis and Palestinians. The form of the workshops or 'Track Two Diplomacy' conferences ranged from the problem-solving approach of Burton (1987) to approaches which aimed primarily at 'initiating permanent change within each participant' as the most effective 'means of affecting the conflict in the long term' (Betts Fetherston 1991: 256). These facilitated workshops have certain conditions in common with both the conflict resolution work of the NCBI and the community building of FCE, and with individual and group therapy. These conditions include the creation of a safe environment for the expression of feelings and an assurance that they will be heard, the development of the ability to listen to others and the acknowledgement of personal responsibility. Such conditions facilitate trust, the achievement of insight and understanding, and a willingness to negotiate. They are essential conditions of both individual and social healing and health.

The example of the Norwegian facilitation that prepared the way for the Oslo accords between Israel and the PLO, as recorded by Jane Corbin (1994), illustrates the application of these conditions in a situation of intense international conflict. The facilitators, Mona Juuls and Terje Larsen, prepared a supportive personal context but made clear their impartiality and the responsibility of the participants for the outcome. There was the opportunity to express past hurts and present fears and to be listened to. The facilitators listened responsively without judgement, although they did not take part in most of the meetings. The participants knew throughout that the product of their meetings had to be handed on to political leaders. They knew that their 'fragile infant' would be 'exposed to the harsh judgement of the whole world' (Corbin 1994: 212). This infant still survives in spite of many anticipations of its death. Its future may be uncertain and its achievement disputed. Nevertheless, it can justifiably be seen as 'a model for mediation in other conflicts' (p. 211) and an example from which there is much to be learnt.

Critics of the Oslo agreement from the Palestinian viewpoint claim that it is fatally flawed because of the power imbalance it represents between Israel, backed by the United States, and the Palestinians. On the Israeli side it is seen as fatally weakening their security and vulnerability to terrorism. In either case they see the facilitation of such an agreement as leading nowhere or even as damaging. This highlights the major problem of facilitative approaches to international problems, and to some extent to all conflicts: the problem of the use of power and violence, with which facilitation must coexist.

Erikson was aware of the problem of power but does not provide an analysis of it. Boulding's *Three Faces of Power* provides a helpful analysis through which the power of the facilitative processes and the use of state power are brought into perspective (1988). He defines three interwoven but distinguishable kinds of power: threat (military or destructive) power; exchange/bargaining (or productive) power; and integrative (or 'love') power, which includes the 'capacity to build organizations, to create families and groups and to inspire loyalty, to bind people together, to develop legitimacy' (Boulding 1988: 25). None of these is simply identified as necessarily bad or good. There seem to be occasions when a degree of threat power is needed for integrative (or productive) power to operate. Integrative power, as Boulding describes it, can be used in a negative way to ensure conformity or as emotional blackmail. Nevertheless, it is generally agreed that too great a reliance on force is bad and that integrative power is generally a positive element. The problem is often one of how to replace threat with integrative power.

In some political situations there seems little room for anything but threat power. In other situations, such as Northern Ireland, the transition from threat to integrative power is a difficult and slow process. In situations such as Kosovo or Bosnia, threat power seemed the determining element, with some bargaining and little integrative power. Yet these very situations also reveal the limits of threat power and the mistakes that follow from a neglect of integrative power. In the longer-term reconstruction of peaceful society, integrative power can and must play a vital role.

Such integrative power is manifested by the 'new forms of communication' described above. Further examples include the work of the 'Women in Black' in former Yugoslavia (Yuval-Davis 1994), the training in the management of conflict provided by the Peace Studies Department of Bradford University, Quaker mediation in Nigeria and in Croatia (Curle 1995), former President Carter's International Negotiation Network and many other voluntary and non-governmental organizations such as the Mediation Network in Northern Ireland. These are the unseen workers who make the headlined political settlements possible and are vital in putting them into practice.

How far such integrative processes are effective depends not just on the imagination and skill of trained or untrained facilitators or the invention of new forms of communication, but also on the ability of society to make use of them. 'The principles', as Menzies Lyth says, 'are not new – it is implementing them which is the problem' (1989: 43). To understand this problem it is essential to take into account the third element to which Erikson pointed when he said that 'society must provide the structure'. This is the subject of the final section of this chapter.

## Psychotherapists' and counsellors' contribution in a changing society

In his early work with the Yurok people Erikson saw Fanny the medicine woman as in many ways similar to a psychoanalyst. He noted, however, that her work was more directly integrated with the immediate social context of the therapeutic activity (1965: 166–9; see Chapter 4, p. 47). His continuing concern was to find ways in which such interaction could be created in modern society.

The central concept which he developed from this concern was that of ritualization. The new forms of communication deriving from the theory and practice of psychotherapy and counselling can be seen as potential new ritualizations in a living culture – or rather in the diversity of cultures, since each individual in the modern world partakes of a diversity of inherited, imposed and self-chosen cultural identities. These new forms are also capable of degeneration into ritualism or moralism. Erikson's greatest concern was that the modern or postmodern world was losing the capacity for ritualization. On the other hand, he also wrote that 'in our day signs of a re-ritualization of everyday life abound . . . and that they can be recognized by their simple vitality – and playfulness' (1978a: 118).

In all societies forms of cultural expression in drama, music, dance, literature, architecture and religious rituals have served to increase awareness, channel strong emotions and reconcile tensions in the community. They provide what Rustin (1991) has called the 'symbolic space' for communication and reflection. The question Erikson raises in the concept of ritualization is how modern society can best nourish and renew its emotional life, its cultural forms and its institutions.

Only a brief survey of an immense field is possible here to illustrate this perspective of a renewal of ritualization in contemporary society and the place of psychotherapists and counsellors in it. On the positive side, in addition to those new forms outlined above, there are many, if sometimes isolated and fragile, examples of new 'creative formalizations' throughout the world. One example is the Truth and Justice Commission in South Africa, which sought to reconcile opposing tensions between the need for justice and the need for a process of grieving and forgiveness. It was based on the therapeutic principle, as Mary Robinson (1999: 5) put it, that 'revisiting the pain of the past can help us to imagine a route to a more secure and inclusive future'. The United Nations also struggles to develop new political forms that can reconcile the opposing tensions between finding peaceful solutions to conflict and managing the realities of power politics and national interests.

In many parts of the world there is a gradual extension of the idea of pluralism, which Samuels describes as 'an attitude to conflict which tries to reconcile differences without imposing a false resolution on them or losing sight of the unique value of each position' (1997: 135). Erikson's concept of ritualization grew out of his contact with the work of ethologists such as Lorenz, who showed how in the animal world aggression was contained and adapted for the benefit of the species through ritual behaviour. Ritualization is another form of such patterns of behaviour, based not only in our human nature but in the nature we share with animal life forms. The commitment of psychotherapists and counsellors to valuing difference, and their skills in listening to others, have a vital contribution to make to the emergence of these new pluralistic forms. Psychotherapy and counselling cross national and cultural borders in spite of intercultural differences. The counsellor in the UK or USA has a common basis of practice and attitude with the counsellor in Uzbekistan listening to the distressed victim of an attempted kidnap marriage.

There is also a gradual extension of the acceptance of hidden or unconscious motivation. For example, in discussions of 'institutionalized racism' the idea is implicit that a person can be a racist without knowing it (Aaronovitch 1999). Concepts such as demonization, dehumanization and denial creep into the language of politicians and journalists, although the latter's wariness of psychological concepts is often indicated by their denigrating it as psychobabble. On another level, politicians, therapists and sociologists participating in the publication of *The Politics of Attachment* attempt to ground political thinking and action in the psychotherapeutic ideas of Bowlby's attachment theory (Kraemer and Roberts 1996).

The idea of 'emotional literacy' (Orbach 1994) promoted by a group of psychotherapists and counsellors in the organization Antidote (Samuels 1997: 132) seems to reflect a changing mood in society. In the public response to the death of Princess Diana could be seen a search for new ways of giving public expression to and valuing of feelings. The culture of television provides a vehicle for the increasing acceptance of the exploration of feelings and relationships in shows such as that of Oprah Winfrey or phone-ins on radio, although these also illustrate the dangers of exploitation.

Samuels has suggested that the citizen may be empowered as 'therapist' of society through affirming the value of 'citizen's subjectivity' (1993: 28). The sharing of feelings of frustration and powerlessness can become a means to greater awareness and self-confidence rather than feelings of helplessness and worthlessness. At another level, the excluded, the ignored and members of a minority can find a voice through new forms of organization such as users' and other community groups. Richards's exploration of the capacity of cultural activities such as music and football to contain and satisfy social tensions through 'disciplines of delight' (1994) has already been noted. Erikson pointed out that the sources of creative change, whether for individuals or society, draw on cultural elements from the past for the regeneration of the present. Some old forms have the capability for renewal and flexible development.

New forms of leadership are being sought to replace what Samuels has called the 'hypermasculine hero' (1998: 32). These too may be able to draw on the facilitative models of group leadership developed in psychotherapy and counselling. They involve, as Samuels says, an ability to accept failure and weakness. The example of the Norwegian Prime Minister Kjell Magne Bundevik's acknowledgement of his depression may be seen as a move in this direction. It was Erikson's hope that new forms of leadership would emerge which depended less on idealization and transferred responsibility. He foresaw a time 'when man will have to come to grips with his need to personify and surrender to "greatness"' (1970a: 99).

On the negative side, and threatening to overwhelm the capacity to create and adapt, is ranged the intractability of prejudice and superstition at all levels from the interpersonal to the international; the persistence of 'pseudo-speciation' as the basis of identity and a source of exploitable power and repeated cycles of violence; primitive totalism in the fundamentalist approaches to religion which split the world into black and white; moralism that judges without understanding and precludes dialogue; the frightening capacity of power and greed to corrupt the most talented and well intentioned; and the still largely hidden tragedies, waste and exploitation of the vulnerable in many forms of child rearing and education. The world seems hopelessly out of balance in its priorities. The juxtaposition of terrible poverty with wealth and exploitation, intergroup violence and the destruction of the planet's capacity to support life are problems which world leaders seem powerless to remedy.

Erikson believed that humanity has the capacity to remedy its own defects and to create something better. His hopes for a facilitative culture of human society depended on the patterns of relationship transmitted through each new generation. 'The great human question', he wrote in *Young Man Luther*, 'is to what extent early child training must or must not exploit man's early helplessness and moral sensitivity to the degree that a deep sense of evil and of guilt become unavoidable' (1972: 256). Erikson's vision lay in the possibility of a conscience that was not tyrannical but disciplined and tolerant. 'The answer lies in man's capacity to create order which will give his children a disciplined as well as a tolerant conscience, and a world within which to act affirmatively' (p. 257).

What might psychotherapists and counsellors do about these concerns? For some, their primary focus is the development of skills of helping, healing and enabling individuals. For others it is to teach these skills. For some it is organizing a facilitating context. Others study and yet others extend the 'job of enlightenment' into direct contact with social issues and political conflicts. Some manage to engage in all these activities. Erikson wrote of the importance of our 'clinical way of work' becoming a part of 'a judicious way of life' (1965: 406).

In considering the possible involvements of the 'socially responsible therapist', Samuels has written of the difference between a committee of therapists addressing some social issue and getting a 'psychotherapist on to every relevant committee' (1998: 28). Erikson's presence at conferences on international conflict or nuclear disarmament, his discussions with the anthropologists and biologists of his time, his talks with political activists such as Huey Newton and students from the USA to India and Cape Town, provide an example of such multidisciplinary participation.

Erikson may be compared to Matthew Arnold, who in the nineteenth century fought 'culture wars' against those he termed the Philistines and the Barbarians. A biographer has commented that Arnold's was 'a recognisably modern voice . . . deeply enmeshed in the messy, contingent detail of modern society, but defending its right to speak freely, pertinently and without being cowed by the conventional wisdom. No society is ever over-endowed with such voices' (Murray 1996: 353).

Erikson's voice, speaking for a tolerant yet disciplined conscience, was formed by his experience of the horrors and the achievements of the twentieth century. *Childhood and Society* is dedicated to 'our children's children'. Erikson's deepest concern and his clearest vision are expressed in the linking of the individual life cycle to the cycle of generations. It is a vision that values differences and looks at prejudice with a rational eye, yet is 'capable of faith and indignation'. The value of his work lies in whatever may be made of this by a new generation, as they face the threats, opportunities and challenges of our world.

# C H A P T E R  **13**

## Epilogue: vitality in old age

Erikson's interest in old age began early, long before he experienced it personally. From the writing of *Childhood and Society* in his late forties, he considered old age as a separate stage with its own task and crisis centred on the struggle for integrity and wisdom in the face of despair. Erikson lived to be 92 and continued writing well into his eighties. It is therefore also possible to have his own comments on this stage as one who experienced it, not just anticipated or observed it in others.

From the publication of *Toys and Reasons* in 1978 until his last publication in 1986, Erikson wrote, co-wrote or edited a number of significant works. In *The Life Cycle Completed* (1985) he undertook a review of the historical development of psychoanalysis in the light of 50 years' hindsight and his own personal experience. As noted in Chapter 2, Erikson distinguishes two 'languages' in the psychoanalysis of the founders. A mechanistic language in the psychoanalytic theory contrasted with the humanitarian and artistic language of clincial practice and the training seminars.

He reviews the life cycle once again but decides this time to review it backwards from old age to infancy! He does this 'to see how much sense a re-view of the *completed* life cycle can make of its whole course' (Erikson 1985: 9). In doing so he puts the emphasis on the final stage as one in its own right, a stage which he says 'acutely demands new attention and concern in our day' (p. 61). His review does not contain any great modifications but he integrates into one chart (pp. 32–3; see Chapter 8, p. 106) all his major concepts as they are linked to the life cycle – including the psychosexual stages, psychosocial crises, basic strengths (or virtues), related principles of social order, benign forms of ritualization and their complementary regressive 'ritualism'. It must be said that many headings on the chart are still only sketchy, leaving many fascinating areas for exploration.

At the end of the work he returns once again to the intricate problems and aspirations that centre on the therapeutic relationship. He questions the classical psychoanalytic relationship as something the patient has to be 'relatively healthy' to undergo (p. 101). He considers the rich possibilities of transference and countertransference interactions and characteristically begins to wonder how rewarding it might be to 'compare the interplay of transferences and countertransferences between analysands and analysts of given sexes and ages in different cultural and historical settings' (p. 103).

The second significant work is the volume *Adulthood* (1978b) that Erikson edited. It consists of studies of the meanings, forms and values attached to adulthood in various cultural and historical settings. In the preface Stephen Graubard writes that 'Erikson provided not only the focus for the discussion but also the intellectual inspiration for many of its more important features'. It was Erikson who recognized the 'advantages of engaging authors from a great variety of disciplines and professions' (1978b: xi).

*Vital Involvement in Old Age* (Erikson *et al.* 1989), the third major work, is also collaborative. It is centred on interviews with 29 octogenarians, all of whom had taken part in the 'Guidance Study' begun in California in 1928, for which Erikson had conducted the 'play configuration' interviews with young teenagers in the 1940s. It is written by Erikson and his wife Joan, both in their eighties, and Helen Kivnick, a clinical and research psychologist nearly 50 years younger than her two colleagues. All three co-writers took part in the interviewing.

The lives of these elderly 'informants' had in various ways encompassed the history of the twentieth century – its two world wars, the Great Depression, boom times and amazing technological changes. Against this background they had in various unique ways lived out the perennial human patterns, through childhood and adolescence, adulthood, parenthood and grandparenthood (for many but not all), a life of work outside and inside the homes they made, illnesses, bereavements and finally old age.

It is therefore an opportunity to explore in some depth Erikson's understanding of how each stage builds on and anticipates the others. The interviewers sought to understand what sustained most of these elderly people in a vital involvement in their own lives and what for each at times, and for a few more chronically, made such an involvement painful, difficult or impossible. 'All of these people are struggling to bring lifelong dystonic tendencies into balance with acknowledged psychological strengths' (1989: 72). There can be seen an overall tension in each life, and in the face of the prospect of death, between an integrity developed through all the stages of life and a despair that such integrity can never be fully complete, that life seems to have been wasted or opportunities have been lost that cannot come again.

> As the elder seeks to consolidate a sense of lifelong wisdom and perspective, he or she endeavours, ideally, not to exclude legitimate feelings of cynicism and hopelessness, but to admit them in dynamic balance with feelings of human wholeness. Later life brings many, quite realistic reasons for experiencing despair: aspects of a past we fervently wish had been different; aspects of a present that causes unremitting pain; aspects of a future that are uncertain and frightening.
>
> (Erikson *et al.* 1989: 72)

Thus the elderly person may achieve an 'ultimate integration' which 'comprises all of those conscious and unconscious processes by which the individual at the end of life seeks to reexperience and to bring again into scale each of the psychosocial themes that have, in turn, given shape to the life cycle' (p. 72).

The interviewers explored in particular how, in the voices of their informants, themes of success and failure are recalled, but also how they are subtly adjusted to the needs of the present. Memory is not just something to be recalled but something to be used. Just one example of such a theme emerging from the richly complex and often poignant glimpses of courage, survival, disappointment, bitterness, cussedness and wisdom is the way in which the earliest struggles between trust and mistrust still resonate in this final stage of life.

> Among our elders' comments are those that reflect exagerrated extremes of trustfulness and mistrustfulness. The first extreme is illustrated by those who assert, in absolute tones that permit no doubt, that they will be taken care of, no matter what – even though instances of need have arisen and the expected caretakers have failed to provide . . . The opposite extreme is illustrated by those for whom the primary mode of experiencing the world seems to be one of blaming, of mistrusting, and of criticizing people and circumstances . . . Any activity seems to represent an opportunity to display apprehension; any encounter becomes an occasion to recall past affronts and injustices. Somewhere between these two extremes lies the expression of a mature faith.
>
> (Erikson *et al.* 1989: 237)

Included in both *Adulthood* and *Vital Involvement in Old Age* are accounts, with a commentary, on Ingmar Bergman's film *Wild Strawberries*. This film tells the story of a day in the life of an elderly Swedish doctor who travels to a ceremony in which he is to be honoured for his life's work and achievement. The two versions are written differently but both have the same purpose: to illustrate themes and concepts of the life cycle through a film of a journey that is both a review of a whole life and an opportunity to revisit and work once more at some of the themes which have dominated and sustained this life. The film was used by Erikson as a basis for seminars on the human life cycle.

The film opens with a justly celebrated dream sequence in which Dr Borg stares at a clock with no hands, listens to the beating of his heart, attends a street funeral which seems to be his and hears what sounds like a baby's cry. He is brought face to face with timelessness, with the ending in time of his own life and with the ongoing time of his own beating heart and the hint of the renewal of birth. There is both emptiness and fullness of feeling. On waking the doctor decides to drive himself to the ceremony, against the remonstrance of his housekeeper of the past 40 years. During the journey he encounters both people close to him and strangers. His daughter-in-law, childless and separated from his son, travels with him; he decides to visit his mother who is struggling with her own cynicism and weariness, but softens a little as they part. The strangers are a trio of students and a bickering couple.

Each of these meetings evokes memories of his life: his youthful first love and disappointment, his broken marriage, the isolation from intimacy that runs from his father and mother through him to his son. These themes are brilliantly interwoven by Bergman through a mixture of flashbacks of real events, fantasies and present day confrontations in which Dr Borg is surprised into finding himself communicating both with the strangers and, in spite of reluctance and difficulty, with those closer to him. Through his encounters with his daughter-in-law Marianne and the student Sara, each involved in her own personal stage and crisis, he experiences a mutuality that helps him to loosen the 'self-restriction' in his 'seeming autonomy of proud withdrawal' (1978c: 2).

The ceremony in the ancient cathedral at Lund is a public occasion. At first it seems to Borg 'meaningless as a passing dream'. But as he stands to receive his doctor's hat he has a revelatory feeling of 'a remarkable causality in this chain of unexpected, entangled events' (p. 16). The ceremony is a ritual affirmation of an important part of his life. It also brings a recognition that that part of his life is over but that it is not everything to him, as perhaps he had feared. It is a 'grand ritual which both seals and permits a transcendence of his over-defined professional existence' (p. 2).

He returns home, not a changed man but a little more aware of and at ease with himself. He is able to be more understanding of his housekeeper, who would nevertheless be horrified if he were to appear to be anything other than the 'Dr Borg' to whom she has grown accustomed and devoted.

There is no substantial evidence of any correspondence between Erikson's intimate life and that portrayed in the film. Nevertheless, Erikson notes his Harvard students' 'friendly suspicions' of an identification with the Swedish doctor, when Erikson chose this movie 'year after year' for the 'human life cycle' course. He makes a connection between the film's setting around Lund and his own Scandinavian origins. Only 20 miles across the Ore Sound from Lund, 'I spent the sunniest summers of my early years visiting my uncles' country houses and being taken for boat rides' (1978c: 4). Friedman identifies a number of other parallels of detail between Erikson's personal life and the events and characters in the film (1999: 445). The place given to this story in these final works and also the loving and perceptive attention to its details does indeed suggest some identification by Erikson with Dr Borg. Certainly Erikson was able to empathize with the elderly doctor, recognizing something perhaps of his doctor father as well as of himself, and the deals each of them made with society and family to achieve a successful career. For Erikson this had meant leaving behind his parents and whatever he could claim as a homeland. He can therefore identify with this doctor whose career contained so much of his adult identity and who, as his career ends, is faced with finding out who he is without it.

It is characteristic of Erikson that he communicates so much of himself in this indirect way, through a commentary on another man's cinematic fiction. With all his perceptiveness and interest in people he is, like Dr Borg, a man who keeps his distance. Like many psychotherapists and counsellors, perhaps, Erikson is more comfortable observing than being observed. There are few records of him as seen by others. Sometimes he is recalled indirectly, as in Coles's account of the young anti-segregationists' enthusiastic response to finding Erikson's books in jail (Coles 1970: xii; see Chapter 8, p. 94). One rare personal glimpse of Erikson is recorded by Coles. Coles was accompanying Erik and Joan Erikson on a journey through Mississippi in 1970. They were there to talk with children and parents engaged in the Headstart programme in the wake of desegregation. 'Toward the end of our stay, as we drove along, past cotton fields ... past the little Delta towns ... I noticed Erik Erikson looking out of the window, observing – but in his face also responding, trying hard to make sense of what he saw, and just as important, trying hard to learn what he believed, where his ethical concerns would require him to go' (1970: 411). Even in this portrait of an observer observed there seems to be something apart and impenetrable in the face of the friend, turned away and looking out of the window.

It is in his observations of others and in his perceptive recording of and reflections on them that Erikson may himself most clearly be identified. Among other writings towards the end of his life are some pieces on special occasions to celebrate or remember friends and colleagues. In 1972 he spoke at a gathering in honour of Robert Knight, who had been Director of the Austen Riggs Center and was responsible for Erikson's move there in 1950. After describing his talents as doctor and leader he adds a description of Robert Knight and another colleague, David Rapaport.

> Among all his colleagues, the most extraordinary one was undoubtedly David Rapaport. In contrast to Bob's tallness, David was small. To see Bob and David come down Main Street together was an experience. In order to keep up with Bob's long steps, David had to hurry along as if on small built-in wheels. Where Bob was calm, David was excitable; where Bob spoke softly and evenly, David alternately shouted and whispered. Bob was the doctor and director; David was the theorist, the encyclopedist and the conceptual conscience of us all ... I think it was Henry Wexler who called Bob the embodiment of the reality principle; so was David that of the superego. This, to be sure, could have been a deadly combination, but the two shared a great sense of humor which made David laugh over Bob's American jokes and Bob laugh in turn, over examples from David's inexhaustible Jewish collection, brought over from Hungary – and nothing can reconcile reality and conscience better than humor.
>
> (Erikson 1987: 737)

In recalling his friends, Erikson the observer reveals perhaps as much as we can know of his gentleness, affection and humour. His account also recreates what can otherwise be desiccated in the pages of dusty tomes. It recalls the personal immediacy, the fellowship laced with competitiveness, the excitement of heady ideas and unlimited horizons, which the world of psychotherapy involved for Erikson and those around him in those days.

How, then, may we suppose that Erikson experienced for himself the final task of reconciling integrity with despair. It is something which only he himself and those closest to him can reliably know. Did it conform to his anticipations or surprise him in unsuspected ways? Probably both. Erikson had written of this stage that 'only an identity safely anchored in the "patrimony" of a cultural identity can produce a workable psychosocial equilibrium' (1965: 402). The word 'patrimony' suggests a degree of ambivalence to be faced in a longing for a father and a fatherland to which some nostalgia still clings. For Erikson there was a lasting shadow of an unknown father, who had not left him a name, and of a German Jewish father who gave him the name Erik Homburger, but whom he left behind to face the brutality of Nazism.

In the New World Erikson found a home and created an identity as therapist, writer, teacher, public figure, American and world citizen, as well as parent and grandparent. In the final stage of life these generative identities have one by one to be relinquished, and the scene is set for the final struggle with life's meaning and whatever resolution can be made of the theme, present from the beginning, of the struggle between despair at individual life's insignificance and the rich promise of existence.

There is a moment in the film when Isak Borg comes to face this dilemma in a way that may reflect Erikson's personal experience. As the travellers relax together halfway through the journey, Dr Borg starts to recite a poem. He begins a line 'When twilight comes', and then falters; it is his daughter-in-law Marianne who completes it: 'I am still yearning.' The young stranger Sara, 'moved to tears ("for no reason at all"), says: "You're religious, aren't you, Professor"' (Erikson 1978c: 12).

In the crisis of old age the individual seeks an integrity that completes and is also beyond identities. There is a longing for what is timeless, mingled with the loss and the celebration of what is ending. As in Isak Borg's dream, there is renewal of life as well as death and the beginning of a new journey. Disgust and despair are part of that journey; so too is hope.

In our own times even the necessity for an ending to life has been challenged and great efforts are made to extend the life-span and delay death. Erikson, however, is more likely to have seen the prospect of an extended life-span in terms of what it might do to the integrity of the old person. It is a view dramatically and movingly portrayed in Janáček's opera *The Makropoulos Case*. Elena Makropoulos was given a potion by her father that enabled her to live for three hundred years. At the beginning of the opera the potency of the potion is running out. Elena has experienced the terrible agony of living too long, repeating experience without desire, with the memories of past joy turned to disgust and bitterness, which she inflicts on her admirers and would-be lovers. She comes to see how the wonder and adventure of life are indissolubly linked to its finiteness. She envies those who find their insignificant concerns so special and important. In the end she is able to recover what she had so desperately and ruthlessly tried to extinguish, her ability to die.

Acceptance of life and death are part of the struggle for integrity that takes place for each individual in a unique time, place and culture. So Erikson wrote of integrity as 'the acceptance of one's one and only life cycle as something that had to be' (1965: 260). In Erikson's time the traditional forms of culture were disintegrating. In such a world the only identities that can sustain integrity and enough wisdom to transmit to the next generation are identities that, while drawing on and acknowledging the past, recreate the multifaceted fragments of our own and others' experience into a new wholeness. Erikson continued through his life to search for such a wholeness. In doing so he has left a rich legacy for all who follow their own search through identity and mutuality to some degree of integrity and wisdom.

# References

Aaronovitch, D. (1999) The person who said I had a funny name is not, of course, a racist. *Independent on Sunday*, 2 March.

Abt, A. F. and Garrison, F. H. (1965) *History of Pediatrics*. Philadelphia: W. B. Saunders.

Adler, A. (1928) *Understanding Human Nature*. London: Allen & Unwin.

Ariès, P. (1962) *Centuries of Childhood*. London: Jonathan Cape.

Arnold, M. (1979) Stanzas written at the Grande Chartreuse. In K. Allott (ed.) *Poems of Matthew Arnold*. London: Oxford University Press.

Bateman, H. and Holmes, J. (1995) *Introduction to Psychoanalysis*. London: Routledge.

Bavington, J. (1992) The Bradford experience. In J. Kareem and R. Littlewood (eds) *Intercultural Therapy*. London: Blackwell Scientific Publications.

Bellah, N. B. (1978) To kill and survive or to die and become: the active life and the contemplative life as ways of being adult. In E. H. Erikson (ed.) *Adulthood*. New York: Norton.

Berman, M. (1975) Review of 'Life History and the Historical Moment'. *New York Times Book Review*, 30 March.

Betts Fetherston, A. (1991) The problem-solving workshop in conflict resolution. In T. Woodhouse (ed.) *Peacemaking in a Troubled World*. New York and Oxford: Berg.

Bhavnani, K.-K. and Phoenix, A. (1994) *Shifting Identities, Shifting Racisms*. London: Sage.

Boulding, K. (1988) *Three Faces of Power*. London: Sage.

Bowlby, J. (1953) *Child Care and the Growth of Love*. London: Penguin.

Brinkley, A., Current, R. N., Freidel, F. and Williams, T. H. (1991) *American History. A Survey*, 8th edn. New York: McGraw-Hill.

British Association for Counselling (1993) *Code of Ethics and Practice for Counsellors*. London: BAC.

Brown, S. (ed.) (1999) *Update No. 1*. Leicester: National Coalition Building Institute.

Burns, R. (1969) To a Louse. In T. Kingsley (ed.) *Burns Poems and Songs*. London: Oxford University Press.

Burton, J. (1987) *Resolving Deep-seated Conflict*. Lanham, MD: University Press of America.

Clarke Stewart, A., Friedman, S. and Koch, J. (1985) *Child Development. A Topical Approach*. New York: Wiley.

Coles, H. (1970) *Erik H. Erikson. The Growth of His Work*. Boston: Little, Brown and Co.

Corbin, J. (1994) *Gaza First*. London: Bloomsbury.

Craib, I. (1998) *Experiencing Identity*. London: Sage.

Craig, Y. (1998) Attitudes to ageing: its social construction, deconstruction and recon-struction. *Counselling*, 9(1), 49–53.

Crosby, F. and Crosby, T. L. (1981) Psychobiography and psychohistory. In S. Long (ed.) *The Handbook of Political Behavior*. New York: Plenum.

Curle, A. (1995) *Another Way: Positive Responses to Contemporary Violence*. London: Jon Carpenter.

*Current Biography Yearbook*. New York: H. W. Wilson.

De Mause, L. (ed.) (1974) *The History of Childhood*. New York: Psychohistory Press.

Demos, J. (1970) *The Little Commonwealth: Family Life in Plymouth*. New York: Oxford University Press.

Dittmar, H. (1992) *The Social Psychology of Material Possessions*. Hemel Hempstead: Harvester Wheatsheaf.

Dryden, W. (ed.) (1996a) *Handbook of Individual Therapy*. London: Sage.

Dryden, W. (1996b) A rose by any other name: a personal view on the differences among professional titles. *Self and Society*, 24(5), 15–17.

Dryden, W. and Feltham, C. (eds) (1992) *Psychotherapy and its Discontents*. Buckingham: Open University Press.

Dryden, W. and Spurling, L. (eds) (1989) *On Becoming a Psychotherapist*. London: Tavistock/Routledge.

Dunn, P. (1974) That enemy is the baby: childhood in imperial Russia. In L. De Mause (ed.) *The History of Childhood*. New York: Psychohistory Press.

Ellenberger, H. (1970) *The Discovery of the Unconscious*. London: Penguin.

Ellis, A. (1997) The future of cognitive-behaviour and rational emotive behaviour therapy. In S. Palmer and V. Varma (eds) *The Future of Counselling and Psychotherapy*. London: Sage.

Erikson, E. H. (1931) Bilderbucher. *Zeitschrift Psychoanalytische für Pedagogik*, 5, 13–19. (English translation as *Children's Picturebooks*, 1986.)

Erikson, E. H. (1940a) On the feasibility of making psychological observations in Canadian internment camps. Unpublished.

Erikson, E. H. (1940b) On Nazi mentality. In S. Schlein (ed.) *A Way of Looking at Things. Selected Essays*. New York: Norton.

Erikson, E. H. (1940c) On submarine psychology. Unpublished.

Erikson, E. H. (1942) Comments on Hitler's speech of Sept. 30, 1942. In S. Schlein (ed.) *A Way of Looking at Things. Selected Essays*. New York: Norton.

Erikson, E. H. (1943) Memorandum concerning the interrogation of German prisoners of war. In S. Schlein (ed.) *A Way of Looking at Things. Selected Essays*. New York: Norton.

Erikson, E. H. (1951) Statement to the Committee on Privilege and Tenure of the University of California concerning the California Loyalty Oath, *Psychiatry*, 14, 243–5. Reprinted in *A Way of Looking at Things*.

Erikson, E. H. (1953) On the sense of inner identity. In *Health and Human Relations*, report on a conference held at Hiddensen, Germany, 2–7 August. New York: The Balkiston Company, pp. 124–43.

Erikson, E. H. (1954a) The dream specimen of psychoanalysis. *Journal of the American Psychoanalytic Association*, 2, 5–56.

Erikson, E. H. (1954b) Identity and totality: psychoanalytic observations on the prob-lems of youth. In *Human Development Bulletin*, Fifth Annual Symposium. Chicago: The Human Development Student Organization, pp. 50–82.

Erikson, E. H. (1955a) The syndrome of identity-diffusion in adolescents and young adults. In J. M. Tanner and B. Inhelder (eds) *Discussion on Child Development*. New York: International Universities Press.

Erikson, E. H. (1955b) Freud's 'The Origin of Psychoanalysis'. *International Journal of Psychoanalysis*, 36, 1–15.

Erikson, E. H. (1956a) The problem of ego identity. *Journal of the American Psychoanalytic Association*, 4, 56–121.

Erikson, E. H. (1956b) The first psychoanalyst. *Yale Review*, 46, 40–62.

Erikson, E. H. (with Erikson, K. T.) (1957) The confirmation of the delinquent. *Chicago Review*, 10(Winter), 15–23.

Erikson, E. H. (1958a) Identity and uprootedness in our time. In *Uprooting and Resettlement*, Bulletin of the World Federation for Mental Health, Vienna.

Erikson, E. H. (1958b) The nature of clinical evidence. *Daedalus*, 87, 65–87.

Erikson, E. H. (1959) Identity and the life cycle: selected papers. In *Psychological Issues*, 1, 1. New York: International Universities Press.

Erikson, E. H. (1961) Reality and actuality. *Journal of the American Psychoanalytic Association*, 10, 451–73.

Erikson, E. H. (1963) The golden rule and the cycle of life. *Harvard Medical Alumni Bulletin*, 37(2).

Erikson, E. H. (1964) *Insight and Responsibility*. New York: Norton.

Erikson, E. H. (1965) *Childhood and Society*. London: Penguin (originally published 1950).

Erikson, E. H. (1966a) The ontogeny of ritualization in man. *Philosophical Transactions of the Royal Society of London*, Series B, 251, 337–49.

Erikson, E. H. (1966b) The concept of identity in race relations: notes and queries. *Daedalus*, 95(1), 145–70.

Erikson, E. H. (1968a) *Identity: Youth and Crisis*. New York: Norton.

Erikson, E. H. (1968b) On the nature of psycho-historical evidence: in search of Gandhi. *Daedalus*, 97(3), 695–730.

Erikson, E. H. (1968c) *Insight and Freedom*. The T. B. Davie Memorial Lecture on Academic Freedom, University of Cape Town, South Africa.

Erikson, E. H. (1970a) *Gandhi's Truth*. London: Faber (originally published 1969).

Erikson, E. H. (1970b) Autobiographic notes on the identity crisis. *Daedalus*, 99(4), 730–59.

Erikson, E. H. (1972) *Young Man Luther*. London: Faber (originally published 1958).

Erikson, E. H. (1974) *Dimensions of a New Identity*. New York: Norton.

Erikson, E. H. (1975a) *Life History and the Historical Moment*. New York: Norton.

Erikson, E. H. (1975b) Conversations with Erik H. Erikson and Huey P. Newton. In Kai T. Erikson (ed.) *In Search of Common Ground*. New York: Norton.

Erikson, E. H. (1978a) *Toys and Reasons*. London: Marion Boyars.

Erikson, E. H. (ed.) (1978b) *Adulthood*. New York: Norton.

Erikson, E. H. (1978c) Reflections on Dr Borg's life cycle. In E. H. Erikson (ed.) *Adulthood*. New York: Norton.

Erikson, E. H. (1981) The Galilean sayings and the sense of 'I'. *Yale Review*, 70(3), 321–62.

Erikson, E. H. (1985) *The Life Cycle Completed*. New York: Norton.

Erikson, E. H. (1987) *A Way of Looking at Things. Selected Papers*, ed. S. Schlein. New York: Norton.

Erikson, E. H. and Erikson, J. M. (1987) Dorothy Burlingham's School in Vienna. In S. Schlein (ed.) *A Way of Looking at Things. Selected Papers*. New York: Norton.

Erikson, E. H., Erikson, J. M. and Kivnick, H. Q. (1989) *Vital Involvement in Old Age*. New York: Norton.

Evans, R. I. (1964) *Dialogue with Erik Erikson*. New York: Jason Aronson.

Feltham, C. (1996) Beyond denial, myth and superstition in the counselling profession. In F. Bayne, I. Horton and J. Biurose (eds) *New Directions in Counselling*. London: Routledge.

Fischer, L. (1997) *The Life of Mahatma Gandhi*. London: Harper Collins.

Fowler, J. W. (1981) *The Stages of Faith: the Psychology of Human Development and Quest for Meaning*. New York: Harper and Row.

Freud, S. (1900) *The Interpretation of Dreams*. Standard edition 4–5. London: Hogarth.

Freud, S. (1901) *The Psychopathology of Everyday Life*. Standard edition 6. London: Hogarth.

Freud, S. (1905) *Fragment of an Analysis of a Case of Hysteria*. Standard edition 7. London: Hogarth.

Freud, S. (1912) *Totem and Taboo*. Standard edition 13. London: Hogarth.

Freud, S. (1921) *Group Psychology and the Analysis of the Ego*. Standard edition 18. London: Hogarth.

Freud, S. (1927) *The Future of an Illusion*. Standard edition 21. London: Hogarth.

Freud, S. (1930) *Civilization and Its Discontents*. Standard edition 21. London: Hogarth.

Freud, S. (1933) *Why War?* Penguin Freud Library 12. London: Penguin.

Freud, S. (1954) *Sigmund Freud. The Origins of Psychoanalysis. Letters to Wilhelm Fliess. Drafts and Notes 1887–1902*, ed. M. Bonaparte, A. Freud and E. Kris. New York: Imago.

Friedman, L. J. (1999) *Identity's Architect. A Biography of Erik H. Erikson*. London: Free Association Books.

Fromm, E. (1942) *The Fear of Freedom*. London: Routledge and Kegan Paul.

Frosh, S. (1987) *The Politics of Psychoanalysis*. London: Macmillan.

Gandhi, M. K. (1927) *An Autobiography or the Story of My Experiments with Truth*, trans. Mahadev Desai. Ahmedabad: Navajivan.

Gellner, E. (1992) Psychoanalysis, social role and testability. In W. Dryden and C. Feltham (eds) *Psychotherapy and its Discontents*. Buckingham: Open University Press.

Giddens, A. (1994) *The Constitution of Society*. Cambridge: Polity Press.

Gilligan, C. (1982) *In a Different Voice*. Cambridge, MA: Harvard University Press.

Gorsuch, N. (1998) Time's winged chariot. *Psychodynamic Counselling*, 4(2), 191–202.

Gould, R. (1978) *Transformations: Growth and Change in Adult Life*. New York: Simon & Schuster.

Graubard, S. (1978) Preface. In E. H. Erikson (ed.) *Adulthood*. New York: Norton.

Grinberg, L. and Grinberg, R. (1989) *Psychoanalytic Perspectives on Migration and Exile*. New Haven, CT: Yale University Press.

Guggenbuhl-Craig, A. (1989) *Power in the Helping Professions*, trans. M. Gubitz. Dallas: Spring Publications.

Gunzburg, J. C. (1997) *Healing through Meeting*. London: Jessica Kingsley.

Hall, S. (1996) Introduction. Who needs identity? In S. Hall and P. du Gay (eds) *Cultural Identity*. London: Sage.

Hartmann, H. (1939) *Ego Psychology and the Problem of Adaptation*. London: Imago.

Hartmann, H. (1956) Notes on the reality principle, in *The Psychoanalytic Study of the Child*, Vol. XI. New York: International Universities Press.

Hartmann, H. (1960) *Psychoanalysis and Moral Values*. New York: International Universities Press.

Haste, H. (1994) Obituary: Erik Erikson. *The Guardian*, 27 May.

Havighurst, R. J. (1972) *Developmental Tasks and Education*. New York: David Mackay.

Hesse, H. (1985) *Wandering*. London: Triad/Panther.

House, R. (1997) Participatory ethics in a self-generating practitioner community. In R. House and N. Totton (eds) *Implausible Professions*. Ross-on-Wye: PCCS.

House, R. and Totton, N. (eds) (1997) *Implausible Professions*. Ross-on-Wye: PCCS.

Houston, G. (1997) The same some time later. *Self and Society*, 25(2), 12–17.

Hunt, D. (1972) *Parents and Children in History. The Psychology of Family Life in Early Modern France*. New York: Harper Torch.

Ignatieff, M. (1994) *Blood and Belonging*. London: Vintage.

Jacobs, M. (1985) *The Presenting Past: An Introduction to Practical Psychodynamic Counselling*. Milton Keynes: Open University Press.

Jacobs, M. (1993) *Living Illusions: a Psychology of Belief*. London: SPCK.

Jacobs, M. (1996a) *Jitendra: Lost Connections*. Buckingham: Open University Press.

Jacobs, M. (1996b) Suitable clients for counselling and psychotherapy. *Self and Society*, 24(5), 3–7.

Jacobs, M. (1998) *The Presenting Past: the Core of Psychodynamic Counselling and Psychotherapy*, 2nd edn. Buckingham: Open University Press.

Jacoby, R. (1983) *The Repression of Psychoanalysis. Otto Fenichel and the Political Freudians*. New York: Basic Books.

Jones, E. (1953) *The Life and Work of Sigmund Freud, Volume 1*. London: Hogarth.

Kamptner, N. L. (1991) Personal possessions and their meanings: a life-span perspective. In F. W. Rudmin (ed.) *To Have Possessions: a Handbook on Ownership and Property*. Special issue of *Journal of Social Behavior and Personality* 6(6), 209–28.

Kareem, J. (1992) The Nafsiyat Intercultural Therapy Centre: ideas and experience in intercultural therapy. In J. Kareem and R. Littlewood (eds) *Intercultural Therapy*. Oxford: Blackwell Scientific Publications.

Kareem, J. and Littlewood, R. (eds) (1992) *Intercultural Therapy. Themes, Interpretations and Practice*. Oxford: Blackwell Scientific Publications.

Kearney, A. (1996) *Counselling. Class and Politics*. Manchester: PCCS Books.

Keenan, B. (1992) *An Evil Cradling*. London: Hutchinson.

Klinefelter, P. (1994) A school counselling service. *Counselling*, 5(3), 215–17.

Kovel, J. (1988) *The Radical Spirit*. London: FA Books.

Kraemer, S. and Roberts, J. (eds) (1996) *The Politics of Attachment*. London: PA Books.

Lago, C. O. and Thompson, J. (1989) *Issues of Race and Counselling in Counselling Settings: Video and Training Manual*. Leicester: University of Leicester Audio Visual Services (video).

Lago, C. O. and Thompson, J. (1996) *Race, Culture and Counselling*. Buckingham: Open University Press.

Lasch, C. (1975) *The Culture of Narcissism*. New York: Basic Books.

Laufer, K. (1974) *Adolescent Disturbance and Breakdown*. London: Penguin.

Levinson, D. J. (1978) *The Season's of a Man's Life*. New York: Knopf.

Littlewood, R. (1992) Towards an intercultural therapy. In J. Kareem and R. Littlewood (eds) *Intercultural Therapy*. Oxford: Blackwell Scientific Publications.

Lowe, G. (1972) *The Growth of Personality*. London: Penguin.

Marcia, J. E. (1966) Development and validation of ego-identity status. *Journal of Personality and Social Psychology*, 3, 551–8.

Maslow, A. (1996) *Future Visions. The Unpublished Papers*, ed. B. Hoffman. London: Sage.

Masson, J. (1992) The tyranny of psychotherapy. In V. Dryden and C. Feltham (eds) *Psychotherapy and its Discontents*. Buckingham: Open University Press.

Menzies Lyth, I. (1970) *The Functioning of Social Systems as a Defence against Anxiety*. London: Tavistock.

Menzies Lyth, I. (1989) *The Dynamics of the Social. Selected Essays Volume 1*. London: FA Books.

Miller, A. (1983) *For Your Own Good*. London: Faber.

Miller, E. (1993) *From Dependency to Autonomy*. London: FA Books.

Montessori, M. (1912) *The Montessori Method*. London: Heinemann.

Montville, J. V. (1990) Psychological roots of ethnic and sectarian terrorism. In V. D. Volkan, D. A. Julius and J. V. Montville (eds) *Psychodynamics of International Relationships Volume 1*. Lexington, MA: Lexington Books.

Montville, J. V. (1991) The arrow and the olive branch. A case for track two diplomacy. In V. D. Volkan, D. A. Julius and J. V. Montville (eds) *Psychodynamics of International Relationships Volume 2*. Lexington, MA: Lexington Books.

Moses, R. (1990a) The leader and the led: a dyadic relationship. In V. D. Volkan, D. A. Julius and J. V. Montville (eds) *Psychodynamics of International Relationships Volume 1*. Lexington, MA: Lexington Books.

Moses, R. (1990b) On dehumanizing the enemy. In V. D. Volkan, D. A. Julius and J. V. Montville (eds) *Psychodynamics of International Relationships Volume 1*. Lexington, MA: Lexington Books.

Murray, N. (1996) *A Life of Matthew Arnold*. London: Hodder and Stoughton.

Naylor Smith, A. (1994) Counselling and psychotherapy: is there a difference? *Counselling*, 5(4), 284–6.

Nesci, D. A. (1991) Collective suicide in Jamestown. In J. Offerman-Zuckerberg (ed.) *Politics and Psychology in Contemporary Psychodynamic Perspective*. New York: Plenum Press.

Newman, C. and Goldfried, M. (1996) Developments in psychotherapy integration. In W. Dryden (ed.) *Developments in Psychotherapy*. London: Sage.

*New York Times* (1994) Obituary: Erik Erikson, 13 May.

Offerman-Zuckerberg, J. (ed.) (1991) *Politics and Psychology in Contemporary Psychodynamic Perspective*. New York: Plenum Press.

Oliner, S. P. (1991) Altruism. In J. Offerman-Zuckerberg (ed.) *Politics and Psychology in Contemporary Psychodynamic Perspective*. New York: Plenum Press.

Orbach, S. (1994) *What's Really Going on Here?* London: Virago.

Palmer, S. and Varma, V. (eds) (1997) *The Future of Counselling and Psychotherapy*. London: Sage.

Pedersen, P. D. and Ivey, A. (1993) *Culture-centered Counseling and Interviewing Skills*. Westport, CT: Praeger.

Pilgrim, D. (1992) Psychotherapy and political evasions. In W. Dryden and C. Feltham (eds) *Psychotherapy and its Discontents*. Buckingham: Open University Press.

Pilgrim, D. (1997) *Psychotherapy and Society*. London: Sage.

Proulx, E. A. (1996) *Accordion Crimes*. London: Fourth Estate.

Richards, B. (1994) *Disciplines of Delight*. London: FA Books.

Rioch, M. (1979) The A. K. Rice Relation Conferences as a reflection of society. In W. G. Lawrence (ed.) *Exploring Individual and Organizational Boundaries*. Chichester: Wiley.

Roazen, P. (1976) *Erik H. Erikson. The Power and Limits of a Vision*. London: Collier Macmillan.

Robertson, P. (1974) Home as a nest. Middle class children in nineteenth century Europe. In L. De Mause (ed.) *The History of Childhood*. New York: Psychohistory Press.

Robinson, M. (1999) The mortal power of affirmation. *New World*, January–March. United Nations Association.

Rogers, B. (1993) Counselling: the heart of an institution. *Counselling*, 4(1), 36–9.

Rogers, C. (1980) *A Way of Being*. Boston: Houghton Mifflin.

Rolland, R. (1924) *Mahatma Gandhi*, trans. C. D. Groth. New York: The Century Co.

Rustin, M. (1991) *The Good Society and the Inner World*. London: Verso.

Sadat, A. el (1993) *In Search of Identity: an Autobiography*. New York: Harper and Row.

Samuels, A. (1992) Foreword. In W. Dryden and C. Feltham (eds) *Psychotherapy and its Discontents*. Buckingham: Open University Press.

Samuels, A. (1993) *The Political Psyche*. London: Routledge.

Samuels, A. (1997) Pluralism and the future of psychotherapy. In S. Palmer and V. Varma (eds) *The Future of Psychotherapy and Counselling*. London: Sage.

Samuels, A. (1998) Responsibility. Part 2. *Self and Society*, 26(3), 28–32.

Samuels, A. (1999) The erotic leader. *Self and Society*, 27(2), 3–5.

Schwartz, B. D. Memorial Library (1998) *Educators, Psychologists and Philosophers. A Bibliography 1982–1992*. http://www.liunet.ed . . . edpeople.htm#Erikson.

Scott Peck, M. (1978) *The Road Less Travelled*. New York: Simon & Schuster.

Scott Peck, M. (1990) *The Different Drum*. London: Arrow.

Searles, H. F. (1965) *Collected Papers on Schizophrenia and Related Subjects*. London: Hogarth.

Stapley, L. F. (1996) *The Personality of the Organisation*. London: FA Books.

Stern, D. (1985) *The Interpersonal World of the Infant*. New York: Basic Books.

Stevens, R. (1983) *Erik Erikson*. Milton Keynes: Open University Press.

Strozier, C. B. (1976) Disciplined subjectivity and the psychohistorian: a critical look at the work of Erik Erikson. *Psychohistory Review*, 53, 28–31.

Sue, D. W. and Sue, D. (1990) *Counselling the Culturally Different. Theory and Practice*, 2nd edn. New York: Wiley.

Symington, N. (1994) *Emotion and Spirit*. London: Cassell.

Thompson, N. L. (1996) Psychoanalytic approaches to history in the era of theoretical pluralism. American Psychoanalytical Association. http://apsa.org/index.htm.

Thorne, B. (1997) Counselling and psychotherapy: the sickness and the prognosis. In S. Palmer and V. Varma (eds) *The Future of Counselling and Psychotherapy*. London: Sage.

Trist, E. and Murray, H. (eds) (1990) *The Social Engagement of Social Science, Volume 1*. London: FA Books.

Volkan, V. (1988) *The Need to Have Enemies and Allies*. New York: Jason Aronson.

Volkan, V. D. (1990) Overview of psychological concepts pertinent to interethnic and international relationships. In V. D. Volkan, D. A. Julius and J. V. Montville (eds) *Psychodynamics of International Relationships, Volume 1*. Lexington, MA: Lexington Books.

Volkan, V. D. (1991) Official and unofficial diplomacy. In V. D. Volkan, D. A. Julius and J. V. Montville (eds) *Psychodynamics of International Relationships Volume 2*. Lexington, MA: Lexington Books.

Walsh, L. (1997) What would the press do without us? *Voice of Counselling*, August.

Wheelis, A. (1959) *The Quest for Identity*. London: Gollancz.

Wilber, K. (1996) *A Brief History of Everything*. Dublin: Gill and Macmillan.

Winnicott, D. W. (1965) *The Maturational Process and the Facilitating Environment*. New York: International Universities Press.

Woodward, K. (1997) Concepts of identity and difference. In K. Woodward (ed.) *Identity and Difference*. London: Sage.

Wright, J. E. (1982) *Erikson, Identity and Religion*. New York: The Seabury Press.

Wrightsman, L. (1994) *Adult Personality Development. Volume 1, Theories and Concepts*. London: Sage.

Yeats, W. B. (1990) The second coming. In D. Albright (ed.) *The Poems*. London: Dent.

Yuval-Davis, N. (1994) Women, ethnicity and empowerment. In K.-K. Bhavnani and A. Phoenix (eds) *Shifting Identities, Shifting Racisms*. London: Sage.

# Index